Doing Away
with
Personal Injury Law

Recent Titles from Quorum Books

Environmentally Induced Cancer and the Law: Risks, Regulation, and Victim Compensation
Frank B. Cross

Legal and Economic Regulation in Marketing: A Practitioner's Guide
Ray O. Werner

Smoking and the Workplace: Issues and Answers for Human Resources Professionals
William M. Timmins and Clark Brighton Timmins

Private Pensions and Employee Mobility: A Comprehensive Approach to Pension Policy
Izzet Sahin

Group Decision Support Systems for Effective Decision Making: Guide for MIS Practitioners and End Users
Robert J. Thierauf

Deregulation and Competition in the Insurance Industry
Banks McDowell

Chemical Contamination and Its Victims: Medical Remedies, Legal Redress, and Public Policy
David W. Schnare and Martin T. Katzman, editors

Statistics for Real Estate Professionals
Rebecca F. Guy and Louis G. Pol

Decision-Aiding Software and Legal Decision-Making: A Guide to Skills and Applications Throughout the Law
Stuart S. Nagel

Regulatory Interventionism in the Utility Industry: Fairness, Efficiency, and the Pursuit of Energy Conservation
Barbara R. Barkovich

The Acceptance of Human Resource Innovation: Lessons for Management
Ellen Ernst Kossek

Doing Away with Personal Injury Law

NEW COMPENSATION
MECHANISMS
FOR
VICTIMS, CONSUMERS,
AND
BUSINESS

Stephen D. Sugarman

Foreword by
Jeffrey O'Connell

Q QUORUM BOOKS

New York • Westport, Connecticut • London

Library of Congress Cataloging-in-Publication Data

Sugarman, Stephen D.
  Doing away with personal injury law : new compensation mechanisms
for victims, consumers, and business / Stephen D. Sugarman.
    p. cm.
  Bibliography: p.
  Includes index.
  ISBN 0–89930–395–1 (lib. bdg. : alk. paper)
  1. Personal injuries—United States.   I. Title.
KF1257.S84   1989
346.7303′23—dc19
[347.306323]   88–38311

British Library Cataloguing in Publication Data is available.

Library of Congress Catalog Card Number: 88–38311
ISBN: 0–89930–395–1

First published in 1989 by Quorum Books

Greenwood Press, Inc.
88 Post Road West, Westport, Connecticut   06881

Printed in the United States of America

The paper used in this book complies with the
Permanent Paper Standard issued by the National
Information Standards Organization (Z39.48–1984).

10 9 8 7 6 5 4 3 2 1

Copyright Acknowledgments

The author and publisher are grateful to the following for granting permission
to use the following materials:

Stephen D. Sugarman, "Serious Tort Law Reform," *San Diego Law Review*
24:4. Copyright © 1987 San Diego Law Review Association. Reprinted with
the permission of the *San Diego Law Review*.

Stephen D. Sugarman, "Taking Advantage of the Torts Crisis," 48 *Ohio State
Law Journal* 329 (1987). Copyright © 1987 by The Ohio State University.

Stephen D. Sugarman, "Doing Away With Tort Law," 73 *California Law
Review* 558–664 (1985).

Stephen D. Sugarman and Robert Cooter, "A Regulated Market in
Unmatured Tort Claims: Tort Reform by Contract," *New Directions in
Liability Law* (1988).

To Karen, who by now probably has
many reasons of her own to hope
for the end of personal injury law.

Contents

Foreword

When I was a young legal academic—now 30 years ago—like most of my ilk, then and now, I fretted endlessly over what field I should concentrate my teaching and research on. And rightly so; such a decision is crucial to an academic career.

Then the retirement of an older colleague opened up two subjects—labor law and torts. My predecessor had concentrated on labor law, teaching torts as an appealing sidelight, allowing one to teach first year students (such fun then or now) in a relative backwater that, unlike labor law, didn't change much and therefore didn't require much keeping up. And that is the priority I thought I'd adopt. But two things became quickly apparent. Labor law was a monster, full of brilliant scholars who seem to have said—or be saying—it all. Preeminent was Archie Cox (my labor law teacher) but including the likes of Willard Wirtz and Ben Aaron. And not only that, cases and rulings cascaded from the NLRB and the courts at a rate to defy assimilation. Who needed it! Torts on the other hand was the opposite: If labor law was a tropical rain forest, torts was a wasteland. Some are able people, but, to speak frankly at the risk of doing so unkindly, many of them seemed most of the time to be poking around or exegeting on a lot of marginal, dry-as-dust doctrinal matters (the intricacies of the last clear chance in Missouri—that sort of thing). Largely ignored was the fact that tort law was, as an *insurance* mechanism, simply a disaster: cumbersome, arbitrary, dilatory, wasteful, and needlessly expensive. But at that point in tort law, insurance was unmentionable, not only in front of jurors, but by appellate judges, and in large measure by academics themselves.

One person above all stood out as an exception to that often dreary pattern: Fleming James of Yale. Almost uniquely, James (along with a few others such as Robert Keeton of Harvard) saw tort law through the lens of liability insurance—and further saw it as part of a pattern (however awkward the fit) of social as well as private insurance. It is easy today to criticize James for urging the expansion of liability insurance to achieve social insurance goals, but few seem to recall that it was James' goal to move tort law toward a workers' compensation-like system. Tort liability insurance, dominated by wasteful and expensive focusing on determinations of fault and value of pain and suffering (as well as payment for the latter), would give way to payment of economic loss, irrespective of fault, thereby in turn doing away with the variables that make tort law so unworkable.

In direct furtherance of James' goal, I was thereupon blessed with the chance to work with Robert Keeton in formulating proposals for no-fault auto insurance. And beyond that I undertook the even more difficult task of applying James' and Keeton's insights to other areas of tort law—principally medical malpractice and products liability. The guiding principle in all this work was to make much better use of liability insurance dollars, taking care not to propose abandonment of tort law completely. Rather my aim was—and is—to use the constraint imposed by the dollars currently being spent on tort liability insurance but to use far more of those dollars to pay for actual monetary losses and thus to spend far less in transaction costs (mostly lawyers' fees) and nonmonetary losses (mostly pain and suffering). (On this point, see O'Connell, *An Alternative to Abandoning Tort Liability*, 60 Minn. L. Rev. 501, 537–40 [1976].)

One disappointment is this work has been how few torts scholars pursue similar efforts. This is not to say there weren't creative efforts along such lines (for example, by Marc Franklin, Roger Henderson, Richard Pierce, to mention a few). But too often scholars addressed only part of this issue, focusing, for example, on the need to cut down on tort recoveries without addressing the resultant shortfalls in compensation for injuries, or insisting that compensation is an entirely separate issue, unrelated to the merits of proposed changes in tort law. Also, scholars interested in fundamental changes too often ignored the details (call it the plumbing) of reform, preferring to skim the treetops. Finally, too many scholars who did address the compensation issue addressed it episodically, ignoring, in the latter case, the dictum that legal reform is not for the short-winded.

So with few exceptions, tort scholars failed to follow James' example of persistently and thoroughly thinking about tort law in insurance terms. To compound the tragedy, as the older generation of tort scholars such as James, William Prosser, Page Keeton, John Wade and Wex Malone gave way, the next generation in large measure found its own desert—also far removed from real problems, often continuing to refuse to face the confusing complexities of insurance. I refer of course to the subject of law and economics. How paradoxical that the first subject (after antitrust) to draw attention from the discipline of law and economics was torts—perhaps the area of law the *least* suited for economists' rigid assumptions of perfect information and perfectly rational behavior. Tort law, dealing as it mostly does with fortuitous, unexpected, relatively unpredictable, rare, accidental events, resists much more than, say, the calculated world of commercial and real estate deals, the rigid assumptions of economics. As a result, tort law now faced a new wasteland—abstract, self-contained, artificial, also often ignoring insurance. The result in turn has been another generation of wasted opportunity—tort scholarship dominated by concerns quite unrelated to reality.

It is Steve Sugarman as a rare exception to all of this that is so impressive. He *does* address the interaction of tort law, insurance and compensation schemes; he *does* delve into the details of his proposals with a subtle appreciation of the literature, as well as testing his own proposals, and he *is* persistent. He has thought long and hard about this field and he stays at it, year after year, article after article (and now, one hopes, book after book).

Of course, with such an ambitious undertaking as his book represents, one can quarrel with some of his thoughts and ideas. Is he sufficiently appreciative of the costs of the private and social insurance substitutes for tort law he proposes? Does it, for example, make (actuarial) sense to include compensation for illness, so little of which is caused by tortfeasors, in his replacement for tort law, with a resultant disparity of costs between his new scheme and that which it replaces? Does it make sense to abandon a long-standing, sophisticated, and, on the whole, well-working scheme such as workers' compensation, rather than build upon it? One can discuss all this at great lengths, and we will all do so greatly aided by Sugarman's command of the literature and his provocative proposals, so deserving of further and close attention.

Jeffrey O'Connell
Charlottesville, Virginia

Acknowledgments

I began teaching Torts at Berkeley in 1972, when I first came into academia, inspired by the refreshing ideas of Guido Calabresi. All the way through, I have received considerable instruction and encouragement from my colleague John Fleming. Although what I propose here is probably too radical for either of them, I trust they both will recognize some of their many insights along the way.

This book has been evolving over several years, and I am grateful to the editors of the *California Law Review*, the *Ohio State Law Journal*, the *San Diego Law Review*, and the Academy of Political Science who have earlier published articles of mine upon which I have drawn here.

My most recent research assistants Karin Immergut, Michael Rochman and Jessie Vapnek have been enormously helpful in this endeavor, as has my longtime secretary Connie Curtin. Finally, I want to thank my dean, Jesse Choper, for his wonderful support, not only financial (through the Boalt Hall Fund), but otherwise.

Introduction

I favor doing away with personal injury law and replacing it with both new compensation arrangements for accident victims and new mechanisms for controlling unreasonably dangerous conduct. This book is an argument for that proposition.

By personal injury law I mean the legal arrangements and surrounding institutions through which people who have suffered bodily injury make claims and file lawsuits against their injurers. These claims are for financial compensation for lost earnings, medical and other expenses, pain and suffering, and, on occasion, punitive damages. Personal injury claims comprise a very large part of the civil justice system. They are the core of, although by no means all of, tort law.

In the past, when the perceived social problem was that individuals were deliberately injuring others, making the injurer pay personally for the harm done seemed only just. It probably was the minimum punishment that a wrongdoer deserved. Furthermore, it may have been necessary to provide a prompt legal remedy in order to calm down the victim, preventing him from retaliating with force. Today, however, we are a long way from that state of affairs.

Currently, most injuries that find their way into the tort system are not cases of intentional wrongdoing; rather, they are the result of accidents. The most common sources of those injuries are automobiles and other forms of transportation, consumer products, medical and related services, workplace accidents, and accidents that occur on other people's property, such as those caused by slips and falls, fires, or other dangerous conditions. Thus, injurers usually are not people the victim is having a feud with; rather, they typically are a motorist that the victim was sharing the road with, the victim's own physician or local bus company, or the maker of an item the victim was using. When someone now makes a tort claim, rather than obtaining swift justice, he or she often will wind up waiting years before the lawsuit is resolved. Moreover, a victim today rarely can expect to recover directly from an individual injurer. Instead, he or she will recover from an insurance company or a large impersonal enterprise, such as a corporation or a governmental entity.

Personal injury law, then, is a form of collective intervention into social and economic affairs. We judge other forms of government action, such as the public transportation system, the Social Security system, the national park system, or any important system of government regulation such as those run by the Food and Drug Administration and the Federal Aviation Administration, by comparing their costs with their benefits. So, too, should we judge personal injury law. Evaluated in this way, I have concluded that this part of tort law generates more perverse behavior than desired safety, that it is an intolerably expensive and unfair system of compensating victims, and that in practice it fails to serve any commonsense notion of justice. In short, I do not think we, as a society, are getting our money's worth.

In the 1960s and early 1970s legal scholars debated exciting proposals to replace parts of tort law with compensation systems tailored to various classes of accidents. The most pressing concern was a no-fault scheme to supplant auto accident law. Initial legislative successes on that front encouraged compensation-minded reformers to grow increasingly bold in their proposals. However, they have not been able to retain center stage.

In the political arena, the auto no-fault movement, which succeeded in less than half the state legislatures, has seemed for the past ten years to be at an impasse. Attention has turned instead to a vigorous, defense-inspired campaign to strip back personal injury law to its traditional core, curtailing the recent judicial expansion of victims' rights, but not providing any alternative forms of compensation.

In academia, tort theory has captured the limelight. Although scholars have written about tort theory from various perspectives, the main thrust of their writing has been to defend tort law's commitment to decentralized private law solutions to accident problems, if not to support the details of the existing tort system. It is time, I believe, to focus academic and political attention once more on doing away with tort actions for personal injury.

Part I of this book examines the justifications advanced in support of existing personal injury law and shows that these goals are either unachieved or inefficiently pursued. I offer a critique of several different kinds of tort apologists, starting in chapter 1 with devotees of law and economics who emphasize the safety goal.

There I argue that it is not tort law, but mainly other existing social forces, that cause people and enterprises to act reasonably. I detail various real world aspects of the personal injury law system that undermine its ability to contribute to safety in the way that its defenders suggest. Then I discuss the substantial negative social effects that personal injury law has on human conduct, such as companies not developing and introducing products that the public wants, vaccines becoming unavailable in adequate quantities, recreational facilities closing down, and competent physicians ceasing to treat some patients. As I explain, tort law further causes the wasteful and unnecessary testing that doctors engage in for the purpose of avoiding lawsuits and that it leads to cover-ups of past wrongdoing, the manufacture of evidence of causation and fault, and the fraudulent staging of injuries. The current system also diverts significant time and attention of high-level executives and professionals away from their main tasks and causes severe demoralization and cynicism among professionals and within enterprises where those responsible for safety feel unfairly maligned.

Chapter 2 addresses enterprise liability advocates who emphasize the compensation goal. In the past thirty years, many academics, as well as judges and lawyers, have embraced personal injury law as a mechanism for compensating accident victims. As I show, however, most disabled people, even most accident victims, are not at all compensated by personal injury law. At the same time, many victims receive excessive compensation, especially those who receive large awards for pain and suffering, those who receive tort compensation for losses that are already covered by other employee benefit and social insurance systems, and those who obtain inappropriate windfall amounts of punitive damages.

The direct and more easily measurable costs of personal injury law, both private and public, are substantial. They are eventually borne by all of us in the form of higher prices for consumer goods and services, higher auto insurance rates, and higher taxes. A recent study conservatively estimated the direct cost of the American tort system in 1984 at $68 billion. For 1988 it is fair to put the direct cost at well over $100 billion. As I explain, the lion's share of this sum does not go to compensating victims, however; instead it is wasted in litigation and administrative expenses. The unwanted indirect costs of personal injury law, if not easily quantified, are also large. They include, most importantly, the already noted socially undesirable consequences that tort law has on people's behavior.

Chapter 3 examines justice and related goals. Is not doing justice to the litigants what the common law is about—resolving disputes between two or more parties by deciding what is fair as to them? That may be the theory, but, in practice, the amount that claimants recover is unlikely to reflect what an objective observer would say they truly deserve. Instead, what count considerably are the talents of the lawyer one happens to have; the tenacity of the defendant (or insurance adjuster) one happens to be up against; whether the defendant happens to be a motorist, a company, or a governmental entity; how attractive (but not too attractive) and how well spoken (but perhaps not too well spoken) the claimant happens to be; what race the claimant is; what state and community the victim lives in; how well one is able to hold out for a larger settlement; the whim of the jury if the case gets that far; and whether one is lucky enough to have available the right sort of witnesses or other evidence of the injury and defendant wrongdoing. As a result, victims frequently come away from the lawsuits far more frustrated than satisfied. Our current personal injury law system is not a system of justice; it is a lottery. Unlike the official lotteries that many states now run, however, the tort lottery is one for which we all are forced to pay.

Part II criticizes the proposals for change that most other reformers have advanced. I start in chapter 4 with tort law reform of the sort pushed by the Reagan administration and defense interests and considered by state legislatures and Congress during the past couple of years. I then turn, in chapter 5, to broader reform proposals for either replacing parts of tort law with tailored compensation systems or substituting for the entirety of personal injury law a general accident or disability compensation scheme. While I find a number of the proposals considered in Part II to be improvements on the status quo, they are not ideal.

Part III offers reforms I do favor. For the long run, I propose that we (1) eliminate tort remedies for accidental injuries, (2) build on existing social insurance and employee benefit plans to ensure generous compensation to all accident victims that is in line with compensation now provided by progressive employers to cover employee income loss and medical expense, and (3) build on existing regulatory schemes both to promote accident avoidance and to provide outlets for complaints about unreasonably dangerous conduct (chapters 6 and 7). For the shorter run, I propose some first steps that might be politically more promising now and that would move us in the right direction for the long term. They include both legislative reform (chapter 8) and reform by private contract (chapter 9).

I

THE FAILURE OF TORT LAW

The Safety Goal

Many try to justify personal injury law on the ground that it promotes socially desirable behavior. Specifically, they claim that it prevents injuries by deterring unreasonably dangerous conduct.[1] Although by no means new, this idea has had a great deal of play of late because it is the cornerstone of the "law and economics" view of tort law, which has been so widely discussed in recent years.[2] If legal liability effectively served this social-engineering purpose, it would be a powerful argument for the retention of tort law. There is, unfortunately, little reason to believe that personal injury law today actually serves an important accident-avoidance function. Worse, to the extent that it does influence behavior, there is good reason to think that much of the result is socially undesirable. Given the tort system's enormous administrative cost, were deterrence its only objective, I believe society would be decidedly better off if it did away with private law damages for accidents.[3]

The argument for tort law as a deterrent can be simply stated. It is first assumed that, absent tort law, people would pursue their own interests, putting their personal desires ahead of the safety of others. As a result, people (and property) would be unreasonably damaged. By contrast, because tort law threatens people with legal liability for the harms they cause, it is seen to force them to take the interests of others into account. In other words, it is assumed that in order to avoid the legal sanction, people will alter their behavior in a socially desirable, less injury-producing way. This perspective rests on a view of man (after Adam Smith) as a fundamentally selfish animal who responds better to calls upon his pocketbook than to calls upon his moral duty to exercise care toward others.

Within this school of thought there is considerable dispute over the best basis for attaching financial liability. Some emphasize the importance of tying liability to fault, defined as failing to avoid accidents that can be efficiently avoided. Others prefer rules of strict liability that force the defendant, rather than the jury, to decide whether there is an efficient way to avoid the accident. Because of these differences of opinion, among others, the law and economics camp is rather divided about what is right and what is wrong about existing tort law. They share, however, a common fear of throwing the baby out with the bathwater whenever abandoning tort law is considered, worrying about extra accidents that may result.

Although law and economics is essentially an academic community (frequently supported by conservative economists who prefer tort law to direct regulation as a form of behavior control), its talk about deterrence parallels that of its otherwise ideologically distant relatives in the plaintiffs' personal injury bar. The bar's arguments, however, are more likely to take the form, not of economic models and supply-and-demand curves, but of examples of wrongdoing inviduals and enterprises that have been caught and brought to account. From the plaintiffs' lawyers' side, these tales illustrate the need for vigilant, independent advocates on behalf of safety, a plausible source of ideas for safer products and services (occasioned by the need to prove at trial that something safer should have been done), as well as the kind of jolt that will shock the individuals or enterprises into changing their ways in the future.

The view of tort law as safety promoter emphasizes the threat of having to pay tort damages. This is not the only cost the tort system imposes, however. Tort law might also deter because of the stigma of an official determination of liability. In addition, tort law might deter because people fear undesirable publicity from reports of official proceedings—publicity beyond that generated by informal assertions backed up by investigative reporting. Finally, tort law threatens large administrative costs of defending one's position, whether one settles or goes to court.

In any event, the general model posited is one in which people and enterprises, like mice put in a psychologist's maze of electrical shocks, are directed away from conduct that brings the sting of tort liability and toward those channels of activity where the sting is avoided. However, this model overemphasizes both the amount of overly dangerous activity that would occur without tort liability and the amount of injury reduction achieved by it.[4]

BEHAVIOR CONTROLS APART FROM TORT LAW

Self-preservation instincts, market forces, personal morality, and governmental regulation (criminal and administrative) combine to control unreasonably dangerous actions independently of tort law. The existence of these forces explains why, if liability for personal injuries were abolished, there would not be the dramatic increase in injuries that the simple tort-as-deterrent model envisions.

Consider first the self-preservation instinct of would-be injurers. Where conduct is likely to be dangerous to oneself as well as others, the drive to protect one's own body will go a long way toward safeguarding others. The attention of airline pilots and motorists to safety well illustrates this point; further examples are efforts by store owners and homeowners to ensure that their premises are free from hazards. I recognize that this pressure is not universally applicable; manufacturers and physicians, for example, mainly endanger others.

Ordinary market forces serve as a second safety control. Clearly, consumers are an important influence in reducing the dangerousness of products and services. Indeed, if buyers have good information and act rationally, the market by itself should provide the goods and services that respond to public willingness to pay for safety.

Beyond the desire to cater to current buyer preferences, most enterprises and professionals have a further interest in attracting new customers. This gives them a financial reason to avoid a reputation for providing dangerous products, premises, or services. Bad reviews by consumer organizations or the media, to say nothing of word-of-mouth complaints, can ruin the further marketing of a particular product or service. In addition, a publicized unsafe product line can besmirch a firm's general standing—a matter of considerable importance in a nation of large, diversified enterprises. Another economic pressure comes from the desire to escape the problems and out-of-pocket expenses that arise when victims complain, threaten to make trouble, or demand their money back. To be sure, because there is good reason to think that many consumers and prospective consumers are neither well informed about dangers nor fully rational actors, and because some products threaten those who are not consumers, market pressures alone do not suffice to achieve the desired level of safety.

Third, moral inhibitions serve to block self-satisfying conduct that would be unreasonably dangerous to others. Even if there were no penalties, or no chance of being caught, many people's own moral sense—their pride in doing right and the accompanying shame of doing wrong—would protect others from harm. Although in today's world it may be empirically difficult to disentangle morally driven from coerced conduct, the former is widespread. In ordinary life, for example, most people neither litter, pick flowers belonging to others, nor toss cigarettes carelessly into the woods, even though regularly presented with such opportunities for anonymous self-indulgence. Frequent illustrations come as well from the world of physicians where "doing good" is internalized as an intrinsic part of one's calling. Engineers and architects also take considerable professional pride in the quality of their work; the safety of a project or product is typically critical to their own self-esteem. Even from the world of highly competitive business come reports of "missionary" chief executive officers, often firm founders, who have bound up their personal identity with the safety and soundness of their product. Of course, not all people have the proper moral inhibitions against behaving unreasonably.

Regulation, in the form of legally binding formal behavioral control mechanisms, is a fourth important force in the realm of accident deterrence. Traditional criminal penalties are but a small part of the overall picture. In recent years there has been a proliferation in collective intervention through national safety agencies such as CPSC, EPA, FAA, FDA, NHTSA, OSHA, and so on through the alphabet. Perhaps even more pervasive are state, local, and professional control regimes as diverse as building codes, highway engineering departments, and medical quality review boards.

These regulatory schemes, combined with the moral, economic, and self-preservation pressures described above, plainly deter considerable undesirable behavior. To be sure, there is much to criticize about regulation. It is neither comprehensive in its reach nor fully effective in its operation. Furthermore, not only can regulation be very expensive, it sometimes ill serves the public interest. Its existence, nonetheless, renders superfluous much of tort law's deterrent potential. To use a common example, what driver would slow down to avoid the imposition of tort liability, in the unlikely event of an accident, who has not already slowed down because of the risk of a lost license and a fine (to say nothing of the fear for one's self and one's moral scruples against such conduct)? As another example, tort law is unlikely to increase airline safety beyond that achieved by FAA pressures, to say nothing of pilot union pressures and carriers' concerns about reputation and saving lives.

The existence of these four safety-promoting forces does not mean, of course, that all drugs, drivers, and drill presses will be as safe as they ought to be. A gap would (and does) remain between how people act and what is socially desirable. It is, of course, understandable that some people would hope that tort law would help close that gap. Yet, considerable unreasonable conduct continues notwithstanding the existence of tort law and there is little reason to believe that the gap is importantly closed because of it. This is because, in practice, many factors undermine personal injury law's potential as a behavioral control mechanism.

WHY THE DETERRENT POTENTIAL OF TORT LIABILITY IS UNDERMINED

In the deterrence model, education and information should warn the potential tort-feasor when the sting will be applied. Where avoidance hurts less than the sting would, he can rationally elect another course of conduct. This is the law and economics view. Its model is decidedly one of general deterrence. People are led to behave properly before they have any personal encounter with the law.

From this perspective, pointing to a series of specific tort cases where personal injury lawyers brought dangerous conduct and products to light hardly proves the "accident protection function or prophylactic purpose of tort law" as Professor Thomas Lambert has argued.[5] Rather, successful lawsuits represent a catalog of tort failures; people behaved in unacceptable ways notwithstanding the threat of liability![6]

Ignorance—Of Law and Facts

The model of general deterrence requires knowledge. Yet many people seem to be ignorant of the threat of tort liability before the first sting. This can be attributed in part to individual inattentiveness and in part to our society's failure to instruct people effectively in their civil obligations. For example, when a state supreme court announces that hosts risk liability for subsequent drunk-driving injuries if they fail to use reasonable care in serving alcoholic beverages to their guests, how many people in the state whose behavior needs modifying even hear of this ruling, let alone remember it? Even in sophisticated enterprises, key actors may remain quite ignorant of their obligations under tort law. In an important empirical study, George Eads and Peter Reuter report they were "struck in the companies we visited by how few changes in law were transmitted to those involved in design decisions."[7] Concerning two manufacturers of potentially highly dangerous products: "[b]oth made substantial efforts to keep their product liability problems separate from their ongoing operating decisions . . . both firms treated the information generated by specific product liability suits as random noise."[8]

Even those with broad awareness of tort liability have many reasons to see it as highly unpredictable. These reasons include rapid legal change, state-to-state variance, the perceived lotterylike nature of secret jury decision making, the vagaries of trials, pervasive rough-and-ready settlement practices, and doctrinal complexity.[9]

It has been argued, however, that uncertainty is an advantage because that is what engenders caution.

Under the present system, it seems reasonable to speculate that any deterrent effect that arises, arises from the specter of huge, perhaps business-crippling, judgments for pain and suffering. . . . Indeed, the virtue of the present system, from a deterrence standpoint, is that the precise magnitude of the costs of malfeasance or nonfeasance is impossible to project. . . . The blows [of tort law] can be financially crushing, and it is those blows of which manufacturers and the medical profession are ever vigilant.[10]

Yet, for most potential defendants, liability insurance, which I discuss later, has largely vitiated this argument. Besides, many parties will simply ignore the tiny possibility of a crushing financial loss in the way that people or companies ignore the chance that they might be killed or destroyed by an unexpected natural disaster. Alternatively, if they dwell on this risk, people are apt to develop socially undesirable defense strategies or to exercise excessive caution and fail to engage in socially beneficial activities. Finally, even if enterprises and individuals were to try to respond to an indeterminate likelihood of crushing liability, they would not know what amount of precaution to take.

Ignorance of legal risk is but one problem. People can also fail to appreciate that they are engaging in excessively dangerous conduct. Sometimes this occurs because people are not sufficiently alert to the consequences of their behavior. But even reasonably attentive people simply do not always analyze all the information necessary to make the "right" decision.[11] Because full rationality often takes too much time, money, or attentiveness, people may be content to rely on shortcuts such as rules of thumb or advice and customs of others. In short, they employ "satisficing" behavior, engaging at best only in bounded rationality that may be unreasonably dangerous.

Finally, the deterrent function of tort law is undermined when parties simply cannot feasibly obtain needed information. In certain situations, people do not become aware that their conduct or product is harmful until long after the harm has occurred. For example, the dangers of many cancer-causing substances and pharmaceutical drugs appear only after a considerable latency period. Even with more ordinary risks, many firms are engaged in such rapidly changing activities that they may no longer be making the product by the time field reports identify it as dangerous.

Incompetence—Individual and Organizational

A second general reason that undermines tort law's ability to deter I will call incompetence. At the individual level, most people, even if aware of the sting, find that, from time to time, they simply cannot make their way safely through the maze. This problem is by no means restricted to the unusually awkward or to those who have unusually bad judgment. Most ordinary people occasionally act clumsily, rashly, or absent-mindedly. We do so even when we know better and will privately admit as much. Virtually no one will claim to act always as the "reasonable person" is supposed to act. Many feel we only have our lucky stars to thank for the fact that our occasional lapses have not seriously hurt anyone, or in some cases, have hurt as few as they have. This is not to suggest that people have no control over their behavior, or that they cannot be broadly influenced to take greater care in their conduct. It is quite another thing to expect tort law to shape basic character, however.

Organizations are faced with a related sort of incompetence problem. As much as management may want to reduce its liability exposure, actually achieving cost-effective changes is often easier said than done. It is not that management lacks strategies to deal with lax or incompetent employees, whether on the assembly line, in the design lab, or on the sales floor. They include better supervision, on-the-job training and education, in-firm incentives, more careful hiring practices, and the creation of separate safety units. But the effective deployment of these techniques is terribly difficult. To quote an experienced observer of corporate safety programs, "[T]here is usually an important difference between issued policy and procedure on product safety and what is actually taking place. No activity is as effective as those responsible for it say it is."[12]

One reason safety receives inadequate attention in enterprises is that individuals and units within the firm have their own agendas and priorities. Managers tend to worry most about their short-run profits, upcoming budgets, and compensation rather than the firm's long-term financial health. And, because there is often considerable delay between when key decisions are made and when tort liability arises, they may well expect to be gone from the firm before the tort problem they ignore comes home to roost.[13]

Discounting the Threat

A further diminution of tort law's effectiveness as a deterrent occurs because people discount the threat of tort liability. From a private economic perspective, some discounting can be quite rational. Some victims with bona fide claims will not sue. The injured parties may be unaware of their legal rights, have an aversion to the idea of litigation, have adequate sources of compensation other than tort damages, or have small individual losses. Or the victims may not even know who their injurer is. Sometimes the judicial system will fail to impose liability for conduct that actually was unreasonably dangerous. This can occur where the victims may have lost evidence, a witness is reluctant, or the fact-finding process works imperfectly. Additionally, sophisticated, potential tort-feasors are likely aware that many cases can be settled for far less than the cost of damages incurred.[14]

Other discounting, while perhaps economically foolhardy, makes psychological sense.[15] Sometimes the risk of harming someone is so small that our mental processes do not know how to deal with it, and it is simply disregarded. Other times, people ignore considerably larger dangers—hoping that miraculously no one will be hurt or that they will not be caught. Some will discount future liability in this way because they are gamblers, others because they are self-destructive, and still others because they put instant gratification ahead of nearly everything else. Finally, some people act rashly out of desperation—which brings me to the next point.

High Stakes in Behaving Dangerously

A fourth factor undermining tort law's effectiveness as a deterrent is that some actors feel they have so much at stake that they satisfy their own immediate needs even though they realize their conduct is dangerous to others and they might wind up subject to legal liability. They conclude that certain safety efforts would place critically at risk important things such as career, family well-being, or self-image, and this risk simply swamps the prospect of a tort penalty. This helps explain why a doctor would continue practicing although aware of his incompetence, why a small-business owner would continue selling a key product despite known safety problems, and why a financially overextended landlord would ignore dangerous condi-tions. Thus, I am unpersuaded by arguments that it is the "marginal, fly-by-night manufacturer [who] might be encouraged by the absence of re-straints against irresponsible conduct."[16] The real fly-by-nights are tempted to act dangerously even with tort law. Indeed, they have little incentive to carry liability insurance.[17]

In sum, people expose others to harm for many selfish or idiosyncratic, high-stakes reasons that are socially unacceptable even though the injurers' private benefits may be great. Put differently, tort law allows people to conclude that the risk of being assessed monetary damages is an acceptable trade-off for the ability to engage in objectionable high-stakes conduct.

Small Penalty

A fifth general factor undermining the effectiveness of tort law as a de-terrent is that it is perfectly rational for most (although plainly not all) actors to conclude that they risk little penalty. One aspect of this is simply the matter of dollars and cents. This is especially true for large enterprises (as contrasted with, say, individual physicians). According to one large survey carried out in 1978—even after large increases in liability insurance pre-miums had been imposed—product, occupier, and general liability costs together typically then amounted to less than .2 percent of sales. This included a burden of .115 percent of sales in the form of insurance costs plus .054 percent of sales in settlement and administrative costs not covered by insurance. These costs varied by industry of course. Hospitals repre-sented the industry with the greatest costs—more than ten times the av-erage—but that still amounted to only 2.35 percent of income. In manufacturing, the highest figure was for rubber and plastics at .58 percent of sales.[18] To be sure, it is now widely realized that after several years of stable costs, liability insurance premiums recently skyrocketed again.[19] Still, even today most enterprises continue to face modest liability insurance costs when compared with total sales; for example, two-thirds of large corporations reported in 1986 that liability insurance adds 1 percent or less to the price of their products.[20]

Moreover, this burden describes the full liability costs for these firms. But the relevant figure for deterrence purposes is how much safety efforts can reduce such costs at the margin. In fact, only rarely can a firm hope to reduce more than a small proportion of its liability insurance costs through accident prevention efforts. The problem is compounded because it may take considerable present cash outlays to achieve accident avoidance that will financially pay off, if at all, only sometime in the distant future. Furthermore, because effective safety efforts show up indirectly as costs avoided, they are often difficult to identify, quantify, monitor, and manage. It should not be surprising, therefore, if enterprises more vigorously pursue other cost-reducing strategies in production, administration, marketing, and finance.

Moreover, it is unlikely that tort-generated publicity and social censure will combine with liability costs to make the economic threat large at the margin. A tort-feasor can almost always avoid an official slap on the wrist by settlement. Cases litigated to the end tend to be those where responsibility is most in dispute, so that many of those held liable in court are not considered wrongdoers by their peers. Finally, for potential injurers the prospect of unfavorable publicity is highly speculative. The popular press selectively publicizes cases with large settlements, titillating facts, or a multitude of victims. Most tort suits never get any significant publicity.[21]

Next I will describe four additional factors minimizing the force of tort law. They revolve around the idea that people are not likely to change their behavior in response to the threat of having to pay for the harm they cause if, in practice, that threat is sharply reduced or eliminated.

First, many individuals have no wealth and hardly any income; many enterprises are woefully undercapitalized. These potential injurers, by virtue of their poverty, have almost nothing with which to pay damages. Therefore, the threat of a tort judgment is not meaningful.

Second, vicarious liability causes victims of employee conduct to sue the enterprise, and in practice, employers do not exercise their legal right to claim indemnity from the employee tort-feasor. As a result, workers are not directly deterred by tort law. Rather, their conduct must be indirectly influenced, if at all. Yet, the ability of firms to threaten employees who impose tort liability on the firms with job loss or some other penalty is limited for many reasons. The frequent delay between bad conduct and a determination of liability will often mean that the person responsible has already moved to another job. In addition, the collective nature of many firm decisions makes it difficult to allocate blame. Moreover, union, morale, and litigation pressures militate against seriously punishing workers, especially where firms have defended themself against liability.[22] Finally, in many instances where a firm penalizes a worker causing tort liability, it would have taken action against him even without a judicial determination of fault. In sum, I do not believe that tort law contributes much to better employee behavior by causing workers to fear losing their jobs or other job sanctions.

A third stakes-reducing factor is the frequent inappropriateness of tort damage awards from the deterrence perspective. The law and economics model requires the correct threat in order to produce the appropriate safety-minded response. Ordinary tort damages are an inaccurate and confused measure of our desire to deter, however. For example, tort law sends out the economic message that one may take less precaution to avoid killing someone than to avoid permanently injuring them because, by the way damages are measured, it is cheaper to kill than to disable. Similarly, tort law tells the rational would-be injurer that he may take less precaution to avoid killing a child than a working adult. Tort law creates these implicit priorities because it awards damages to compensate rather than to deter. But from the perspective of accident avoidance, these priorities do not reflect our social values.

Liability insurance is a final factor contributing to a reduced torts sanction. Indeed, Professor John Fleming suggested more than twenty years ago that "the deterrent function of the law of torts was severely, perhaps fatally, undermined by the advent of liability insurance."[23] However, this subject is of sufficient importance to require separate discussion.

Liability Insurance and Deterrence

Complete liability insurance protection shifts the direct economic deterrent pressure of tort law from would-be tort-feasors to insurance companies. This shift complicates tort law's potential for behavioral control.[24]

Most American enterprises, professionals, and drivers are protected by liability insurance (or else the victim does not bother to sue). Liability insurers, however, rarely choose to use significant deductibles or coinsurance provisions to put economic pressure on individual insureds in the way that first-party insurers do. That alone should breed skepticism about the role of insurers and insurance in promoting safety.[25] There are, nevertheless, four factors that might serve to reintroduce some of the safety pressure that liability insurance removes: (1) insurance pricing, (2) the cancellation and nonrenewal of coverage, (3) safety measures required as a condition of coverage, and (4) contractual provisions of the insurance policy.

Before considering such complexities, it should be understood that the arguments that follow apply much less to the giant American enterprises because they typically are self-insured.[26] Alternatively, they buy insurance either covering only extremely large losses or else containing "retrospective" premium-setting provisions that cause liability costs generally to reflect actual experience. In the latter case, insurers are used largely to process claims.

Large enterprises tend to be sophisticated profit maximizers; many have separate safety and loss control units. Of course, because these giant firms are so visible, they are subject to reasonably close scrutiny by regulatory authorities and consumers. Thus, they have good reason to promote safety independent of tort law. On the other hand, these same firms may make allies of regulatory agencies, thereby blunting the effect of administrative control. Although the picture is a complex one, I will concede that the behavior-influencing potential of tort law is probably greatest for giant enterprises. Unfortunately, as I will discuss later, these economic giants often respond to such pressures in perverse rather than socially desirable ways.

Insurance Pricing

For those would-be defendants who do insure, there is plainly some potential for insurance pricing to reestablish economic incentives for safe conduct. For example, suppose insurance pricing were highly sensitive to risks insureds created. Carried to its extreme, one's premium would exactly reflect the harm one were going to cause, although at that point we are no longer talking about insurance. Indeed, in order for insurance to work there must be some uncertainty—about future conduct and/or the amount of liability. While that in turn prevents fully accurate individualized premiums, still under a system of individual, risk-based pricing, alert insureds would recognize immediate financial incentives: can X dollars in our premiums be avoided by a lower cost investment in safety? Alternatively, suppose at the other extreme that liability insurance premiums were indifferent to the safety efforts or records of insureds. In that case, insureds would have no incentive to increase safety in order to lower insurance costs.

In theory, one might expect the pressure of competition to encourage insurers to individualize pricing wherever possible. They could break the market into finely tuned categories and set different premiums to reflect the injury potential of each category. The insured, in turn, would have an economic incentive to get into a lower-priced category. Pricing practices could thus make enterprises sensitive to the dangers they create.

In practice, however, only a very small proportion of insureds pay premiums that are importantly sensitive to changes in the dangerousness of their conduct. This is not to say that insurance rates in no respect reflect the likelihood of tort liability. For example, young males, city dwellers, and those who drive a lot typically pay higher auto liability insurance premiums. But these price differences do not relate to how carefully the individual actually drives. To be sure, such price differences could influence decisions at the "activity level," such as whether to drive when young and whether to drive less frequently. However, they are not designed to influence the manner in which the driving is performed. In the same vein, many enterprises pay greater premiums because their industry has a record of more frequent or more costly accidents. Yet, once again, so long as individual firms pay on the same basis (e.g., on sales volume or floor space), individual accident records and safety measures will have no impact on premiums.

It would appear, so far, that insurance-pricing practices drastically dampen any potential for tort damages to stimulate individual safety efforts. However, the insurance practice known as experience or merit rating remains to be discussed. Even here, because of actuarial requirements, under current practices only a modest proportion of firms qualify for experience rating. For smaller firms, past experience is too uncertain a guide to future risk. Besides, insurers wish to avoid the administrative costs of individualizing premiums for such small firms. Only when firms are large enough can insurers use individual past records as predictors of future claims when setting premiums.[27] Experience rating holds greatest promise for large enterprises with broad insurance protection. As already indicated, the largest firms dominating this group tend to self-insure—the ultimate experience rating. Nevertheless, focusing on those who do insure, I doubt that experience rating serves as an important promoter of safety.[28]

In theory, experience rating gives prompt and accurate economic feedback on the efficacy of safety investments; in practice, it does not. One difficulty is delay. Because of concerns about the credibility of the data, experience rating usually involves basing premiums on multiyear moving averages. As a result, on top of the delay between the time investments in safety are made and a lower accident rate is experienced, there is a further lapse before those fewer losses are reflected in lower premiums. If those who made safety decisions had the firm's long-run profit in mind, these delays would not be such a problem. However, as already noted, there is good reason to think that such a perspective is unusual.

Second, experience rating yields premium adjustments that only loosely reflect an individual firm's safety record. Much of the premium depends on insurer overhead costs rather than the insured's experience. In addition, in setting new premiums, insurers usually must only roughly estimate past losses that are incurred but not yet reported—thus further dampening the impact of the firm's actual experience. Finally, pricing leeway and current competitive practices among insurers further weaken the connection between actual loss and premium levels. According to Eads and Reuter, most liability insurance rates "are determined judgmentally, not on the basis of actuarial experience."[29] Most insurance companies allow their underwriters to authorize reduced premiums for companies with good safety programs and good management. Although lacking solid actuarial justification, this price flexibility, at least in theory, could influence a company to improve safety because it turns in part on factors under the insured's control. In practice, however, there is reason to think that this underwriting flexibility is not actually used to promote safety but rather that it provides the leeway for vigorous price competition at times when there is a soft market for liability insurance.

Moving away from firms, because individuals have a low frequency of prior claims and accidents, there is considerable doubt whether past experience can reliably predict future liability. Still, I admit that both motorists and some professionals face the prospect of higher insurance rates based on their past experience. Here, however, experience rating seems more a marketing strategy, appealing to a vague sense of fairness, than an effective deterrent.

For drivers, for example, I remain unable to see how the fear of $100–200 more in insurance premiums will yield safer driving habits where moral qualms, self-preservation interests, and fear of fines or losing a license have not. A concern about higher insurance rates surely will cause nonreporting and private settlement of small accident claims once crashes occur. But this is hardly the same thing as driving more safely in the first place.

My views concerning professionals are similar. Experience rating at least partially reintroduces the economic threat of tort law. Yet is it really plausible that experience rating will be effective where other control mechanisms have failed to overcome inhibitors such as discounting and incompetence? Anyway, for the most important group of professionals—physicians—experience rating appears to be a relatively trivial factor in determining the insurance premium the doctor pays; instead, speciality and location are the key determinants.[30]

Nonrenewal Threats

Even if a premium hike mattered little, the threat of cancellation might be more effective in promoting care. But, once again, given the realities of the insurance market, the risk that an insurer will drop an individual policyholder on safety grounds is small. Most reasons why insurers decide not to renew are irrelevant to individual deterrence. For example, nonrenewals occur because an insurer has decided to withdraw from a geographic market or to stop insuring a certain class of customers. These decisions, of course, are not made on an individual customer basis.

Occasionally, all standard insurers may suddenly adopt a broad nonrenewal stance toward a class of past customers. This happened in the 1970s, for example, both to physicians in certain geographic areas and to manufacturers of certain products. Again in the mid–1980s, a serious shortage of both product liability insurance and general-enterprise liability insurance developed. Midwives, child-care centers, municipal governments, and others suddenly found no one wanting their insurance business. While those disruptions can be exasperating, fear of them does not stimulate safer practices. This instability is largely unpredictable, and no single enterprise can do much to prevent it by improving its own safety record.

Any safety incentive must stem from the risk of nonrenewal that particular individuals and firms face because of their accident record. Even in the infrequent case where this threat is real,[31] insureds can usually find alternative comparable insurers. At worst, commercial customers will have to buy at higher rates in the "surplus and excess" market and motorists will have to use the higher cost "assigned risk" pool.

The prospect of having to buy in high-cost markets probably causes some firms to absorb small claims without involving their insurance companies. This behavior parallels the response of individual drivers to merit rating; they privately pay off small claims to avoid possibly increased premiums. As already noted, this response is hardly the same as modifying conduct to avoid harm in the first place.

Safety Requirements

Insurance companies themselves can take safety measures such as inspecting premises. More importantly, they can demand safety measures of insureds. For example, they can require employee-training courses and fire-control systems. Here, too, I am skeptical whether tort law significantly increases accident avoidance.

Apart from driver education, insurance companies rarely make safety-related demands before providing individual liability insurance. Professionals such as doctors, for example, are not regulated by their insurers. Likewise, insurers require enterprises to adopt few significant safety measures. Indeed, in the late 1970s the Interagency Task Force on Product Liability found that while the majority of insureds received some loss-prevention services from their insurers, most felt that the changes suggested were of "quite limited utility."[32] Eads and Reuter asked the firms they investigated whether they "received help from insurance companies in spotting underlying product safety problems. The universal responses were that they did not."[33] The most common examples in the literature come, not from liability insurance, but from first-party casualty (e.g., fire) insurance—sprinklers and fireproofing—or from workers' compensation—plant safety.

One explanation for insurer inaction is that individual insurance companies fear free riders. After determining how an insured could lower its tort exposure, a company might lose the business to a competitor who takes advantage of the results of such a study but can offer lower rates because it did not make the initial outlay. It is not easy for companies to legally protect the results of such surveys. In addition, insurers may conclude that government agencies have already uncovered most safety opportunities. Indeed, there is reason to believe that insurance inspectors rely on government safety standards rather than create their own. Finally, in many circumstances, product design problems, for example, the firms are usually far more expert than the insurers. Insurers may sometimes have better data, or earlier warning, than do individual firms about the accidents that competitors are experiencing with similar products or activities. But in view of widespread industry publications and conferences, this information advantage is most likely to arise only with small clients where the account size rarely warrants individualized safety attention.

This is not to say that insurers do not review safety practices before they decide to underwrite new business, at least when the enterprise is large. For example, insurers usually investigate quality-control practices, past recalls, and safety units. Nevertheless, no good evidence suggests that insureds take precautions in anticipation of these reports, or that rates significantly depend on them.

Recently, in a replay of the experience of the mid–1970s, now that the big rate increases of 1986–1987 have been absorbed, there is much less panic about product liability insurance. Again, competitive insurers have begun to reenter the market. In both the late 1970s and mid–1980s, a common complaint was that many insurers were primarily interested in reaping the benefits of investment income that the then high interest rates offered and were less concerned about underwriting losses. While that condition may not currently hold, it remains that insurance sales forces usually work on a commission basis, thus putting underwriters under enormous internal pressure to write any business—without requiring customers to incur extra safety expenses.

Contract Terms

Insurers can seek to influence the conduct of their insureds by the terms of the insurance contract. For example, policies typically provide that the insurance is unavailable if the insured fails to cooperate in the defense of a suit against him. With respect to preaccident conduct, policies might provide that insureds must maintain, say, product safety units; but I have seen nothing to indicate that policies actually contain such provisions.

Rather, the main thing that insurance contracts do that is relevant to safety is to exclude coverage, thereby making buyers self-insured to that extent. Deductibles have already been mentioned. Coinsurance (where the insured bears, for example, 20 percent of its liability) do not appear to be a common feature of liability insurance, although this is rather common in first-party health insurance, for example. Most significantly, insurers may either cap the amount of coverage they will offer or else exclude certain kinds of risks altogether. An important example of the latter is the risk that the insured will be held liable for pollution; this sort of protection is now nearly unavailable. Unfortunately, the most visible impact of exposing people and organizations to open-ended risks of liability, as I will discuss next in more detail, is the withdrawal of individuals and enterprises from socially productive activities. For example, many reputable enterprises will now go nowhere near the hazardous-waste disposal business (or related businesses where the risks of pollution liability are considerable) for fear that one slip (real or alleged) could bring financial ruin. This, of course, risks leaving such activities, not to the well-established firm with a reputation to protect and a large laboratory to draw on, but rather to the lightly capitalized newcomer, in it for a quick buck and hoping to get out before causing (or at least before getting into) trouble.

SOCIALLY UNDESIRABLE RESPONSES TO TORT LAW

By Injurers

I turn now to a general discussion of why the pressures the tort system creates have a socially negative impact. Perhaps the greatest concern is overdeterrence—that people may not enter into socially desirable activities that risk injury to others. The fear of lawsuits can cause well-trained and qualified people to avoid or flee the work they otherwise would prefer to do, or at least to resist innovation and reasonable risk taking on the job. For example, during the malpractice crises of the mid-1970s and the mid–1980s some competent doctors appear to have chosen to not enter or to have withdrawn from undersubscribed specialties where the risk of a malpractice suit was great. Obstetrics, where malpractice costs are rising especially fast, is the most prominent example.[34] There are also persistent reports of companies holding back new consumer products (such as child car-safety seats), or attempting to restrict the use of products, or ceasing to manufacture products (such as private light airplanes or football helmets), not because it is thought the products are or would be unreasonably dangerous, but because the firm chose to minimize the risk of getting caught up in what was perceived to be the tort lottery.[35] The uncertainty of tort liability seems a likely culprit here.

A second serious problem is that tort stimulates defendants and would-be defendants to take perverse action. Doctors are again a good example. They engage in an enormous amount of defensive medicine in the form of ordering more tests, gathering more information from patients, and making more records with a view toward creating ironclad defenses in the event of later malpractice suits. This probably wastes billions of taxpayer and insurance dollars annually.[36] Our payment system for financing medical care facilitates such abuse by giving neither patient nor doctor an incentive to curb costs. Although some defensive medicine may be desirable and actively improve patient care in an effective way, conduct motivated solely by fear of unwarranted lawsuits is not.[37] Moreover, it may actually result in injuries, as patients suffer side effects from unneeded tests and as nurses fail to attend patients while they are caught up in filling out forms. A parallel phenomenon is excessive product warnings that probably serve only to confuse the user. Indeed, Eads and Reuter found some drug companies knew they were overwarning in ways that reduced effectiveness; but they also believed such practices would reduce their exposure to suit.[38]

Besides resource waste through defensive strategies, injurers conceal their bad conduct after the fact.[39] Plaintiffs' lawyers tell many stories of conspiracies of silence, of shredding or hiding of crucial documents, and of dissembling in depositions. I concede that all such cover-ups do not occur in response to tort threats; there are many reasons for hiding your errors. Still, to the extent that tort does represent an additional threat, it presents an additional incentive for cover-up. A cover-up to avoid tort liability is not only morally objectionable, but it interferes with processes that correct behavior. Hence, a torts-motivated cover-up can block internal efforts of the enterprise, as well as efforts by regulatory agencies, to avoid injuries in the future.

Tort law can also discourage safety improvements in the face of pending liability. In product liability cases, defendants' safety improvements are clearly admissible in many jurisdictions.[40] And proof of a safer alternative is probably sufficient for plaintiffs' verdicts. In negligence cases, defendants fear that such efforts will suggest additional measures that could have been taken at the time of the accident. At a minimum, this fear breeds delay until old claims are disposed of.

Furthermore, defendants and their insurers have a strong financial interest in fighting claims, however meritorious. Giant enterprises who are repeat-player defendants may view aggressive litigation as a strategic investment aimed at avoiding a reputation of being an easy mark. Reviewing a broad survey of firms' attitudes toward tort law, Eads and Reuter concluded that most firms "consider the product liability problem serious enough to have taken specific organizational steps to deal with it."[41] It turns out, however, that much of the effort was directed at litigation control. Eads and Reuter report two additional litigation-driven strategies: keeping the firm's name off component parts to avoid identification and producing wasteful internal documentation that engineers thought unnecessary—but lawyers insisted on.[42]

Yet another consequence of plaintiffs' right to sue in tort is that defendants often perceive litigation as unjustified. As a result, managers and professionals become demoralized by participation in discovery and trial as well as by unfavorable outcomes. They often claim the tactics of plaintiffs' lawyers and the findings of uninformed jurors unjustly impugn their integrity, their product, or their reputation. To guard against this, "firms may choose to litigate for reasons of internal morale."[43]

Such demoralization occurs, for example, where workers are injured by machines whose safety features were disengaged at the workplace, often by the workers themselves, and then the workers sue the machine manufacturers. It is easy to see why the defendants in such cases feel abused. So, too, the demoralization problem is easy to appreciate when governmental agencies are liable for virtually all the damages in a case where they are a minor defendant. That happens to the Federal Aviation Administration, for example, when the air controllers are held negligent but the prime fault clearly lies with a not adequately solvent pilot of a private plane. To take another example, hospital staffs are acutely aware that parents of children born with unexpected birth defects tend to claim the medical team was responsible. From the hospitals' perspective, for medical advances that have saved the lives of a great many babies, instead of thanks, the profession gets many unwarranted suits—products of exaggerated expectations.[44] In general, malpractice law seems to have depressed or made cynics out of many doctors and has probably hurt doctor-patient trust relationships.[45]

To be sure, many would-be and actual defendants do not act in the undesirable ways I have described, and new measures might be taken to control some of this perverse behavior—such as an altered medical expense reimbursement system to combat unnecessary testing. Nonetheless, a vigorous tort system seems inevitably to carry with it the sorts of negative consequences I have discussed.

Some might wonder why I confidently point to negative responses to tort law while dismissing the prospect of positive behavior. My reasons are of two sorts. First, the existence of these costs seems well documented, even if their dimension is in considerable doubt. Second, and perhaps more important, the incentive structure is different. For tort law to work positively, a very imperfect control mechanism vaguely threatening ambiguous extra costs sometime in the future must achieve safety results beyond those already attained from many other forces working in the same direction. By contrast, the perverse conduct I have described largely occurs when someone is able to make a rather discretionary decision directly related to his job function that vividly promises the actor a clear gain in the short run.

By Victims

From the deterrence perspective, tort law's use of fault principles is also meant to stimulate safer conduct by would-be plaintiffs. Although some economic models predict overly dangerous victim conduct would result from eliminating the contributory fault rule,[46] their assumptions fail to account for real world factors. For example, these models ignore self-preservation instincts, which surely would have a far greater effect than a potentially reduced recovery. Moreover, the factors of ignorance, incompetence, discounting, and high stakes will affect victims' conduct just as they impact on injurers' behavior.[47]

Of even greater concern is that tort law creates perverse incentives for victims to exaggerate their injuries. In order to document such pretended harms, unscrupulous lawyers send clients to unethical doctors who run up large bills to certify phantom injuries. The victims may thus obtain better wage-loss settlements. More importantly, such medical expenses may lead to substantially enhanced payments for pain and suffering. Even without prompting, victims malinger because they can charge the costs to defendants and because they believe that a longer convalescence will increase their chances at trial.

Finally, some victims simply lie to create liability against an innocent defendant, manufacturing evidence of causation and fault. Indeed, the complete and apparent widespread fabrication of accidents is one of the unhappy products of the tort insurance industry. Of course, fabrication and exaggeration of what happened is not a problem unique to tort law, and any compensation or insurance scheme is likely to encounter this problem. Yet, given its lotterylike features, and the fact that a once-and-for-all determination is made, personal injury law is especially enticing on this count.

EMPIRICAL EVIDENCE ON TORT LAW AND SAFETY

My arguments have shown that the behavioral model connecting tort law and private conduct is more complicated and far less promising than usually suggested by apologists for the tort system as a deterrent. Yet, these arguments are not definitive. I have already conceded that existing regulatory, economic, moral, and self-preservation pressures fail to control all dangerous conduct that society would like to deter. Maybe in the end there are safety gains at the margin—small as I think they are—that outweigh the substantial negative consequences and the enormous administrative costs of the system. Thus, how much impact personal injury law has is an empirical question. Unfortunately, it is enormously difficult to design and execute research to answer this question.

Based on a review of the literature, I conclude that theorists who defend torts on deterrence grounds have no convincing empirical support for their position. As late as 1979, reviewing articles on the impact of tort law, Professor Robert Rabin discussed the promise of empirical work in terms indicating considerable dissatisfaction with anything yet produced.[48] Writing in 1981, professors Richard Posner and William Landes—the leading defenders of the tort-as-deterrent position—surely would have cited at least all the available favorable evidence. However, what they offer is thin.[49] By 1987, when they published their book, *The Economic Structure of Tort Law*, Landes and Posner had little to add; what they do present is rather one-sided, and, I believe, they are too optimistic in their interpretation of much of what they cite, most of which I next discuss.[50]

Two fairly recent survey research efforts involved large-scale investigations into the impact of specific, celebrated torts cases on professionals—

eye doctors and therapists. On balance, their findings on the impact of legal changes on behavior are inconclusive.[51] Eads and Reuter's research design, as earlier noted, involved intensive interviews at a small number of large firms. They claim their research showed that "the product liability system is probably the most fundamental determinant of the incentives for product safety"; yet, they found that "product safety officers were unable to identify more than a few relatively minor legal decisions that had directly impinged on design and production criteria for the firm."[52] Even more striking, Eads and Reuter found that "[a]ll the firms viewed product liability litigation as essentially a random influence, generating no clear signals as to how to adjust design behavior."[53] If big firms respond to the risk of product liability in this manner, one should despair over tort law as a deterrent because this is the very context where tort is most promising.

Of course, with many business leaders engaged in a campaign to modify products liability law in their favor, interviewees in the Eads and Reuter study had reason to downplay the role of tort in shaping their behavior. This problem plagues any survey research. Therefore, rather than relying on interviews, a few researchers have looked at external evidence of behavior.

Of greatest interest here are the few empirical studies on the impact of tort law that have used econometric techniques. Interestingly enough, all such studies I have found have sought to investigate the impact of tort law in the auto accident area where I would predict the prospects for stimulating safer conduct are extremely weak. Nonetheless, three authors have claimed positive results. Elizabeth Landes investigated highway fatalities in states where auto no-fault plans were enacted and found that, holding other variables constant, auto fatality rates rise as no-fault plans do away with an increasingly large share of tort suits.[54] Richard Grayston probed the impact on drivers of auto liability insurance-pricing practices and found that, other things being equal, states with higher average liability insurance rates have fewer cars registered.[55] Professor Marc Gaudry studied Quebec's introduction of a sweeping auto no-fault plan and linked Quebec's shift to no-fault with a sharp increase in auto accidents.[56]

There are two deeply unsatisfying things with studies such as these. First, their results (suggesting that eliminating tort liability will lead to more accidents) have not been confirmed by other studies. These include one by Paul Zador and Adrian Lund that, in effect, redid the E. Landes effort using what they believe is a better model and that discredited Landes's findings.[57] Another study that found no support for the proposition that no-fault plans lead to more auto fatalities and injuries was prepared by the U.S. Department of Transportation as part of its 1984 follow-up study on auto no-fault insurance.[58] Finally, Paul Kochanowski and Madelyn Young found that there was "no foundation whatsoever" for the fears that no-fault insurance leads to a "dramatic escalation of fatal accidents."[59]

Second, and for me ultimately more important, the studies by E. Landes, Grayston, and Gaudry are incapable of providing proof that people drive worse as the law and/or their auto premiums become less fault based. Rather, these studies at best could well be showing that when the price of driving decreases, people drive more and, in turn, have more accidents. In Quebec, for example, the auto no-fault plan sharply lowered the driving costs of teenagers. Presumably, we already know about the impact of price on the quantity of driving, not only from common sense, but from the two big OPEC-induced oil price rises of the recent past. However, this is not what interests us here. After all, if we want to reduce auto accidents by discouraging driving, we could tax gasoline more or raise car registration fees (and such fee increases could be targeted at those we want most to discourage, such as teenagers). The issue is the quality of driving—whether tort law with traditional insurance arrangements causes individuals to drive more safely. No study I have found has demonstrated this to be true.

My skepticism about the effectiveness of current tort law in influencing the accident rate was recently confirmed by a simpler, yet equally telling, empirical examination of product liability law by Professor George Priest. Noting the tremendous recent growth in the scope and cost of product liability law, Professor Priest hypothesized that if this branch of tort law were well tuned to accident reduction, the change in tort law should show up in various time series data concerning deaths and injuries. However, having examined those data that are available (concerning deaths by accident type, worker job deaths and disabling injuries, and product-related injuries requiring emergency room treatment), he could find no such impact.[60]

CONCLUSION

I have provided many explanations for why tort law is unlikely to promote significantly more desirable behavior than that which would occur in its absence. These impugn the usual economic models, because they indicate those models do not adequately take account of many important factors. I have also described various bad consequences of tort law. In the absence of convincing data on deterrence, there is no reason to conclude that personal injury law and its baggage yield a net social gain. Given its enormous administrative costs, it is reasonable to conclude that the system is operating in the red. To be sure, the points I have made apply more to some areas than to others. Yet tort has its greatest theoretical potential where regulation is already most concentrated. In short, I do not advocate that society abandon behavior control, but rather that new nontorts approaches be tried. For example, as I will discuss later, society might try trading five lawyers for a highway engineer and a dangerous-product public information officer. We would not only save money, but we might get considerably better accident protection to boot.

In this vein, it is perhaps worth speculating how much accident avoidance would have to be achieved to make the costs of the tort system worth its benefits on safety grounds. Writing in the medical malpractice field, Professor Patricia Danzon suggests, as a rough approximation, a one-for-one relationship. That is, for torts to pay, there would have to be one medical accident (of equal severity) avoided for every one compensated by the tort system.[61] She arrives at her estimate on the basis that, whereas eighty cents of each first-party insurance dollar reaches victims as compensation, only forty cents, she says, of each malpractice liability insurance dollar does. The extra forty cents in transactions costs, equal to the forty cents of compensation benefits paid from malpractice insurance premiums, yields her one-for-one conclusion.

Yet if different, and I believe more reasonable, assumptions are made, the ratio quickly looks altogether different. For example, if more pessimistic estimates of malpractice insurance overhead costs are made, and payments for pain and suffering and duplicate payments for economic loss otherwise compensated from other sources are disregarded, then one can conclude that only about 10 percent of medical malpractice premium dollars reach victims as compensation for out-of-pocket losses, as compared with Danzon's 80 percent figure for traditional first-party insurance. On this basis, presumably, seven accidents must be avoided for every one compensated in order for deterrence to pay. But this is just the start. In addition, there must be added all of the previously described noninsurance and undesirable social costs that tort law causes, plus the otherwise socially desirable costs of accident avoidance, if any, that are incurred as a result of tort law. Altogether, this could easily double the ratio to fourteen to one or more—that is, fourteen or more medical accidents avoided because of malpractice liability fears for every one compensated. Similar calculations could be made for other sectors of tort liability and the ratios there are likely to be equally bad. Moreover, in other areas, relatively speaking, more victims are now compensated by tort, thus requiring even more effective deterrence by Danzon's test. The idea that tort law might deter that many medical or other accidents seems to be very much wishful thinking to me.

NOTES

1. It is not suggested that society should deter conduct on the basis of danger alone; some risks, because of the benefits they create, are socially acceptable. Safety at any cost is an empty slogan. Avoiding all accidents would restrict our behavior and lower our standard of living in unacceptable ways, for example, by forcing a ban on automobiles and airplanes.

2. One giant in this movement is Dean Guido Calabresi. Although a critic of many aspects of existing tort law, he advocates decentralized, cost-internalizing tort reform or tortlike mechanisms that depend for their justification on their deterrent effect. *See* his enormously influential book, G. CALABRESI, THE COSTS OF

ACCIDENTS (1970). Professor, now judge, Richard Posner is another giant in the law and economics field. Most take his writing to represent a broad defense of current tort law on deterrence grounds. In fact, Judge Posner's writings have undergone some change. By now it is no longer clear whether his "theory" is (1) as most have assumed, a largely positive model of how tort law actually shapes behavior, (2) a normative model of who deserves to bear the costs of accidents, (3) a predictive model intended to explain how judges have decided and will decide cases, and/or (4) a descriptive model that allows one to imagine much of tort doctrine as having been shaped as if it were trying to promote an efficient level of accidents. *Cf.* Posner, *A Theory of Negligence* 1 J. LEGAL STUD. 29 (1972) with Posner, *The Ethical and Political Basis of the Efficiency Norm in Common Law Adjudication*, 8 HOFSTRA L. REV. 487 (1980) and Landes and Posner, *The Positive Economic Theory of Tort Law*, 15 GA. L. REV. 851 (1981). *See generally* W. LANDES and R. POSNER, THE ECONOMIC STRUCTURE OF TORT LAW (1987). Other important recent contributions to this literature include S. SHAVELL, ECONOMIC ANALYSIS OF ACCIDENT LAW (1987) and R. COOTER and T. ULEN, LAW AND ECONOMICS 326–476 (1988). For an important earlier discussion of tort law and deterrence, *see* Williams, *The Aims of the Law of Tort*, 4 CURRENT LEGAL PROBS. 137, 144–51 (1951).

3. The reader should bear in mind that some commentators accept my criticisms yet argue, not for the abolition of personal injury law, but for its increased effectiveness as a behavioral control mechanism. Others, while favoring abolishing the current system insist on replacing it with one or more accident compensation schemes whose financing is linked to the sources of injuries in order to promote safety. For reasons detailed later, I reject both these reforms. Still others, of course, rest their defense of tort on considerations other than deterrence; hence, they are largely indifferent to this issue.

4. Others have also cataloged factors undercutting tort's role as a deterrent. Together these writings evaluate tort law in the United States and other common law countries. *See* for example D. HARRIS, M. MACLEAN, H. GENN, S. LLOYD-BOSTOCK, P. FENN, P. CORFIELD, and U. BRITTAN, COMPENSATION AND SUPPORT FOR ILLNESS AND INJURY 328 (1984) ("Deterrence of carelessness operates in a random way."); T. ISON, THE FORENSIC LOTTERY 89 (1967) ([T]he value of tort liability as a deterrent . . . is thought on the whole to be negligible."); Brown, *Deterrence and Accident Compensation Schemes*, 17 U.W. ONT. L. REV. 111, 153 (1978) ("[T]he tort liability system appears to offer at most minimal deterrence."); Fleming, *Is There a Future for Tort?*, 58 AUSTL. L.J. 131, 134 (1984) ("[O]ne must be skeptical about the effectiveness of tort law in promoting accident prevention."); and E. BERNZWEIG, BY ACCIDENT NOT DESIGN 65–71 (1980).

5. Lambert, *Suing for Safety*, TRIAL, Nov. 1983, at 48. Professor Lambert is one of the most ardent defenders of tort law. His spirited writings for the publications of the Association of Trial Lawyers of America unmistakably paint plaintiff lawyers as the good guys in white hats—leaders of a populist revolution against the excesses of large-scale organizations that dominate American capitalism.

6. Professor Lambert, perhaps conscious of this methodological problem, makes this odd statement: "An error does not become a mistake unless you refuse to correct it," *id.* at 56. But surely he is not suggesting that in any of his examples the defendants

were blameless; surely, he believes that all these harms were reasonably foreseeable and easily correctable before any injury occurred.

I recognize, of course, that once conduct is determined to be unreasonably dangerous, it is socially desirable for it to stop. Hence, a fall-back defense of tort as deterrent would argue that at least it functions to identify and halt such ongoing activity. This is perhaps closer to what Professor Lambert had in mind because the practices in his examples did change. Nevertheless, there are problems of proof here, because he cannot show from his evidence that it was tort law that induced these changes. It is certainly possible that general publicity and customer feedback prompted such improvements. Consider his discussion of a Parker Brothers toy that included small rubber parts on which two children had choked to death. After the second death, Parker Brothers recalled the product. Professor Lambert says,

The company was sensitive not only to the constraints of the law . . . but also to the imperatives of moral duty and social responsibility, and the commercial value of an untarnished public image. . . . The commendable conduct of Parker Brothers in this case is one of the most striking tributes we know to the deterrent value and efficacy of Tort Law, *id.* at 55.

I find this wholly unpersuasive. What proves tort law mattered at all in this case?

In the same vein, without providing evidence of its impact, Professor Joseph Little sees tort law as a mechanism society uses to "regulate behavior predictably and guard its members against the ravages of extreme antisocial conduct," Little, *Up with Torts*, 24 SAN DIEGO L. REV. 861, 863 (1987).

Although the posture of the plaintiffs' bar is predictable, that advocates on behalf of consumer interests should also support tort on deterrence grounds is disheartening in view of the lack of evidence in support of this position. *See for example Hearings Before the House Econ. Subcomm. on Stabilization of the House Comm. on Banking, Fin. and Urban Affairs*, 99th Cong., 2nd Sess. (Aug. 6, 1986) (testmony of Ralph Nader). An accompanying report by Nader's Public Citizen, *The Assault on Personal Injury Lawsuits: A Study of Reality Versus Myths*, Aug. 1986, also broadly claims that tort deters while at the same time providing evidence that the liability insurance industry, in fact, now makes precious little effort to promote safety.

7. G. EADS and P. REUTER, DESIGNING SAFER PRODUCTS: CORPORATE RESPONSES TO PRODUCT LIABILITY LAW AND REGULATION ix (1983) (Rand Corporation Institute for Civil Justice). The Eads and Reuter monograph presents both a review of prior work and the results of their own research. Eads and Reuter interviewed executives concerned with safety at some twelve large enterprises. The interviews lasted for at least an hour, often for several hours. They report that they decided not to expand their sample because after a dozen interviews they "seemed to be traversing worn ground," *id.* at 90.

8. *Id.* at 94. By contrast, operational decisions in these firms were quite responsive to regulatory commands.

9. Even professionals, who are generally aware of their potential liability, may be unaware of specific, required standards of conduct. Professor Daniel Givelber and his colleagues confirmed this point through an empirical study of the California Supreme Court's decisions in Tarasoff v. Regents of University of California. Tarasoff v. Regents of the Univ. of Cal., 13 Cal. 3d 177, 529 P.2d 553, 118 Cal. Rptr. 129 (1974) [*hereinafter cited as Tarasoff I*]; Tarasoff v. Regents of the Univ. of Cal., 17 Cal. 3d 425, 551 P.2d 334, 131 Cal. Rptr. 14 (1976) [*hereinafter cited as Tarasoff*

II]. *See* Givelber, Bowers, and Blitch, *Tarasoff, Myth and Reality: An Empirical Study of Private Law in Action*, WIS. L. REV. 443 (1984). The case involved the duty of a therapist to protect a would-be victim at risk from a dangerous patient. The authors recognized that their survey of therapists could not tell us what the respondents did in actuality, but rather only what they said they did. Nonetheless, they tried to minimize this potential gap between reported and actual behavior. In addition, they employed a large sample: more than 1700 therapists responded to their questionnaire. Professional awareness of the *Tarasoff* case was, in the authors' view, astoundingly high. Over 75 percent of therapists had heard of *Tarasoff* or a case like it. Nevertheless, the authors found that the typical therapist did not understand the case in two important respects. First the professionals seemed to equate the law with the subsequently withdrawn Tarasoff I, interpreting tort law as requiring them to warn the victim. In fact, in the revised *Tarasoff II,* the court held that "reasonable conduct" was the appropriate standard. In other words, the therapist's duty might be met through other behavior, such as warning the police. Second, some therapists seemed to believe the *Tarasoff* court required action whenever the patient made a threat. In fact, the *Tarasoff II* opinion adopted the lawyerly, perhaps nebulous, idea of a duty to act reasonably in the face of impending danger. This duty might exist without an actual threat and might not exist even if a threat were made. The California law in this area has since been altered by statute, *see* Cal. Civil Code §§ 43.92 (West 1986 Supp.)

10. Campbell, *Enterprise Liability—An Adjustment of Priorities*, 10 FORUM 1231, 1235–36 (1975).

11. *See* Latin, *Problem-Solving Behavior and Theories of Tort Liability*, 73 CALIF. L. REV. 677, 682–696 (1985). For another effective and more recent attack on the lack of reality of many law and economics models, *see* Latin, *Activity Levels, Due Care, and Selective Realism in Economic Analysis of Tort Law*, 39 RUTGERS L. REV. 487 (1987). I note, however, that Professor Latin would do away with less of tort law than I would.

12. Manuele, *Product Safety Program Management*, 2 J. PROD. LIAB. 98 (1978). For an admission of the past ineffectiveness of risk management strategies in the hospital setting and a call for better efforts, *see* AMERICAN HOSPITAL ASS'N, MEDICAL MALPRACTICE TASK FORCE REPORT ON TORT REFORM 12–13, 44–46 (1986). Further evidence comes from a study by professors Twerski and Weinstein and their colleagues who carefully examined the design process in four firms selected because of their reputation for product safety. *See generally* A. WEINSTEIN, A. TWERSKI, H. PIEHLER, and W. DONAHER, PRODUCTS LIABILITY AND THE REASONABLY SAFE PRODUCT (1978) and Twerski, Weinstein, Donaher, and Piehler, *Shifting Perspectives in Products Liability: From Quality to Process Standards*, 55 N.Y.U.L. REV. 347 (1980). Their purpose was to explore the utility of a process defense in product liability cases. Even in these firms, the authors were disappointed in what they discovered. None of the companies' processes included every element the authors saw as important. Of course, maybe the authors were too demanding; perhaps the extra elements they sought would make no real difference in terms of outcomes. They did not explore that issue. Indeed, they could not even tell us whether the processes in place were responsive to tort law.

13. *See* Siliciano, *Corporate Behavior and the Social Efficiency of Tort Law*, 88 MICH. L. REV. 1820, 1844–45 (1987).

14. In a recent survey of large U.S. corporations, the Conference Board found that 20 percent were subject to more than thirty suits annually and 14 percent were sued more than 100 times annually. N. WEBER, PRODUCT LIABILITY: THE CORPORATE RESPONSE 8 (1987) (Conference Board Report No. 893).

15. *See* Calabresi and Klevorik, *Four Tests for Liability in Torts*, 14 J. LEGAL STUD. 585, 617 (1985).

16. Ford, *The Fault with "No Fault,"* 61 A.B.A.J. 1071, 1072 (1975).

17. For further discussion of the puny power of the tort system against irresponsible producers, *see* Siliciano, *supra* note 13, at 1849–50.

18. G. EADS and P. REUTER, *supra* note 7, at 30–31. Consistent with this finding, Professor Patricia Danzon (then Munch) found in 1976, after sharp rate increases, that "even an upper bound estimate of full product liability costs" was "less than 0.5 percent" of "net domestic income of the non-financial corporate business sector," *see* P. MUNCH, COSTS AND BENEFITS OF THE TORTS SYSTEM IF VIEWED AS A COMPENSATION SYSTEM 12 (1977) (Rand Corporation Institute for Civil Justice). Eads and Reuter concluded that in 1984 "for most large manufacturing firms, product liability costs . . . probably amount[ed] to much less than 1 percent of total sales revenue," G. EADS and P. REUTER, *supra* note 7, at 121. Eads and Reuter also report that product liability premium income was about $1.3 billion in 1980 versus $23 billion in workers' compensation premium income that year, *id.* at 136.

19. *See generally* Harrington, *Prices and Profits in the Liability Insurance Industry* in LIABILITY: PERSPECTIVES AND POLICY (R. LITAN and C. WINSTON, eds.) 42 (1988).

20. WEBER, *supra* note 14, at 13.

21. Professor Peter Bell reports studies that negate the supposition that a doctor will lose substantial numbers of patients because he or she has been sued for malpractice and/or lost a malpractice case, *see* Bell, *Legislative Intrusions into the Common Law of Medical Malpractice: Thoughts about the Deterrent Effect of Tort Liability*, 35 SYRC. L. REV. 939, 957 n. 84 (1984). On the other hand, Bell explains why doctors have an exaggerated fear of the malpractice threat, *id.* at 975–90. Whether this fear gets translated into socially desirable or undesirable conduct, of course, is another question. I will shortly discuss what I see as the undesirable consequences.

22. The Conference Board recently found, for example, that "in only one out of ten companies is the performance rating of a department head dependent, even in part, on product-liability claims brought against the firm," *id.* at 20.

23. Fleming, *The Role of Negligence in Modern Tort Law*, 53 VA. L. REV. 815, 823 (1967).

24. It is useful to consider why liability insurance is permitted at all. Without insurance, the fear of an enormous judgment could have socially undesirable impacts. Many individuals, for example, might abandon driving because of the risk that they might be held liable for an enormous injury despite their care. In addition, the risk of losing one's capital as a result of an enormous tort liability might deter the formation of small businesses. Most would agree that these examples represent overdeterrence—the undesirable squelching of socially acceptable behavior.

At the same time, were there no insurance, other segments of the population might engage in even more discounting. These actors would either disregard the prospect of tort liability or else rashly assume that they could somehow maneuver out of any lawsuits. This denial approach to potential liability undermines its role as a deterrent. Besides, many would find it socially objectionable for risk averse people to shoulder the behavioral consequences of such a system.

By contrast, large enterprises could deal sensibly with the unavailability of liability insurance through self-insurance. Some could absorb even the largest losses they might plausibly anticipate. One probable consequence, therefore, would be the formation of more large enterprises. Doctors might form huge partnerships. Many individual store owners would seek to become chain store outlets. Yet such structural changes motivated solely by risk-spreading concerns may be socially unwelcome. Indeed, American economic policy for many reasons has favored small- and medium-size enterprises. Thus, liability insurance is probably thought important simply because it counters such pressures toward economic concentration.

There is also a fairness argument for allowing liability insurance. Bad luck, rather than bad conduct, often generates enormous liability. Thus, absent insurance, people would pay damages out of proportion to their wrongdoing. In addition, it would be thought unfair by many to preclude insurance when liability is imposed on a nonfault basis, as, for example, in many product injury cases.

25. Corporate liability insurance, however, is frequently sold with a deductible, and the amount of the typical deductible appears to be growing. *See* N. WEBER, *supra* note 14 at 6.

26. Some have estimated that, in terms of dollars, a third or more of the commercial liability insurance market is self-insured. *See* Priest, *The Current Insurance Crisis and Modern Tort Law*, 96 YALE L.J. 1521, 1527 n. 34, 1570 n. 193 (1987).

27. Eads and Reuter's study suggests that 43 percent of premium income (obviously representing the great bulk of insureds) comes from policies that are not experience rated, G. EADS and P. REUTER, *supra* note 7, at 25. Generally speaking, a firm must have annual liability insurance premiums of more than $2500 before experience rating can even begin to apply, *see* INSURANCE SERVICE OFFICE, GENERAL LIABILITY EXPERIENCE AND SCHEDULE RATING PLAN 1 (1983). This generally requires annual sales of more than $2.5 million. In the analogous field of workers' compensation insurance, it has been estimated that one-quarter of employers have experience-rated premiums, J. CHELIUS, WORKPLACE SAFETY AND HEALTH 26 (1977).

28. In 1977, the Interagency Task Force on Product Liability concluded that insurance rates provided inadequate incentives for firms to undertake liability-prevention programs. *See* 1 INTER-AGENCY TASK FORCE ON PROD. LIAB., FINAL REPORT OF THE INSURANCE STUDY (1977). Professor Terrence Ison has argued that "there is no real evidence that experience ratings have been beneficial in reducing accident rates," T. ISON, *supra* note 4, at 93. For detailed descriptions of liability insurance rating and pricing practices, *see* AMERICAN INS. ASS'N, PRODUCT LIABILITY INSURANCE: UNDERWRITING, RATES, RESERVES, BUSINESS CYCLES 34–53 (1979) and TASK FORCE ON PROD. LIAB. & ACCIDENT COMPENSATION, U.S. DEP'T OF COMMERCE, REPORT ON PRODUCT LIABILITY INSURANCE RATEMAKING, 32–96 (1980) [hereinafter cited as TASK FORCE].

29. G. EADS and P. REUTER, *supra* note 7, at 110. For Bernzweig's comments

on the many unscientific facts that influence insurance pricing *see* BERNZWEIG, *supra* note 4, at 124–33.

30. Professor Danzon found, for example, that specialty alone accounted for half the variation in doctors' premiums. P. DANZON, WHY ARE MALPRACTICE PREMIUMS SO HIGH—OR SO LOW? 31–33 (1980) (Rand Corporation Institute for Civil Justice).

See also Bell, *supra* note 21, at 954–57. Professor Bell found that even those medical malpractice insurers he found in New York State who had a policy of surcharging doctors with bad records only rarely did so. He concluded: "Thus tort law gives the doctor no financial incentive to behave more safely," *id.* at 957. Bell suggests that malpractice insurance is not experience rated because doctors do not want it to be, and that their objection may be rooted in "the widely held belief [by doctors] that malpractice suits and awards bear little relation to the existence of negligence by the defendant doctors," *id.* at 964.

For an up-to-date report on Florida where malpractice insurance rates do not take into account a doctor's past record, *see* Nye, Gifford, Webb, and Dewar, *The Causes of the Medical Malpractice Crisis: An Analysis of Claims Data and Insurance Company Finances*, 76 GEORGETOWN L.J. 1495, 1530–36 (1988). The authors of that article also found that nearly half of the total payout for medical malpractice claims between 1975–1986 was accounted for by the 4 percent of Florida physicians (867 in total) with two or more paid claims. They noted that 3229 physicians experienced one paid claim during this period, *id.* at 1558.

31. A *Consumer Reports* survey found that only a tiny proportion of auto insureds—1 percent—faced nonrenewal in the past three years for any reason. *See Auto Insurance: Which Companies Are Best*, 49 CONSUMER REPORTS 506, 508 (Sept. 1984). Admittedly, the respondents to Consumer Union's 1983 Annual Questionnaire probably face nonrenewal less frequently than the public at large.

32. G. EADS and P. REUTER, *supra* note 7, at 28.

33. *Id.* at 111.

34. A report of the American Medical Association (AMA) claims that a substantial portion of physicians are now turning away high-risk patients and are refusing to do high-risk procedures. The Florida Medical Association reported that 25 percent of the state's obstetrician–gynecologists no longer deliver babies for fear of malpractice claims, the national figure is said to be 12.3 percent. According to one survey, more than 60 percent of all obstetrician-gynecologists in the country have been sued at least once, 20 percent of them more than three times, *see The 'Crisis' in Medical Malpractice Suits*, *San Francisco Chron.*, Jan. 18, 1985, at 46, col. 3 and ALLIANCE OF AMERICAN INSURERS, CIVIL JUSTICE REFORM DATA 7 (1986). For physicians generally, there were 17.8 malpractice claims per 100 doctors in 1985 (up from 7.9 in 1976), AMERICAN HOSPITAL ASS'N, *supra* note 12 at 1. In California, claims per 100 physicians increased to 26 in 1984 and exceeded 50 per 100 doctors in four specialities—obstetrics-gynecology, orthopedic surgery, neurosurgery, and plastic surgery, GENERAL ACCOUNTING OFFICE, MEDICAL MALPRACTICE: CASE STUDY ON CALIFORNIA 13–14 (1988). According to the General Accounting Office (GAO), annual malpractice premiums for obstetrics-gynecology rose nationally 72 percent between 1982 and 1984 to $16,800, GENERAL ACCOUNTING OFFICE, MEDICAL MALPRACTICE: INSURANCE COSTS INCREASED BUT VARIED AMONG PHYSICIANS

AND HOSPITALS 27 (1986). For 1986 in California, according to the GAO, basic rates for such doctors were being quoted in the $36,000–43,000 range, GAO, CASE STUDY ON CALIFORNIA, *supra* at 12–13. In Dade and Broward counties in Florida, average insurance rates for obstetrics jumped to nearly $100,000 in 1986 and to over $165,000 by July 1987. For the rest of the state, the numbers were about $60,000 and over $87,000 for the two periods. *See* Nye, Gifford, Webb, and Dewar, *supra* note 30 at 1501. Yet another GAO study shows that obstetrics accounts for 10 percent of the malpractice claims and 27 percent of the indemnity payments made, GAO, MEDICAL MALPRACTICE: CHARACTERISTICS OF CLAIMS CLOSED IN 1984 39, table 3.1 (1987). *See also* Shavell, *Theoretical Issues in Medical Malpractice*, in THE ECONOMICS OF MEDICAL MALPRACTICE (S. ROT-TENBERG, ed.) 35, 52 (1978) (concerning the problem of patient selection bias); Zeckhauser and Nichols, *Lessons from the Economics of Safety*, *id.* at 25 (explaining the phenomenon of doctors who do not perform certain treatment). Of course, if poor or inefficient doctors were selectively driven from practice by tort law, that would be another matter. But there is no good evidence that this is so.

Bell, *supra* note 21, at 961–62 discusses the lack of evidence on this issue and the conflicting surmises that can be drawn about safety if high malpractice premiums (1) cause part-time doctors to retire (or practice full-time) and/or (2) cause doctors to concentrate their practice more than they would otherwise, with some leaving high-risk specialities for other types of practice.

35. Priest, *supra* note 26 at 1565–68; G. EADS and P. REUTER, *supra* note 7, at 4, 107; S. CARROLL and N. PACE, ASSESSING THE EFFECTS OF TORT REFORMS 33 (1987) (Rand Corporation Institute for Civil Justice); and INTER-AGENCY TASK FORCE ON PRODUCT LIABILITY, BRIEFING REPORT 9–10 (1977). But perhaps too much has been made of the product withdrawal claim; *see* WEBER, *supra* note 14 at 14–15, who found that, while a quarter of large firms said they withdrew a product or service because of product liability considerations, the actual amount of reported firm revenue lost as a result was quite small.

36. *See* for example Rottenberg, *Introduction*, in THE ECONOMICS OF MED-ICAL MALPRACTICE (S. ROTTENBERG, ed.) 1, 11 (1978) and Shavell, *id.* at 49 (for an economist's explanation of this phenomenon). For an empirical description *see* Greenwald and Mueller, *Medical Malpractice and Medical Costs*, *id.* at 83. AMA reports put the cost of defensive medicine at between $15 and $40 billion annually, *see* AMERICAN MEDICAL ASSOCIATION, COMMITTEE ON PROFES-SIONAL LIABILITY, STUDY OF PROFESSIONAL LIABILITY COSTS (1983) and STUDY OF PROFESSIONAL LIABILITY PROBLEMS (1984). *See also* AMERICAN HOSPITAL ASS'N, *supra* note 12, at 5.

37. Professor Jerry Wiley conducted a study in which he sought to measure the impact of the Washington Supreme Court's decision in Helling v. Carey, 83 Wash. 2d 514, 519 P.2d 981 (1974), superseded by statute, as stated in Meeks v. Marx, 15 Wash. App. 571, 550 P.2d 1158 (1976). *See* Wiley, *The Impact of Judicial Decisions on Professional Conduct: An Empirical Study*, 55 S. CAL. L. REV. 345, 369 (1981). The Washington court had held that it was malpractice not to test for glaucoma in patients under forty years of age, despite prevailing medical practice.

The case was celebrated both because it rejected medical custom as the standard for malpractice and because of a concurring opinion suggesting that the case was better seen as imposing strict liability on doctors. Wiley saw this as a good occasion to test whether a well-publicized, high court opinion aimed at a well-defined target group influenced conduct. However, the survey showed that, contrary to the court's belief, the practice of testing patients under forty for glaucoma was widespread in Washington before the *Helling* decision. This drastically reduced the potential for the case to influence behavior.

In any event, Wiley found that while testing for the under forty group did increase somewhat in Washington after *Helling*, it also increased in states not governed by *Helling*. Indeed, after *Helling*, Washington's testing rate was less than that of many states. And it seems clear from Wiley's findings that after *Helling*, the under forty group in Washington and elsewhere is still tested less often than is the over forty group. Wiley further concluded that he could not show that *Helling* had caused an increased proportion of Washington opthalmologists to test younger patients routinely for glaucoma. Wiley believes that *Helling* did increase the amount of testing that Washington opthalmologists did, but only in quite minor ways. He concludes, "The survey data seem to cast doubt on the assumption that appellate court decisions are able to change the standard of practice," *id.* at 385. Moreover—and this is the key point here—it remains uncertain whether the minor increase in testing in fact was socially desirable or merely another defensive response.

38. G. EADS and P. REUTER, *supra* note 7, at 107–09. The study of the impact of the *Tarasoff* decisions, discussed earlier, suggests this same overwarning problem in a professional setting. The authors conclude that as a result of *Tarasoff*, therapists now give warnings contradicted by their clinical judgment, *see* Givelber, Bowers, and Blitch, *supra* note 9, at 470.

39. *See* for example, Delgado and Vogel, *To Tell the Truth: Physicians' Duty to Disclose Medical Mistakes*, 28 U.C.L.A. L. REV. 52 (1980).

40. For the two leading California decisions, see Shelbauer v. Butler Mfg. Co., 35 Cal. 3d 442, 673 P.2d 743, 198 Cal. Rptr. 155 (1984) and Ault v. International Harvester Co., 13 Cal. 3d 113, 528 P.2d 1148, 117 Cal. Rptr. 812 (1974).

41. G. EADS and P. REUTER, *supra* note 7, at 74.

42. In 1978, the Conference Board received 300 responses to a survey on products liability and product safety. The respondents came from the 2000 largest companies in the country. Although the survey found that many big firms recently had set up formal product safety programs, the programs' primary responsibilities were managing litigation and interacting with regulatory agencies, *id.* at 107, 109.

43. *Id.* at 133.

44. *See* AMERICAN HOSPITAL ASS'N, *supra* note 12, at 4–5.

45. *See id.* at 8, discussing Dr. Sara Charles's study of doctors who have been sued.

46. *See* Landes and Posner, *The Positive Economic Theory of Tort Law*, *supra* note 2, at 876, 77, 880–83; *see also* Schwartz, *Contributory and Comparative Negligence: A Reappraisal*, 87 YALE L.J. 697 (1978).

47. *Cf.* Priest, *Modern Tort Law and Its Reform*, 22 VALPARAISO L. REV. 1, 10–14 (1987). Professor Priest argues, and I agree, that in many circumstances the consumer is better able than the product manufacturer to prevent accidents. He is also right to assert that current tort doctrine too often seems based on the opposite assumption. But it is an altogether different thing to believe, as Priest seems to, that, by denying victims compensation, tort law can importantly influence them to exercise more care in their use of products.

48. *See* Rabin, *Impact Analysis and Tort Law: A Comment*, 13 LAW & SOC'Y REV. 987 (1979). As Rabin ably shows in his review, much of the research on tort law's impact has little relevance to our question.

49. Posner and W. Landes refer to two "unpublished" studies, one by R. Grayston, Deterrence in Automobile Liability Insurance (1971) (unpublished Ph.D. thesis, University of Chicago Graduate School of Business), the other by E. Landes, Insurance, Liability and Accidents: A Theoretical and Empirical Investigation of the Effect of No-Fault on Accidents (1980) (University of Chicago Center for the Study of the Economy and the State). In 1985, Posner was still citing only those two studies. Posner, *Can Lawyers Solve the Problems of the Tort System?*, 75 CALIF. L. REV. 747, 749 nn. 12–13 (1985). Both studies have been published and are discussed shortly. *See also* Bruce, *The Deterrent Effects of Automobile Insurance and Tort Law: A Survey of the Empirical Literature*, 6 LAW & POLICY 67 (1984), which, although it reports on lots of other kinds of empirical study, finds only the Grayston and E. Landes study looked at the connection between tort law (more precisely auto insurance premiums) and conduct.

50. W. LANDES and R. POSNER, THE ECONOMIC STRUCTURE OF TORT LAW 10–11 (1987).

51. *See* Givelber, Bowers, and Blitch, *supra* note 9 (therapists); Wiley, *supra* note 37 (opthalmologists). For a discussion of Wiley's work and other surveys that sees in them more powerful evidence than I do for the proposition that the threat of tort liability promotes desirable behavior by physicians, *see* Bell, *supra* note 21, at 965–73.

For example, when, according to one survey Professor Bell reports, 91 percent of doctors who say they increased the frequency of amniocentesis testing for pregnant women over age thirty-five say they did so because of the patient's best interest, and when 70 percent of these same respondents say they did so because they believed they would be liable in a malpractice suit if they did not, I am highly skeptical that this fear of malpractice liability is an important cause of any doctor's behavior.

52. G. EADS and P. REUTER, *supra* note 7, at ix. More precisely, Eads and Reuter say, "[W]e encountered only one case in which the loss of a major suit might have been the proximate cause for the firm's establishing its product safety effort," *id.* at 106. Perhaps even more damning was their finding that no product safety officer "cited any instance in which a particular case caused a safety-enchancing change in design behavior," *id.* at 107.

53. *Id.* The Conference Board, however, in response to a survey in 1986, found that a third of firms reporting said they improved designs in response to product-liability concerns, and a fifth of those (about 7 percent overall) reported lowered accident rates, WEBER, *supra* note 14, at 14. I suspect, however, that a more careful probing of the sort Eads and Reuter did would confirm their original findings.

54. Landes, *Insurance, Liability and Accidents: A Theoretical and Empirical Investigation of the Effect of No-Fault Accidents*, 25 J.L. & ECON. 49 (1982).

55. Grayston, *Deterrence in Automobile Liability Insurance—The Empirical Evidence*, 40 INS. COUNS. J. 117 (1973).

56. M. GAUDRY, MEASURING THE EFFECTS OF THE 1978 QUEBEC AUTOMOBILE INSURANCE ACT WITH THE DRAG MODEL (1986). Gaudry's paper is discussed in Trebilcock, *The Social Insurance-Deterrence Dilemma of*

Modern North American Tort Law: A Canadian Perspective on the Liability Insurance Crisis, 24 SAN DIEGO L. REV. 929, 991 (1987).

See also Swan, *The Economics of Law: Economic Imperialism in Negligence Law, No-Fault Insurance, Occupational Licensing and Criminology?*, AUSTRALIAN ECON. REV. (3rd Qrtr. 1984), who found (after expressing skepticism about E. Landes's study) that the introduction of New Zealand's no-fault scheme led to an increase in the highway death rate, but had no effect on the accident and injury rate.

57. Zador and Lund, *Re-Analyses of the Effects of No-Fault Auto Insurance on Fatal Crashes*, 53 J. OF RISK AND INSURANCE, 226 (1986). E. Landes's study is also harshly criticized in O'Connell and Levmore, *A Reply to Landes: A Faulty Study of No-Fault's Effect on Fault?*, 48 MO. L. REV. 649 (1983).

58. U.S. DEPT. OF TRANSPORTATION, COMPENSATING AUTO AC-CIDENT VICTIMS Appendix B. (1985).

59. Kochanowski and Young, *Deterrent Aspects of No-Fault Automobile Insurance: Some Empirical Findings*, 52 J. OF RISK AND INSURANCE 269 (1985).

60. Priest, *Products Liability Law and the Accident Rate*, In LIABILITY: PER-SPECTIVES AND POLICY (R. LITAN and C. WINSTON, eds.) 184, 194, (1988).

61. Danzon, *Medical Malpratice Liability, id.* at 101, 117–18.

2

The Compensation Goal

Over the past three decades, it has become increasingly popular to view victim compensation as the central purpose of tort law. Because neither Congress nor our state legislatures have adopted a comprehensive social insurance scheme, personal injury law has been viewed in some quarters as a progressive alternative.

This idea has particularly infected the courts,[1] and it is easy to appreciate why courts find "compensation" so appealing. The torts system typically must choose between a single plaintiff who may have suffered greatly and a defendant who is a giant enterprise or is backed by an insurance company. Judges and juries assume that such defendants can readily absorb and widely distribute this loss. The phrase *enterprise liability* expresses the idea that tort law can relieve the suffering of individual victims by spreading those losses through the mechanism of the price system or through liability insurance.[2]

In other words, compensation advocates argue that accident costs should not remain where they first fall in a lump on accident victims. Rather they should be shifted onto the society at large. From this point of view, personal injury law is viewed as a growing success.

The emphasis on compensation rests on the assumption that significant gaps exist in first-party protection, even apart from compensation for pain and suffering. Certainly in individual cases it often appears that the victim will not be able to absorb the loss very well; the claimant's expert can often show that the financial burden of a serious accident will amount to a sum that most people will find crushing if they had to pay for it themselves. Moreover, because the actors in the judicial process usually do not have access to evidence of plaintiffs' collateral benefits such as insurance (traditionally this is inadmissible), one can appreciate why they would play it safe and assume the worst—no health insurance, no sick leave, no Social Security, etc. Besides, at the appellate level, even though a particular victim may be well off, courts must formulate doctrines that apply to all, including the less fortunate victims. In sum, given (1) the general compassion for accident victims, (2) a belief in the superior loss-spreading abilities of tort defendants, and (3) the activism of today's judiciary, tort law has become a dynamo for doling out compensation to meet presumed need.

Even defense lawyers typically will concede, when confronted by badly injured victims, that, of course, something should be done for them. Indeed, let me assume that most Americans agree that when people become disabled and face unexpected income losses and medical expenses that leave them in financial straits, there is a collective duty to help them.

But is it through tort law that they should be helped? Inside enterprises that make consumer products or directly serve the public, among doctors, and within local governments, this compensation-oriented view of personal injury law is often derisively termed "the search for the deep pocket." As these groups see it, many defendants are being forced to pay for injuries for which they are not justly responsible.

My objections are deeper, however. Even if other compensation sources are inadequate,[3] there are serious shortcomings in trying to use the common law as a substitute mechanism. No matter how passionately they wish to compensate victims, judges are stuck with the administrative apparatus of tort law, the rules of damages, and an obligation to maintain a modicum of fidelity to principles of private adjudication. Because of these constraints, tort law fails as a sensible general system for accident-victim compensation.

Moreover, while some praise creative judicial expansions of the existing structure, one result is that tort law becomes harder to supplant. The need for a better approach to compensation becomes less urgent because at least some victims are helped. More important, vested interests entrench and multiply. As the system grows, the stakes increase, and these interests find more reasons to fight the displacement of tort. At the same time, liberalizing tort law takes time, talent, and attention away from work on superior compensation plans.

I will discuss the deficiencies of tort as a compensation system in four categories. Three have to do with benefit problems, while one has to do with costs.

UNCOMPENSATED AND UNDERCOMPENSATED VICTIMS

Tort law cannot provide compensation to enormous numbers of accident victims. Our jurisprudence requires a causal link between the plaintiffs and the defendants and some notion of defendant responsibility even where fault is no longer relevant. This problem is not limited to the rather unusual

"DES daughters" sort of litigation, where plaintiffs cannot identify which of many pharmaceutical manufacturers provided the damaging drug to their mothers. At least there, a causal connection does exist between the plaintiff group and a limited number of DES manufacturers, and many courts have creatively adapted common law principles to serve what they see as the ends of justice. But in many accidents there simply is no plausible defendant.

For example, if a driver's mind wanders after a hard day at work, who can be held responsible if he loses control of the car for a minute and crashes into a tree? The object of his thoughts? The tree owner? The car manufacturer? The owner of the road? His boss? Are supermarkets to be held liable for those who trip over their own feet in the parking lot? Are ladder, gutter, or patio makers to be liable for those who fall off ladders onto patios while cleaning gutters? Are beach operators to be liable for those who drown despite heroic efforts of lifeguards? And who is going to be liable for the thousands of injuries that occur every year when people are hit by lightning, to say nothing of the myriad of other accidents that, viewed figuratively, amount to being hit by lightning? In short, there are many accidents where the plaintiffs cannot identify a credible defendant with superior loss-spreading ability. One-car mishaps, most in-home accidents, and recreational accidents are all good examples of this point.[4] Yet, these victims, like other victims, need compensation. A recent British survey found that no more than 12 percent of all British accident victims obtain tort damages—and there, unlike in the United States injured workers are not routinely barred from suing their employers as a quid pro quo for workers' compensation benefits.[5] Even if the American claims frequency were double or triple the British experience, the point would be clear. Indeed, Professor Patricia Danzon has recently estimated that of those injured by medical malpractice only one in twenty-five, at most, recovers through the tort system.[6]

Besides, even after recent liberalizations of American tort law, the circle of liability is narrower than it might be. Expansive strict liability is not the rule. Absent fault, airline and bus companies are not liable to passengers, doctors are not liable to their patients, and property owners are not liable to their guests.[7] Although courts could have adopted stricter liability in these areas in the name of victim compensation, thus far they have not. In short, both the reality of how many accidents occur and current doctrine combine to create a substantial liability gap. In consequence, tort law refuses compensation to many victims who, from the perspective of their need, are as deserving as those who succeed through the system.

To further widen the compensation gap, many tort defendants are judgment proof. Enterprises living on a financial shoestring often go without liability insurance. Many individuals have no funds to satisfy tort judgments. This group includes a distressingly large number of motorists who drive without liability insurance or who carry the bare statutory minimum.

Moreover, plaintiffs often settle cases for less than their full losses because of delay, lack of proof, urgent financial need, contributory negligence, and limited defendant insurance. Even then, large legal fees and expenses must be deducted. Other victims get nothing because their injurer is unidentified or out of judicial reach. Thus, can it be surprising that the tort system leaves a large proportion of seriously hurt victims uncompensated or substantially undercompensated? Many studies document this result, including even those restricted to cases where claims are actually filed, and then to actual economic loss.[8]

THE ARBITRARINESS OF TORT COMPENSATION

Personal injury law too often compensates in an arbitrary, perhaps whimsical, way. People receive lump sums instead of payments as they need them. And, they often receive their money long after the accident. Moreover, lawyers' talents, plaintiffs' demeanor, defendants' grit, and the idiosyncrasies of jury composition combine to hand similar victims altogether dissimilar results.[9]

Geographical bias also pervades the system. In an empirical study of malpractice claims, Professor Danzon found that "[u]rbanization is the single most powerful predictor of both frequency and severity of claims, even after controlling for higher physician and lawyer density in urban states, more pro-plaintiff common law and the frequency and severity of claims in other liability lines."[10] Likewise, states have adopted dramatically different attitudes toward the currently gigantic problem of asbestos injuries, even though the problem surely is national. Some states construe the statute of limitations so as to block nearly all claims while others cut off virtually no one.[11] It is no wonder, then, that many people view tort law as a lottery.[12]

EXCESSIVE AMD UNNECESSARY COMPENSATION

Although ineffective as to many victims, tort law is at the same time too generous to other victims in both small and large injury cases. Studies have regularly shown that most tort claims are small claims.[13] To be sure, many small injuries result in no claim at all. However, many others yield substantially more compensation than they warrant because injurers (and their insurers) find buying off nuisance claims cheaper than litigation.[14]

Similarly, some badly injured tort victims fare fabulously better than do others in our society who have similar needs, but claim against other compensation systems. Indeed, a relatively few claimants win an extraordinary amount of the total sum paid out in personal injury cases. For example, based on a sample of medical malpractice claims, Professor Danzon found that 2 percent of all cases (those involving awards more than $100,000 in pain and suffering) accounted for more than 40 percent of all the payments made to claimants.[15] Similarly, the General Accounting Office (GAO) has found that 2 percent of malpractice claimants, those paid more than $200,000 for pain and suffering, obtained 60 percent of all the payments made for pain and suffering.[16] In the same vein, it has been estimated that of medical malpractice claimants who obtain more than $100,000 in damages for pain and suffering, the portion of their award that goes for pain and suffering amounts to 80 percent.[17] And these high-stakes winners are gaining an even larger share of the pie.[18] For example, million dollar verdict winners in Cook County, Illinois, jumped from two, who obtained 4 percent of total awards in 1960–1964, to 67, accounting for 85 percent of awards in 1980–1984.[19]

Yet, if we put fault aside and concentrate on the need for compensation alone, tort victims who obtain big recoveries are not more deserving than the sick, the congenitally disabled, the elderly, people injured at work, wounded soldiers, and perhaps the unemployed as well, all of whom are compensated through other social mechanisms.

Basic compensation arrangements, such as the disability insurance program in Social Security, do not compensate for what tort law calls general damages—essentially pain and suffering. Even though workers' compensation often pays moderate sums for serious disfigurement, the judgment in a torts case with similar injuries dwarfs the scale of these awards. As Professor George Priest has recently estimated, perhaps nearly 50 percent of all tort awards now go for nonpecuniary losses.[20]

In addition, tort law aims to replace 100 percent of lost income, which is more than typical compensation schemes provide.[21] Tort law is also unusual because it refuses to consider the victim's other sources of compensation. Nowadays, most, although unfortunately not all, accident victims are able to look to compensation arrangements attached to their employment (or to that of another member of the family). These arrangements include health insurance, disability insurance, sick leave, Social Security, and the like. As a result, many people, including many with legitimate tort claims, do not need personal injury law as a compensation mechanism for lost wages, medical expenses, and other out-of-pocket losses.

For those victims, tort law's main function (apart from providing a double payment that may or may not have to be reimbursed to the insurer who paid first) is to provide money for pain and suffering. Yet as already noted, compared with how our society compensates accident victims through other modern arrangements, personal injury law pays accident victims excessively for their pain and suffering. In short, if victim compensation is the social goal, surely the legislature can fashion a far more efficient and complete mechanism than the judges have.

EXTRAVAGANT ADMINISTRATIVE COSTS

Finally, the tort system is fabulously expensive to operate in comparison to modern compensation systems. As a result, a shockingly small share of the money paid in for liability insurance ever finds its way back out and into the hands of victims. First, there are large insurance commissions and other marketing costs that come with privately marketed, often individualized, insurance policies. Next, highly individualized and unpredictable tort law rules promote exorbitant claims administration, including investigation costs and lawyer fees. Although precise estimates are difficult to come by, it seems widely agreed that typically half or more of liability insurance premium payments are ground up in transaction costs. When payments for losses already covered by collateral sources and for pain and suffering are subtracted, one finds that only about 10–15 percent of the costs of the tort system go to compensating victims for out-of-pocket medical expenses, lost income, and the like.[22]

In addition, both plaintiffs and defendants incur substantial uninsured costs (including lost time) in the processing of a tort claim. Finally, the tort system imposes a great deal of public expense in the form of judge, jury, and administrative time.[23] Therefore, compared with health insurance and with various social insurance schemes such as Social Security and workers' compensation, personal injury law appears extravagantly wasteful. For example, in New Zealand's accident compensation scheme, of which more later, about 90 percent of expenditures go to or on behalf of injured people; administrative and other transaction costs claim only 10 percent.[24]

This general picture is confirmed by a recent study by the Institute for Civil Justice that examined the total costs of the tort system and the share going to plaintiffs as compensation (i.e., after their attorneys' fees and other costs). James Kakalik and Nicolas Pace estimated the expenditure on tort litigation in 1985 at between $29 and $36 billion, of which the sum paid as compensation amounted to between $14 and $16 billion, less than half.[25] Plaintiff and defendant legal fees and expenses together amounted to about $12 billion. The value of plaintiffs' and defendants' time lost to participation in litigation, public expenditures on the judicial system, and other claims-processing costs generated the rest of the transactions costs. This study, which does not capture costs and compensation paid out where claims are made but no lawsuit is filed,[26] also does not separately account for the portion of the net compensation received by plaintiffs that goes to duplicate other compensation sources or for pain and suffering, as compared with the share that replaces net economic loss.

Professor Priest has recently leveled an additional charge against tort law as a compensation system. According to Priest, it is, ironically, the very decision by courts to turn the common law into an insurance mechanism that is responsible for the recent liability insurance unaffordability and unavailability crisis. As he sees it, with expanding liability, insurance loses some of its economic advantages. In turn, safer companies are driven to self-insure, leaving the most dangerous risks left in the insurance pool. This forces either a steep increase in insurance costs or the unraveling of the pool altogether. One important consequence is undesirably higher costs of goods and services that are disproportionately burdensome to low income consumers, who are, as well, disproportionately lesser beneficiaries of the tort system.[27] This critique strikes at the heart of the basic assumption of "enterprise liability" that the tort law/liability insurance system can be used as a workable compensation mechanism. In short, Priest concludes, "our society would benefit if the insurance features of modern tort law were excised."[28]

MASS TORT CASES

Another way to appreciate the weakness of tort law as a compensation mechanism is to examine some of the highly publicized "mass tort" cases with which American courts have recently been grappling. In these cases, a large number of victims claim to have been hurt in essentially the same way by the defendants' conduct. Sometimes they bring claims as class actions; other times defendants seek to consolidate suits against them. Judges often try to work out settlements that create a claim-processing agency to distribute a fixed sum among the victims. In operation, tort law serves as a grotesquely expensive and terribly slow compensation scheme providing unpredictable and uneven benefits. Moreover, its beneficiaries are people who, although typically innocent, are no more deserving than other victims who are not fortuitous enough to have access to the mechanism.[29]

Agent Orange

Vietnam veterans brought a class action against seven chemical companies, foremost among them Dow Chemical, who produced the herbicide Agent Orange (AO).[30] The number of claimants in the case was nearly 250,000 when a settlement was reached in 1985. Plaintiffs asserted a wide range of injuries arising from when the American military sprayed large amounts of AO contaminated with dioxins on suspected Viet Cong bases. Many U.S. troops were exposed to the herbicide in various ways, although the extent of exposure is extremely hard to determine in individual cases.

One grave weakness in the plaintiffs' case concerned whether AO actually injured American soldiers. Although animal studies associate substantial doses of dioxin with numerous disorders and birth defects, rather little is known about the effects of dioxins in general, and AO in particular, on humans.[31] Judge Jack Weinstein, presiding over the matter, lent much support to the chemical companies' position that, while the claimants may have disabilities, there is to date little reason to think AO is responsible.[32] Indeed, for those who failed to join the settlement described below, he dismissed their suits on, among other grounds, the failure to provide adequate evidence of causation.[33]

Even if AO were the culprit, is it equitable to allow these veterans to recover in tort but not allow recovery to tens of thousands of others who were killed and injured in the war—many surely because of someone else's fault? Normally, our soldier-victims of a war effort do not sue the military, makers of military equipment and weapons, or the enemy. Rather, like other workers injured on the job, they are supposed to file claims under the veterans' disability compensation plan—the military counterpart to workers' compensation. Of course, in the AO setting the government also rejected the plaintiffs' statutory compensation claims on the ground that the alleged injuries are not caused by AO.[34] The vets in that respect, however, are like masses of other Americans who suffer partial, often severe, disabilities, but cannot link them to their work. Where disability is total, Social Security benefits are generally available. However, the United States unlike many other nations, does not have a broad income-protection scheme for partial disability that would cover nonwork-connected harms. As I will later argue, it would be far preferable to reform our compensation schemes to address the needs of all such partially disabled people rather than to continue to award torts benefits on an *ad hoc* basis to some of them.

A $180 million settlement of the AO cases was reached on the eve of trial. In one sense this is an enormous figure—certainly for a torts settlement. In another sense, however, it is a rather trivial sum. It amounts to an average of only $3600 per plaintiff when spread over an estimated 50,000 claims that will actually be paid (to use a frequently employed figure). As *Newsweek* put it, "The defendants . . . continued to insist that [AO] . . . had not harmed anyone, but privately chortled that they had walked away after paying on"10 cents on the dollar.' "[35] On the other hand, in view of the apparent weakness of the lawsuit, one might wonder why the defendants settled at all. The explanation lies with the defendants' exorbitant legal costs—allegedly $75 million with no end in sight—together with the risk, however small, of losing more than a billion in court. It is tragic to spend such enormous sums in litigation in order to produce such a relatively puny compensation fund. In approving the settlement that Judge Weinstein worked out, the court of appeals treated the plaintiffs as, in effect, receiving "nuisance value" for their claims.[36]

With the causation issue generally in doubt, and in view of the proof problems individual claimants would face, even if it were assumed that AO causes certain kinds of injuries, Judge Weinstein faced a very difficult problem of deciding how the $180 million should be distributed. It is quite understandable that Judge Weinstein, wisely working to minimize the administrative costs involved and seeking to spread the funds reasonably widely, would select criteria for distributing the bulk of the fund that do not require a showing that links AO to an individual's injury.

Thus, he essentially adopted a three-part test: (1) the claimant Vietnam veteran or his survivors must show some evidence of exposure to AO—this is most commonly meant to be achieved by meshing the veteran's military records with the government's computerized records of AO spraying locations, (2) the claimant veteran must be either deceased or totally disabled within the meaning of the Social Security Act—favorable Social Security Administration (SSA) findings will be binding, but unfavorable SSA decisions or the failure to apply for Social Security will not necessarily bar a claim, and (3) so as to exclude claimants whose disabilities or deaths are "unquestionably unrelated" to AO, they must not have been "predominately caused by truama"—for example, "automobile accidents, homicides, suicides and war wounds."[37] Notice how this scheme goes part way toward accepting the plaintiffs' theory of the case—requiring AO exposure and excluding obviously non-AO caused injuries—even though Judge Weinstein rejected the connection between AO and veteran injury on the merits. But that, of course, is inherent in such settlements. At the same time, there are plainly many who are meant to recover from the settlement pool who also unquestionably were not injured by AO, but whose injuries were not traumatic. Yet Judge Weinstein realized that going down that trail, e.g., sorting out certain heart attack victims, or victims of diseases plainly contracted outside Vietnam, would lead to a hopeless quagmire, to say nothing of enormous administrative costs. In short, prongs (1) and (3) together create a class that is larger than the plaintiffs' theory would envision.

On the other hand, prong (2), by requiring severe disability or death, narrows the class considerably. In 1985, Judge Weinstein estimated that about 50,000 of the 250,000 claims that had been filed will be paid. This was done to provide more than a token sum to each claimant. Under the plan, later approved by the court of appeals, the maximum award is estimated to be $12,800 and would be paid over time to a totally disabled veteran who was totally disabled by 1970 and was then under age thirty-five. Two-thirds of the total payment of compensation benefits are meant to go to an estimated 14,000 eligible veterans (at an average payment of $9,600 each) who were totally disabled as of the time of the settlement. Another 10 percent are aimed at the survivors of an estimated 6,000 eligible veterans who had died by the time of the settlement, with the remainder scheduled for those becoming totally disabled or dying after time of the settlement.

As of late–1988, however, no compensation benefits had yet been paid out. Hence, the upshot for many veterans who were totally disabled by 1970 is that, about twenty years later, starting in 1989, if they are lucky, they might begin to receive payments, eventually amounting to $12,800, for twenty-five years worth of disability (i.e., between 1970 and 1995).[38]

While this award is not nothing, in most cases it will be relatively small in comparison to the Social Security benefit these claimants are already receiving for the same impairment plus any regular veteran's pension they may be receiving. The same clearly may be said of the AO settlement death benefit, which has an estimated maximum of only $3,400. While this is no way detracts from Judge Weinstein's inventive way of handling the settlement sum, it shows how unsuccessful tort law is as a compensation device even in a more than $200 million (with interest) case such as this—and especially when we think about what now must be more than $100 million in legal fees and related expenses on both sides.

Bendectin

The Bendectin litigation is in some ways analogous to the Agent Orange litigation. Dow Chemical, the defendant in this action as well, is the parent corporation of the acquired enterprise Richardson-Merrell, now Merrell Dow, the maker of Bendectin.[39] Bendectin is an antinausea drug that was marketed in the United States between 1957 and 1983. It was commonly prescribed during pregnancy. Thirty million women worldwide have taken the drug, including, according to some sources, as many as 10–25 percent of pregnant American women during this twenty-five-year period. It has been claimed that Bendectin causes birth defects.

Since 1977, hundreds of suits have been brought against Merrell Dow. Most of them were consolidated, and a $120 million settlement agreement was tentatively reached. It unraveled, however, when the U.S. Court of Appeals for the Sixth Circuit concluded that the supervising federal judge impermissibly created a class with no opt-out rights.[40]

As with Agent Orange, there is great doubt as to defendants' liability. Many believe that existing evidence does not prove Bendectin harmful— that the birth defects resulted from other causes. Indeed, the defendant is generally winning cases outright on the causation issue—including, most importantly, one major case that arose from the attempted class action settlement and consolidated about 1200 claimants.[41] As with AO, it was defense costs and the potential of enormous liability sufficient to exhaust insurance coverage that seem best to explain why the defendant would have been willing to pay more than $100 million to get rid of the problem.

Apart from its trial court victory in the one major case, the defendant has had to do battle at trial with a large number of mostly individual claimants, and about 300 cases were pending nationally as of May 1988.[42] The defense has been winning most, but not all, trials. As of May 1988, for example, plaintiffs (frequently represented by Barry Nace, the leading claimant attorney in the Bendectin saga) had prevailed in five of seventeen cases, including one case in which the jury awarded $20 million in compensatory and $75 million in punitive damages, and another in which the claimant was awarded about $1.2 million. In a third case, the first plaintiff Bendectin victory nationwide, the District of Columbia Court of Appeals had reinstated the claimant's $750,000 verdict after it had been set aside by the trial court on the ground that it was against the great weight of evidence.[43] More recently, however, the trial court granted the defense a new trial in that case on the ground that one of the plaintiff's key experts had lied about his professional status. Because this expert has testified in several of the successful Bendectin lawsuits, their standing may also be in jeopardy.

Meanwhile, Merrell Dow has been involved in an enormous amount of litigation over strategic and other issues such as federal removal, *forum non conveniens*, the statute of limitations, the availability of consortium rights to parents of children alleged to be injured by Bendectin, and so on.

In the end, perhaps Bendectin does cause birth defects; perhaps not. What we have seen, however, is that claimants, by demonstrating a weak causal connection to a product, nearly extracted a large settlement from an available defendant that would have meant an average payment of $150,000 each. At the same time, most equally innocent children with birth defects go uncompensated by tort law. As it turns out, now most Bendectin claimants will also probably wind up with nothing. Yet a few (who knows, possibly a few hundred) could wind up with very substantial awards. As a compensation system, this makes no sense. Meanwhile an important drug has been forced from the marketplace that the Food and Drug Administration (FDA) never recommended withdrawing.

Asbestos

By 1984, after nearly ten years of litigation, more than 25,000 personal injury claims had been made against companies in the asbestos industry.[44] By mid–1988, there were more than 60,000 active personal injury claims, and more than 25,000 had been settled. The potential for additional claims is enormous. Some have predicted that as many as 350,000 Americans might eventually die from their past exposure to asbestos. In contrast to AO and Bendectin, there is no doubt that asbestos is dangerous. Still, an individual claimant may encounter considerable difficulty showing a health problem was caused by asbestos, rather than by, say, smoking. Moreover, because of desires for cash now and fears that delay will mean no compensation later (the statute of limitations will run out or the defense will run out of money), in the last couple of years a new type of claimant is increasingly common. Victims who are still working full-time seek immediate tort compensation once X rays or other indications predict future trouble, even though the timing and extent of their ultimate disability from asbestos is quite unclear. In such cases, the settlement obtained now is quite unlikely to match future needs.

Asbestos injuries are essentially job related. Under sensible workers' compensation schemes, victims should receive benefits for what is an occupational disease. But unlike workers who lose limbs because of the conduct of fellow employees, or who contract occupational diseases but can point only to their employer, asbestos victims discovered the possibility of a more generous recoupment in tort. Workers' compensation is no longer the exclusive remedy for job injuries, as had been envisioned. Indeed, for some it has become a war chest for a protracted tort case against a third party where one can be found. This trend is not unique to asbestos plaintiffs, however, and in fact, a substantial share of all payments in product injury cases these days are for work-related claims.[45] This pattern, which leads to severe inequality as among workers, also renders rather inapt the consumer injury paradigm around which the doctrine of strict liability in tort developed, where the otherwise uncompensated product buyer was of central concern. On the other hand, for a variety of reasons, including proof problems and inadequacies of state workers' compensation laws, not all asbestos victims have access to any compensation mechanism other than tort law[46]— and some that do forego their workers' compensation claim on the advice of counsel for fear that evidence these produced will weaken their tort claim.

Administrative overhead alone, however, makes the tort system a disgraceful forum for dealing with the asbestos problem. As of 1984, claimants had received somewhat more than $236 million. Their lawyers, however, had earned $164 million and the defendants had incurred more than $600 million in expenses.[47] Surely this expense-to-payout ratio is outrageous for a compensation mechanism. It is hoped that victims are now gaining a larger share of the defense payout as the settlement process becomes more streamlined.

Differing laws from state to state have caused asbestos victims to be treated quite differently. As noted earlier, some states such as New York, for example, had statute of limitations policies that were far more favorable to defendants than in many other places. When the New York State legislature, in response, finally opened a one-year "window," from mid–1986 to mid–1987, to allow claims that had otherwise been barred, an estimated 10,000 plaintiffs filed suit.[48]

The major defendant (although there are enormous numbers of parties involved in this litigation) Johns-Manville has gone into bankruptcy at a time when its net worth was more than $1 billion. Some will contend that litigation teaches asbestos makers, and industry in general, a lesson. Evidence that Johns-Manville officials deliberately covered up early danger signals encourages such arguments. But current shareholders and insurers—not bad actors from the distant past—will be the ones to suffer financially. As Archibald Cox puts it,

Does it really make sense to have the compensation awarded to those whose health was injured turn upon exhaustive investigation and trial of the question whether a particular manufacturer or user knew or should have learned about the dangers of working with asbestos twenty, thirty, and forty years ago? After exhaustive inquiries and protracted trials, will the verdict and judgment really turn upon careful, reasoned findings upon such questions? Is the method developed for the negligence of the nineteenth century suited to such cases? Have we done anything but make it more cumbersome and more expensive with the outcome more uncertain?[49]

IUD

The A. H. Robins company bought the rights to produce and market the Dalkon Shield in 1970 and eventually marketed 4.6 million of these birth control devices worldwide.[50] Even though considerable evidence has linked the device to serious health consequences, Robins all along denied any wrongdoing. Although spokesmen for the company argued that Robins never would have recklessly chanced liability with a product accounting for such a small part of their business (the Dalkon Shield generated only $500,000 in profit), plaintiffs charged the firm with failure to test the product adequately initially and, more damning, with a deliberate cover-up of its dangers once discovered.

As in other mass tort cases, serious causation issues have arisen. Other factors cause the same injuries said to be caused by the Dalkon Shield, and Robins won outright victories in about half of the fifty-odd cases that had actually gone to trial by 1984. At the same time, however, Robins was settling what then seemed like an enormous number of claims; by August 1985, it had paid out about $500 million to resolve 9500 claims (an average of more than $50,000 per claim). These settlements often involved protracted negotiations. Robins claimed many IUD wearers actually contracted their problems from their "lifestyle." Much to the plaintiffs' annoyance, the defense frequently probed the claimants' sexual practices at considerable lengths.

The amount that victims obtained for similar injuries varied considerably. This was partly caused by differences in available evidence, representation, and state law. In addition, the settlement value of the IUD cases relentlessly increased, due to accumulating evidence against Robins and higher jury awards, including a $6 million punitive damages verdict. In late 1984, therefore, plaintiffs who previously would have settled for $15,000 were settling for $100,000.

As would be expected, a distressingly small share of Robins's costs actually went to compensate victims. For example, by August 1984, Robins's insurers had paid out $132 million. Presumably, less than $100 million went to the victims themselves. To that point Robins had paid $101 million in its own litigation expenses. In short, torts as a compensation mechanism is once more shown to be highly uneven and terribly inefficient.

In August 1985, Robins declared bankruptcy and sought reorganization.[51]

Amid charges of prodefendant bias, federal district Judge Robert Merhige, as of this writing, has been supervising the reorganization negotiations for three years. A $4 million advertising campaign to uncover potential claimants was first launched, and in response, 232,000 claims were filed. Owing, for example, to many claimants' failure to follow up on information requests and other factors, the number of potential claimants was trimmed to 193,000 by the end of 1987.

In April 1987, Robins filed its first plan of reorganization that proposed a total fund for the IUD victims of an amount not to exceed $1.75 billion. By the end of 1987, Judge Merhige determined that the fund would have to be at least $2.475 billion. By the summer of 1988, the claimants had voted to support this solution (about three-quarters of claimants voted and nearly all favored the plan).[52] Still by the fall of 1988, more than three years after Robins first sought the protection of bankruptcy, no damages had yet been paid out to any of the claimants beyond the 9,500 or so with whom settlements had been reached prior to the bankruptcy declaration, and appeals against the reorganization plan were pending. During this period, of course, the defense legal fees and related costs continued to mount, and the claimants' lawyers' clocks continued to run.

Assuming the $2.475 billion dollar figure will stick, this averages less than $15,000 per potential claimant (on the basis of 193,000 claimants), from which the costs of administering the fund (including the victims' lawyers' fees) are to be subtracted. As with the Agent Orange and asbestos experience, it is extremely doubtful whether, in the end, most IUD victims will receive anything like the kind of individualized attention to their claims that the tort system promises, or even as compared to what the workers' compensation and Social Security systems deliver.

CONCLUSION

Do we need torts for compensation purposes? When I consider my own situation, I know that if I were hurt in an accident, my medical bills would be paid. If I missed a week or a month or more of work, my wages would be continued. If I were disabled and no longer able to work as a law professor, I would have a generous disability pension. Hence, I do not need the tort system to compensate me for my economic losses arising from accidents. What's more, my protection does not depend on my being able to prove anyone was at fault or sold me a defective product. It does not matter whether I was careless in injuring myself, and it does not even matter whether or not an accident put me out of commission—sickness and other disabling causes are equally covered. That is how it should be. What I want, and what I assume most people want, is basic protection against income losses and for medical expenses that are incurred for whatever reason. The current tort system clearly does not provide this protection. I realize that I have what some might term a progressive employer—the University of California and ultimately the state of California. And, of course, not everyone has the kind of protection that I have. But this is the very problem that tort reformers should address.

In short, compensation of accident victims is a proper social concern, but it should be furthered through means other than tort law. Later, I discuss my own approach to the compensation goal.

NOTES

1. Good examples of liability-expanding opinions by the California Supreme Court with candid statements about the compensation goal are Sprecher v. Adamson Co., 30 Cal. 3d 358, 636 P.2d 1121, 178 Cal. Rptr. 783 (1981) and Rowland v. Christian, 69 Cal. 2d 108, 443 P.2d 561, 70 Cal. Rptr. 97 (1968). On the instrumentalism of today's judiciary, *see* Schuck, *The New Judicial Ideology of Tort Law*, in NEW DIRECTIONS IN LIABILITY LAW (W. OLSON, ed.) 4 (1988).

2. *See generally* Priest, *The Invention of Enterprise Liability: A Critical History of the Intellectual Foundations of Modern Tort Law*, 14 J. LEGAL STUD. 461 (1984).

3. I later show that this assumption is often exaggerated.

4. Consumer Product Safety Commission (CPSC) studies show that the most frequent injury-causing activities include (1) using stairs, (2) bicycling, (3) playing baseball, (4) playing basketball, (5) playing football, (6) using cutlery, (7) using nonglass doors, (8) using chairs and sofas, (9) using tables, and (10) using nails. Although the list probably includes some defective products and some instances of someone else's negligence, most of these injuries simply will not lead to tort claims. The CPSC reports that the products producing the most severe injuries include (1) cigarette lighters, (2) gasoline, (3) batteries, (4) drain and oven cleaners, (5) heating equipment, (6) stoves and ovens, (7) swimming pools, (8) power lawn equipment, (9) home chemicals, and (10) money. Once again, however, injuries arising from these products are also dominated by careless usage by victims rather than product defects. It is important to note that cigarettes, alcohol, automobiles, drugs, and firearms fall outside the CPSC's jurisdiction.

5. D. HARRIS, et al., COMPENSATION AND SUPPORT FOR ILLNESS AND INJURY 317 (1984). Less than one in three vehicle accident victims obtained damages, less than one in five work-related accident victims obtained damages, and less than one in fifty victims of all other accident types obtained damages.

6. Danzon, *Medical Malpractice Liability*, in LIABILITY: PERSPECTIVES AND POLICY (R. LITAN and C. WINSTON, eds.) 116 (1988). For a discussion of many reasons why tort victims fail to file claims and evidence of the class-related pattern of claims, *see* Abel, *The Real Tort Crisis—Too Few Claims*, 48 OHIO ST. L.J. 443 (1987).

7. Some would argue that the reluctance of judges to direct verdicts for defendants, together with the doctrine of *res ipsa loquitur* and proplaintiff rules of evidence, make many such defendants strictly liable in fact, if not in law. Yet, based on my conversations with practitioners, I conclude that tort settlement practices show that, while both sides consider juries proplaintiff, the lawyers still base their negotiations on the fault requirement.

8. R. KEETON and J. O'CONNELL, BASIC PROTECTION FOR THE TRAFFIC VICTIM 34–69 (1965) discuss many such studies.

9. "A growing body of evidence . . . indicates that some jurors may fail to comprehend as much as 50% of the judge's instructions regarding the law," R. MAC-COUN, GETTING INSIDE THE BLACK BOX: TOWARD A BETTER UNDERSTANDING OF CIVIL JURY BEHAVIOR 21 (1987) (Rand Corporation Institute for Civil Justice). *See also* Blum, *What's a Leg Worth? It Depends*, NAT'L L.J., August 1, 1988, at 1, col. 1.

10. Danzon, *The Frequency and Severity of Medical Malpractice Claims*, 27 J.L. & ECON. 115, 143 (1984).

11. J. KAKALIK, P. EBNER, W. FELSTINER, and M. SHANLEY, COSTS OF ASBESTOS LITIGATION 5 (1983) (Rand Corporation Institute for Civil Justice) [hereinafter cited as COSTS OF ASBESTOS LITIGATION].

12. It is sometimes argued that tort law serves (or should serve) the function of redistributing income from the rich to poor. *See generally* Epstein, *The Social Consequences of Common Law Rules*, 95 HARV. L. REV. 1717, 1717–44 (1982). Although ordinary people receive payments from richer corporations and insurance companies, these payers are not individuals but institutions. Indeed, tort law's commitment to full income replacement disfavors the poor. In addition, the wealthier the victim, the higher the medical expenses for similar injuries. Furthermore, despite the contingent fee arrangement under which the plaintiffs' bar works, rich victims have better access to lawyers. To the extent that lawyers benefit from the system, this is hardly a progressive redistributive transfer. Even if torts disproportionately injure the poor, there would still be significant target inefficiency considering all the tort victims who are not poor. Indeed, because such a large proportion of damages goes to only a few victims, the idea of torts as an engine for income redistribution seems altogether inapt.

13. Professor Danzon (then Munch), using Insurance Service Office data, reports that in 1976, 89 percent of product liability personal injury claims involved economic losses of $5000 or less. Although these 89 percent of the cases involved 6 percent of economic loss, they received 24 percent of the payments, P. MUNCH, COSTS AND BENEFITS OF THE TORTS SYSTEM IF VIEWED AS A COMPENSATION SYSTEM 14 (1977) (Rand Corporation Institute for Civil Justice). *See also id.* at 38–39 (for similar data on auto claims) and *id.* at 76–81 (for similar malpractice data). Another study of product injury cases found that more than 90 percent of those claims closed with a payment involved claimants with either no disability or a temporary disability only, *see* Viscusi, *Occupational Accidents and Illness* in LIABILITY: PERSPECTIVES AND POLICY (R. LITAN AND C. WINSTON, eds.) 173 (1988).

14. For example, a recent General Accounting Office (GAO) study of malpractice claimants found that those who had merely external, insignificant, or temporary disabilities received (by mean or median measures) indemnity payments that averaged more than their economic losses, whereas the opposite was true in case of major permanent disability cases, GAO, MEDICAL MALPRACTICE: CHARACTERISTICS OF CLAIMS CLOSED IN 1984, 46–47, tables 3.7 and 3.8 (1987).

15. MANNE, et al., MEDICAL MALPRACTICE POLICY GUIDEBOOK (Florida Medical Ass'n) 139 (1985).

16. GAO, *supra* note 14, at 50, table 3.11.

17. GAO, MEDICAL MALPRACTICE: A FRAMEWORK FOR ACTION 27 (1987).

18. D. HENSLER et al., TRENDS IN TORT LITIGATION 21 (1987) (Rand Corporation Institute for Civil Justice).

19. Litan, Swire, and Winston, *The U.S. Liability System:Background and Trends*, in LIABILITY: PERSPECTIVES AND POLICY (R. LITAN and C. WINSTON, eds.) 9 (1988).

20. Priest, *The Current Insurance Crisis and Modern Tort Law*, 96 YALE L.J. 1521, 1554 (1987). Professor Gary Schwartz suggests that as much as "sixty-five percent of all payouts for uninsured motorists claims are in fact attributable to victims' pain and suffering," Schwartz, *A Proposal for Tort Reform Reformulating Uninsured Motorist Plans*, 40 OHIO ST. L.J. 419 (1987).

21. Economists have argued that, viewed as a matter of "optimal compensation," tort's goal of making a person whole is wrong. Given a choice, most fully informed people would not buy insurance designed to completely replace their losses in the event of a disabling accident, because the marginal benefit of money otherwise spent on premiums would exceed that of the insurance. This analysis rests on the assumption that money is less useful to one who is disabled. *See* for example Calfee and Winston, *Economic Aspects of Liability Rules and Liability Insurance*, in LIABILITY: PERSPECTIVES AND POLICY (R. LITAN and C. WINSTON, eds.) 22 (1988).

22. Earlier Professor Danzon (then Munch) estimated that products liability and medical malpractice plaintiffs who pay litigation expenses receive only about 30 percent of the liability insurance premium dollar in tort payments. *See* P. MUNCH, *supra* note 13, at ix. A recent estimate put the proportion of malpractice premiums paid to victims at between 28 and 40 percent, Bovbjerg and Havighurst, *Medical Malpractice: An Update for Noncombatants*, 2 BUSINESS AND HEALTH (Sept. 1985). These figures, of course, include payments for pain and suffering and duplicate payments covered by other sources. Rand Corporation's 1984 study of asbestos cases found that in order to deliver $236 million to victims, the system has had to expend $770 million in litigation expenses. This included $164 million in plaintiff expenses, $420 million in defendant legal expenses, and $186 million in other defendant expenses. COSTS OF ASBESTOS LITIGATION, *supra* note 11, at 39. *See generally* O'Connell, *Alternatives to the Tort System for Personal Injury*, 23 SAN DIEGO L. REV. 6 (1986) and O'Connell, *An Alternative to Abandoning Tort Liability: Elective No-Fault Insurance for Many Kinds of Injuries*, 60 MINN. L. REV. 501 (1978).

23. *See* J. KAKALIK and R. ROSS, COSTS OF THE CIVIL JUSTICE SYSTEM: COURT EXPENDITURES FOR PROCESSING VARIOUS TYPES OF CIVIL CASES (1983) (Rand Corporation Institute for Civil Justice).

24. ACCIDENT COMPENSATION CORP., 1986 ANNUAL REPORT 15 (1986). Professor Priest, *supra* note 20, at 1560, notes that in the United States private health insurance typically spends 10 percent on administrative costs, and that such costs are 8 percent in Social Security disability and 21 percent in workers' compensation.

25. J. KAKALIK and N. PACE, COSTS AND COMPENSATION PAID IN TORT LITIGATION (1986) (Rand Corporation Institute for Civil Justice).

26. In medical malpractice cases, for example, it has been estimated that 37.5 percent of cases are settled without a lawsuit being filed. *See* GAO, MEDICAL

MALPRACTICE CHARACTERISTICS OF CLAIMS CLOSED IN 1984 37, table 2.20 (1987).

27. Priest, *supra* note 20, at 14, 1550–51 and following.

28. Priest, *Modern Tort Law and Its Reform*, 22 VALPARAISO U.L. REV. 1, 20 (1987).

29. For a good description of the growing number of multimillion dollar toxic tort settlements arising out of environmental hazards claimed to injure, or threaten the future injury of, large numbers of people, *see* Huber, *Environmental Hazards and Liability Law*, in LIABILITY: PERSPECTIVES AND POLICY (R. LITAN and C. WINSTON, eds.) 132–39 (1988). Peter Huber concludes that the growing threat of tort liability for diffuse environmental hazards, in which courts engage in overinclusive presumptions about causation, are leading to settlements "detached from any objective measure of harm," *id.* at 145. This portends a serious loss of social welfare.

For a criticism of the expansion of tort law to cover victims in mass tort cases through weakened fault and weakened causation requirements, *see* Abraham, *Individual Action and Collective Responsibility: The Dilemma of Mass Tort Reform*, 73 VA. L. REV. 845 (1987).

30. *See in re* "Agent Orange" Prod. Liab. Litigation, 597 F. Supp. 740 (E.D.N.Y. 1984) and *in re* "Agent Orange" Prod. Liab. Litigation, 611 F. Supp. 1223 (E.D.N.Y. 1985). *See generally* P. SCHUCK, AGENT ORANGE ON TRIAL (1986).

31. *See generally* Fox, *Agent Orange Study Is Like a Chameleon*, 5 SCIENCE 1156 (Mar. 16, 1984); Lyons, *Study of Vietnam Veterans Finds No Increased Risk of Birth Defects*, N.Y. Times, Aug. 17, 1984, at 1, col. 4; Riley, *A Silver Bullet—Or Merely a Dud?*, Nat'l L.J., Aug. 23, 1984, at 1, col. 1.

32. *See* Fried, *Judge Tentatively Approves Pact to Settle Agent Orange Lawsuits*, N.Y. Times, Sept. 26, 1984, at 16, col. 1. Weinstein has been quoted as saying, "I have serious doubts about whether this case should have been brought at all . . . you have shown no factual connection of any substance between the diseases and the alleged cause," 6 AMICUS J. 46 (Fall 1984) (statement to Plaintiffs' Management Committee, Sept. 26, 1984, reported in the editor's reply to a reader's letter). Of course, future studies might demonstrate this alleged link.

33. *In re* "Agent Orange" Prod. Liab. Litigation, 611 F. Supp. 1223 (E.D.N.Y. 1985). This decision was affirmed by the court of appeals on the so-called government contract defense. *In re* "Agent Orange" Prod. Liab. Litigation, 818 F.2d 187 (2d Cir. 1987).

34. For a discussion of government-funded research on the causation issue, *see* Lyons, *U.S. Embarks on $100 Million Study of Agent Orange*, N.Y. Times, Sept. 25, 1984, at 21, col. 1.

35. *A Fast Deal on Agent Orange*, 103 NEWSWEEK 56 (May 21, 1984). *See generally* Fox, *Tentative Agent Orange Settlement Reached*, 5 SCIENCE 849 (May 25, 1984) and Flaherty and Lauter, *Inside Agent Orange*, Nat'l L.J., May 21, 1984, at 1, col. 1. The defendants had hoped to recover all their costs from the government, who, they say, knew what it was getting—exactly what it ordered. But the government was found to be immune, *in re* "Agent Orange" Prod. Liab. Litigation, 611 F. Supp. 1221 (E.D.N.Y. 1985) *aff'd* 818 F.2d 204 (2d Cir. 1987).

36. *In re* "Agent Orange" Prod. Liab. Litigation, 818 F.2d 145, 171 (2d Cir. 1987).

37. *In re* "Agent Orange" Prod. Liab. Litigation, 611 F. Supp. 1396, 1412 (E.D.N.Y. 1985). This is Judge Weinstein's opinion that sets out the details of how the settlement fund is to be distributed. It was largely approved by the second circuit in *in re* "Agent Orange" Prod. Liab. Litigation, 818 F.2d 179 (2d Cir. 1987).

38. *See* Blum, *Agent Orange Funds Are Released*, Nat'l L.J., July 18, 1988, at 17, col. 1 ("it will be at least the end of the year before the checks go out").

39. *See generally* Mekdeci v. Merrell Nat'l Laboratories, 711 F.2d 1510 (11th Cir. 1983) and Kolata, *How Safe is Bendectin*, 1 SCIENCE, 518 (Oct. 31, 1980). In the 1960s Richardson-Merrell manufactured MER–29, a drug that lowered cholesterol but also caused cataracts. The company paid out $200 million in damages in 500 lawsuits. In addition, it was fined for making false statements to the FDA. Richardson-Merrell also marketed Thalidomide in North America. About 200 Canadian and 20 U.S. children with limb defects successfully sued the company. An FDA ban prevented worse results.

40. *See in re* Richardson-Merrell Inc. "Bendectin" Prods. Liab. Litigation, 533 F. Supp. 489 (J.P.M.D.L. 1982); *in re* Bendectin Prods. Liab. Litigation, 749 F.2d 300 (6th Cir. 1984); *see also* Lauter, *Bendectin Pact Creating Furor*, Nat'l L.J., July 30, 1984, at 1, col. 1; and Lauter, *Confusion Reigns Over Bendectin*, Nat'l L.J., Nov. 12, 1984, at 3, col. 1.

41. *See* Kaufman and Lauter, *Bendectin Verdict Doesn't End Suits*, Nat'l L.J., Mar. 25, 1985, at 3, col. 2 and *in re* Richardson-Merrell Inc. "Bendectin" Prods. Liab. Litigation, 606 F. In September, 1988, the U.S. Sixth Circuit Court of Appeals upheld the defense victory at trial. *See Bendectin Verdict Upheld*, Nat'l L.J., Sept. 12, 1988, at 6, col. 2.

42. *See generally* Strasser, *Bendectin Award: $95 Million*, Nat'l L.J., July 27, 1987, at 29, col.1 and Strasser, *Key Testimony Questioned in Bendectin Case*, NAT'L L.J., May 9, 1988, at 9, col. 1.

43. Oxendine v. Merrell-Dow Pharmaceuticals, Inc., 506 A.2d 1100 (Dist. Col. Ct. of Apps.) (1986).

44. *See generally* Chen, *Asbestos Litigation Is A Growth Industry*, 254 ATL. MONTHLY, 24 (July 1984), and Carter, *Asbestos Coalition Falling Apart*, Nat'l L.J., Apr. 25, 1988, at 3, col. 1.

45. For data suggesting that workplace injuries accounted in 1977 for 11 percent of product liability claims and 42 percent of payments for bodily injury, *see Product Liability Reform: Hearings Before the Subcomm. for Consumers of the Senate Comm. of Commerce, Science, and Transportation*, 97th Cong., 2nd Sess. 106 (statement of E. McCarthy) (March 12, 1982).

46. For a discussion of the shortcomings of our existing workers' compensation system in dealing with occupational diseases and some proposals for reform, *see* REPORT TO THE PRESIDENT AND THE CONGRESS, WORKERS' COMPENSATION: IS THERE A BETTER WAY? 11–13, 23–27 (1977). For other critical reports of the existing workers' compensation system's handling of occupational disease and proposals for new compensation plans, *see* Schroeder, *Legislative and Judicial Responses to the Inadequacy of Compensation for Occupational Disease*, 49 LAW & CONTEMP. PROBS. 151 (1986); Solomons, *Workers' Compensation for Occupational Disease Victims: Federal Standards and Threshold Problems*, 41 ALB. L. REV. 195 (1977); and Note, *Compensating Victims of Occupational Disease*, 93 HARV.

L. REV. 916 (1980). *See generally* J. STAPLETON, DISEASE AND THE COM-PENSATION DEBATE (1986).

47. *See* COSTS OF ASBESTOS LITIGATION, *supra* note 11, at 39.

48. Adams, *Courthouse Doors Are Reopened*, Nat'l L.J., Sept. 14, 1987, at p. 1. col. 2.

49. Chen, *supra* note 44, at 32 (quoting Cox's statement to the American Bar Association Annual Meeting in Atlanta, Aug. 1983).

50. *See generally* Palmer v. A. H. Robins Co., 684 P.2d 187 (Colo. 1984); Klein-field, *Ongoing Problems for Robins*, N.Y. Times, Aug. 1, 1984, at D1, col. 3; "Morning Edition," National Public Radio (Nov. 15, 1984); Middleton, *Robins Mounts Drive to Settle Dalkon Suits*, Nat'l L.J., Dec. 24, 1984, at 1, col. 3, and 10, col. 2; and "All Things Considered," National Public Radio (Jan. 16, 1985).

51. *See generally* the ongoing coverage in the *National Law Journal* by Alan Cooper, for example, *Plaintiffs' Lawyers Fault Robins' Plan*, May 4, 1987, at 3, col. 1; *Robins Amends Bankruptcy Plan*, June 1, 1987, at 3, col. 1; *New Robins Plan is Filed*, Sept. 7, 1987 at 14, col. 1 and *Robins Fund: $2.5 Billion*, Dec. 28, 1987, at 3, col. 1.

52. *See* Cooper, *It's Over: Robins Plan Gets the Nod*, Nat'l L.J., Aug. 1, 1988, at 10, col. 1. For reports of squabbles among the fund's trustees, *see* Cooper, *Dalkon Shield Trusts Off to a Rocky Start*, Nat'l L.J., Sept. 12, 1988, at 4, col. 1.

3

The Justice Goal and Other Illusionary Goals

One traditional view of common law judges and juries is that they decide whether fairness dictates that the injurer or the victim should bear the loss. This justification for tort law derives from moral values: e.g., when X negligently injures Y, it is only morally right that X, not Y, bear the loss. A century ago Oliver Wendell Holmes endorsed this view of tort law in his famous lectures, *The Common Law*. With personal injuries, victims can not in actuality be made whole. Therefore, tort law has developed the device of monetary damages to serve the goal of corrective justice.

The defense bar rarely resists this idea. When it is fair for our clients to pay, they say, then they should pay. Our job is to ensure that they are not made to pay at other times. Recognizing that the issue is often a close one, many defense lawyers, like their opponents at the other counsel table, are fierce defenders of the jury system as the mechanism for resolving these disputes.

Although the corrective justice theme had receded from academic writing in the face of modern instrumentalist justifications for tort law, such as deterrence and compensation, it has reappeared in recent scholarship.[1] But the idea that tort law actually serves to compensate the deserving by those who deserve to pay is a mirage.

THE INJUSTICE OF TORT LAW IN ACTION

Those who defend tort law on corrective justice grounds emphasize the highly individualized justice of a traditional courtroom. But this is thoroughly unrealistic today. First, liability insurance and the doctrine of respondeat superior vitiate individualized corrective justice on the defendant side. Plaintiffs are simply not compensated by their injurers. Instead, the burden is diffused. Indeed, in the absence of insurance or deep pockets, victims usually do not sue, so that those who are usually most clearly thought obliged to provide compensation—those who commit violent crimes—are touched hardly at all by tort law. At the same time, without loss-spreading mechanisms, tort damages would often be out of proportion to any sense of blame.

Turning to the plaintiffs, it is unrealistic to view the victims' personal injury awards as the basic source of compensation. Instead, victims increasingly recover their out-of-pocket loss from some other source before they sue. Does it serve corrective justice when the defendants' employers or insurers pay a second time? Considerations of fairness might suggest to some that the defendants (or successful plaintiffs) reimburse the collateral source. This now often happens. But it means that, in practice, tort law becomes a process for having one insurer pay another; this is far removed from any meaningful sense of individual justice. In short, exponents of corrective justice often have a naive air about them. Like the formal rules traditionally binding on judges in the courtroom, they are blind to the vast systems of insurance on both sides of the tort equation.

The typical corrective justice vision compounds the unreality by imagining that victims naturally want legal redress from their injurers,[2] that people sue to remedy their sense of injustice. Yet surely very many people file claims today, not to make sure their injurer gets his just deserts or to soothe their own outrage, but because of the lure of substantial financial rewards that their friends or their lawyers told them they would be foolish not to claim. Thus, it is by no means evidently right to say that tort suits respond to a deeply felt need for redress; aided by plaintiffs' attorneys, the legal remedy generates its use by virtue of its very existence.[3]

Worse, corrective justice devotees assume that people actually obtain real justice through tort law. To the contrary, in large numbers of cases, the current system functions whimsically and not in accord with anyone's sense of justice. Many people find the idea of "going to law" extremely distasteful and do not—or else they do and have their fears confirmed.

Looking at the entire process, where more than 90 percent of all cases are settled, rather than fine-tuned, individualized justice, what we see is more like a lottery. Rather than a system in which settlements are entered into in the shadow of a fundamentally just set of legal requirements, Lady Luck plays an all too prominent role. Was your injurer insured? Do you happen to have (or did the other side make up or destroy) the right evidence? Do you have the right lawyer, the right expert, and the ability to endure the settlement process? Do you look like you will make a good witness? Who happens to be the insurance adjuster or lawyer with whom the settlement is being negotiated? Moreover, many find the jury process itself a very chancy proposition—reflecting not so much justice as the odd factor that happens to catch the attention of one or more persuasive jurors, the luck of who happens to sit on the jury, the location of the trial (e.g., rural or urban), the status of the defendant (individual, corporate, or governmental), the race and appearance of the victim, and so on.

Professor James Henderson articulates a fall-back defense of tort law as creating "the appearance, at least, of trying to reach individualized results that are fair to all concerned."[4] But where is this apparent? Not among the public, ordinary tort plaintiffs, or candid lawyers.

Because organized communities of potential defendants (product makers, professional service providers, and the like) are hard pressed to deny that some bad apples among their ranks do exist, they usually find it difficult (or inexpedient) to reject outright the notion that tort liability is required by justice. They typically retreat, therefore, to the position that, in practice, far too many innocent defendants, who could not reasonably have avoided the accident in the first place, are now being punished—and that even where proof of defendants' negligence is a formal legal requirement, juries are still allowed to make determinations of causation and fault on flimsy and unconvincing evidence, pursuant to jury instructions containing weak standards of proof. But there is a deeper problem.

THE LACK OF A SATISFYING THEORY OF JUSTICE

Even apart from these realities, we have no clear and convincing theory of corrective justice. No one argues for tort liability wherever the words *injurer* and *injured* describe the parties at bar. The problem comes in deciding when liability should attach.

According to Holmes's formulation of corrective justice, only a valid claim that they have been wronged may entitle plaintiffs to damages.[5] Holmes, however, did not insist that the injury must be the result of the defendants' moral culpability. Rather he argued that defendants should be held to community standards of reasonable conduct even when they were incapable of meeting them owing to some personal shortcoming. To be sure, Holmes invoked administrative convenience in support of this view— he thought it would be too difficult to decide about the moral culpability of many defendants. But he emphasized even more strongly that victims were entitled to proper conduct, and that when they did not get it, they deserved payment of damages from their injurer, regardless of his personal fault. Modern negligence law reflects this ideology.

The cogency of Holmes's theory of liability for what I'll call "objectively unreasonable conduct" is quite another matter. The principle of objective unreasonableness fails to explain much of tort law—as it stood at Holmes's time and as it stands today. It cannot account for cases in which defendants are liable despite the reasonableness of their conduct, or for cases in which defendants escape liability notwithstanding their unreasonable conduct. Had

Holmes rejected such decisions as "wrong," at least he would have formulated an elegantly simple normative theory, albeit one that had little
predictive value (i.e., as a positive theory). As the Holmesian argument
developed, however, the plaintiffs in some cases seemed wronged even by
reasonable conduct. In other cases, practical considerations, problems of
proof, and other administrative reasons prevailed in determining the outcome. Yet in others, either plaintiffs were seen to have invited harm or it
seemed excessive or inappropriate for some other reason to make the defendants pay for the harm they unreasonably caused. The upshot is an
approach to tort liability that sharply deviates from the simple principle of
objective fault that Holmes had initially articulated and defended. As em-
bodied today in the *Restatement of Torts* it has become a complex notion of
corrective justice with justifications rendered into doctrinal lingo—"duty,"
"proximate cause," "assumption of risk," "immunity," and the like. No
satisfactory overarching theoretical vision has yet emerged. Instead, we are
told that it comes down to a matter of "expediency" or "experience" rather
than "logic."

Professor George Fletcher advanced a new rights-based theory of tort
liability in 1972. He was unhappy on moral grounds with the utilitarian
flavor of the objective unreasonableness paradigm and dissatisfied with its
weak predictive powers. Fletcher advocated the principle of imposing liability for "nonreciprocal risk taking" as the basic norm of corrective justice.[6]
Under Fletcher's approach, for example, a careful dynamite blaster subjects
a nearby farmer to a nonreciprocal risk; two private plane pilots, however,
subject each other to reciprocal risks unless one flies carelessly, thus making
the risk nonreciprocal. These examples also illustrate how Fletcher tries to
handle with one principle those problems, such as the dynamite case, that
current tort law masters only by rejecting the normal negligence standard
in favor of strict liability. To date, however, Fletcher's view has found few
adherents.

Although the apparent simplicity of Fletcher's principle makes it initially
attractive, in fact, the core concept is not easy to apply. First, what about
risks makes them nonreciprocal? For example, what about crashes between
bicyclists and motorcyclists? Or what about two adjacent landowners where
one dusts crops and the other owns cattle that wander outside their proper
territory? Second, like Holmes, Fletcher bases his theory on the decided
cases. He devotes much effort to demonstrating that his is a powerful
positive theory: he tries to show that a wide variety of decided cases would
have the same outcome under his test as they do now under more complex
rules. But Fletcher's theory, like Holmes's formulation, is incomplete. The
nonreciprocal risk test leaves too much of torts unexplained. Cases involving
preexisting relationships, such as nonnegligent motorist-passenger and
doctor-patient injuries, are clear examples. Both involve nonreciprocal risks
even when the doctor and driver act carefully. Yet under current tort law,

liability in those cases requires a finding of negligence.[7] Third, and most important for my purposes, as a normative matter Fletcher does not supply convincing reasons why the essence of justice is receiving money after having been the victim of nonreciprocal risk.

Fletcher argues that when one exposes another to a nonreciprocal risk "it seems fair to hold him liable for the results of his aberrant indulgence."[8] Later he argues that "all individuals in society have the right to roughly the same degree of security from risk," analogizing to John Rawls's first principle of justice about liberty.[9] And still further on, Fletcher says in his attack on the notion of reasonableness that underlies modern negligence law, that an individual "cannot fairly be expected to suffer . . . in the name of a utilitarian calculus."[10] To me these are descriptions or conclusions but not arguments. Fletcher does suggest that the unfairness he sees arises from the benefit that the actor gained at the victim's expense.[11] But this point is not developed, and I do not see what confines it to nonreciprocal risks rather than all risks.[12]

Professor Richard Epstein, in turn, has offered a moral theory of liability that rests on the principle of causation.[13] Essentially, Epstein argues that all cases where A should be liable to B reduce to fact patterns corresponding to the causal paradigms of either A hit B or A created a dangerous condition resulting in harm to B. This approach is meant to express the moral intuitions of ordinary people by relying on the plain meaning of the word *caused*.

Epstein too has earned considerable criticism. In many cases he is forced to fall back on more complex considerations when it is simply unclear how the layman would resolve the causation issue. As Professor Fletcher has pointed out, Epstein provides no real guidance for distinguishing cases in which the harm should be seen as inflicted by the defendants from cases in which the harm is better seen as caused by circumstances (forces of nature or third parties).[14] Other times he compromises the simplicity of his theory by introducing defenses in order to reach solutions he desires but that the causation principle would contradict. More importantly, Epstein too gives little explanation why corrective justice demands that the victims recover damages from the injurers whenever the injurers "caused" the harm. Epstein says, "[b]riefly put, the argument is that proof of the proposition *A hit B* should be sufficient to establish a prima facie case of liability."[15] Epstein cites Leon Green's statement about "a deep sense of common law morality that one who hurts another should compensate him."[16] These statements are far too "brief" or "deep" to count as arguments with me.

In a later article, Epstein says that his theory has implicit philosophical premises that are "tied to a preference for equal liberties among strangers in the original position. . . . [T]he limitation upon that freedom of action is that he cannot 'cause harm' to another. . . . The justification . . . is quite simply a belief in the autonomy and freedom of the individual."[17] But, again, merely invoking a dubious analogy to Rawls does not demonstrate that such preferences and justifications cannot equally be applied to other non-strict liability theories of tort such as liability for unreasonably dangerous conduct. As Professor Ernest Weinrib has put it, if autonomy with respect to others is the goal, why, for example, focus "on the results of the defendant's behavior," as does Epstein's formulation, instead of on the conduct itself?[18]

Epstein also says, "I attach a good deal of importance to the 'natural' set of entitlements that I think are generated by a concern with individual liberty and property rights."[19] But calling them "natural" avoids the problem. Indeed, Epstein seems to recognize this when he concedes "by defining property rights as I have done, I have foreordained a system of strict liability."[20]

Perhaps the reader will imagine that the three theories of corrective justice I have considered—unreasonable conduct, nonreciprocal risk taking, and causing harm—only conflict at the boundaries of tort law. Perhaps Holmes, Fletcher, and Epstein would at least agree on ordinary cases, despite their differences in phrasing and their possible differences in opinion about exotic cases. Consider, for example, routine accidents such as careless drivers running down pedestrians, careless doctors injuring their patients, and careless manufacturers injuring their consumers. Yet these commonplace examples provoke disharmony from our three moralists: Fletcher is ambivalent about the car injury case, especially when the pedestrian is himself a regular driver;[21] Epstein would relegate medical malpractice to contract law where patients would agree not to sue for ordinary negligence;[22] and Holmes wrote *The Common Law* when the privity doctrine protected negligent manufacturers.

Professor Glanville Williams has made a more severe attack on the use of tort law to serve justice goals. He distinguishes what he calls ethical retribution from ethical compensation.[23] The former rests on a punishment notion Williams rejects as "an ultimate value-judgment."[24] I will take up the punishment theme in the next section. Ethical compensation concerns what I have been calling corrective justice. Williams argues that although a tort victim deserves compensation, the tort-feasor ought to pay only if there is no other source, such as the state, an employer, or an insurance company. On this view, corrective justice should not worry about whether the injurer does the compensating. The defendant should be liable only as a matter of last resort.

Professor Jules Coleman, a persistent and insightful critic, echoes these themes. He argues that two notions require careful separation—the grounds for rectification and the mode of rectification.[25] For Coleman, corrective justice concerns the grounds, and his underlying principle is that wrongful gains and losses should be annulled. As for the mode of rectification, however, that could be through tort law or other mechanisms.

This approach readily leads him to distinguish two sorts of fact situations. The first class is illustrated by my wrongfully taking your book or money. Because, according to Coleman's scheme, I have a wrongful gain and you a wrongful loss and because the law can compel the object's return, corrective justice can be nicely served by using tort law to restore the status quo ante. Otherwise, the appropriator will be specially and personally enriched at the victim's expense.[26] However, most tort cases fall outside this category. The common auto accident is Coleman's best example. Although someone has been hurt, the injurer has nothing to return. Perhaps the injurer benefited (for example, by gaining a thrill or profiting financially from driving too fast), but this benefit is unrelated to the harm imposed. After all, most bad driving does not injure anyone and that which happens to do so is not likely to have been unusually bad; moreover, where the injurer was clumsy or inattentive, he probably did not benefit from having so acted.

As I see it, Professor Coleman's view would confine tort law—where injurer pays victim—to the restitutionary setting. There the most sensible mode of rectification would require a specific defendant to disgorge a wrongful gain appropriated from a specific victim, as in the stolen book example. Elsewhere, such as in the auto accident, even if the victim has suffered a wrongful loss and hence deserves compensation, Coleman joins Williams in doubting whether tort law should be used to make the injurer alone pay. Rather, he advocates a wider responsibility as might come about through an auto no-fault plan. Thus, under Coleman's theory we could readily dispense with most of tort law without sacrificing corrective justice.

According to Professor Weinrib, corrective justice concerns, not the grounds of rectification, in Coleman's terms, but rather it is a matter of structure, the mode of rectification, as Coleman put it. That is, corrective justice is what tort law does when it requires one to compensate another. On this approach, one must look elsewhere than to the meaning of corrective justice for a normative theory of when, if ever, tort law should require compensation. For Weinrib, like Epstein, the content of corrective justice is found in the ideas of Immanuel Kant. But whereas Epstein draws on Kant's objection to using others as objects (or giving yourself a preference over others) as the basis for a strict liability theory, Weinrib finds in Kant the core of negligence law—objectively unreasonable conduct. As Weinrib sees it, the question to be asked is whether you would have chosen to act as you have were the plaintiff's interests or property your own.[27] It is difficult to know how to mesh this formulation with Williams's point about the availability of other sources of compensation, except to note that were you to own the plaintiff's property and it was insured, then you might well choose to sacrifice it in furtherance of the objective you seek.

In sum, people are fundamentally divided over what the standard for imposing liability should be (even where the facts are not in dispute). Candid people will agree that there is often no unambiguous answer to the question: Does justice demand that the defendant pay the victim in this case? In the past, questions of this sort were often met with the response that the answer may be found by researching "the law." But today there are few followers of the view that there is a single just result out there that can be found by consulting legal books and past decisions. For one thing, the common law, especially tort law, has changed dramatically in recent years. These abrupt changes have been made by judges—indeed, often by judges on a sharply divided state supreme court—who, while no doubt believing themselves properly within the path of the common law, are plainly driven by their own personal views of justice rather than by a disinterested search for some scientific or moral truth. In sum, it is probably better to say that, rather than one, there are often many satisfactorily just results.

I conclude that where most victims can obtain reasonable compensation from another source, cutting off access to defendants' insurers does little disservice to such corrective justice norms as we collectively hold. Adequate alternative sources of compensation would exist in the world-without-tort-law that I envision. Therefore, I find the pursuit of corrective justice through ordinary torts cases is an extravagance primarily benefiting lawyers and the insurance industry.

THE FAILURE TO PUNISH WRONGDOERS OR TO PROVIDE VICTIM SATISFACTION

Somewhat akin to the notion of corrective justice are two interrelated justifications sometimes given for tort liability: punishment and vengeance. The frequent cry of the plaintiffs' bar comes vividly to mind. Tort is necessary in order to strike back at and hurt wrongdoers. Whatever their theoretical appeal, these goals also are seldom achieved.

The point of punishment is that a wrongdoer should suffer. Yet in most accident cases, the tort-feasor simply does not pay. Either the insurance company or the employer bears the loss. Usually, the actual bad actor suffers little consequence. In a great number of cases the active tort-feasor does not even know the outcome,[28] or learns that the insurance company paid up simply to close the books, whatever the insurer's real opinion of the insured's conduct. This hardly constitutes punishment. Moreover, because nearly all cases are settled, even individuals who know they have been at fault rarely receive an official reprimand.[29]

Although higher insurance rates and job penalties punish some tort-feasors, these unofficial punishments are uneven and unpredictable. Advocates of torts as a method of punishment can hardly be satisfied with such horizontal inequity.

Moreover, there are fundamental theoretical problems with viewing our tort system as a punishment scheme. For one thing, the system holds many people liable who do not seem deserving of punishment. Two examples are defendants whose conduct fell below community standards but could not have done better and defendants who are held strictly liable. Furthermore, because tort demands compensatory damages, the award is often a poor measure of the wrongfulness of the defendants' conduct. Some juries try to punish by adjusting pain and suffering awards to reflect wrongdoing. But this practice is unpredictable as well as futile so long as insurance companies or shareholders pay.

Vengeance is the flip side of punishment. Although many consider revenge to be an inappropriate value, some conclude that many victims have a psychological need for satisfaction.[30] However, the present system ill serves the vengeance goal. First, it is hard to see how plaintiffs can get much satisfaction when their personal wrongdoers do not pay. Second, the victims who sue often find more aggravation than satisfaction or revenge. Countless plaintiffs report that if they did experience any emotion, it was exasperation, hostility, and continual discomfort.[31] To be sure, there are occasional plaintiffs (and certainly some plaintiffs' lawyers) who derive elation from the humiliation of an adversary at trial. But this kind of satisfaction comes to only a minute proportion of the people who actually file claims.

The related peace-keeping claim is that tort law is necessary in order to vent victims' steam and ensure they do not resort to violent self-help.[32] Tort law is unlikely to mollify victims of personal assault. Money will not soothe those victims who have a strong urge to retaliate and are physically able. Moreover, when the defendant is plainly judgment proof, as is the case in many bodily assault cases, tort can have little peace-keeping potential. In such instances, only swift action by the criminal authorities can assuage plaintiff anger.

The realistic case for torts on this rationale must rest on the belief that tort suits keep people from acting in socially undesirable ways toward accident-causing corporations, professionals, and motorists. However, such reasoning flies in the face of a general awareness by those who know anything about the tort system that the road to legal victory is often long and treacherous. It also suggests that we would regularly hear about victims beating up uninsured and careless motorists involved in accidents. Surely, a more powerful peace-keeping force is that most people realize that they would risk criminal liability if they deliberately inflicted harm on a tortfeasor.

If, indeed, the victims' need to retaliate is an important problem, then a better social strategy is to provide other outlets for such revenge. For example, well-handled appearances before traffic courts, medical review boards, and regulatory agencies promise more psychological benefit to victims. Many such appearance rights now exist, and this is an avenue I will later develop further.

SETTING MEANINGLESS STANDARDS

Can tort law be justified as an important signaling device? Of concern here is the alleged moralizing or educating function of torts. A number of notions together comprise this possible function of personal injury law. The common law, it has been argued, uses the tort process to establish community standards for reasonable conduct. In turn, people learn what is expected of them.

In a related claim, some argue that society uses tort law to insist on proper conduct by reaffirming social norms (that are elsewhere established) through the mechanism of holding those who fail to conform financially responsible for the consequences.[33] Under this view, without tort penalties social norms might lose their force and become ignored and people might become disillusioned and angry if they conformed to proper standards while others who did not went unpunished. Unlike the corrective justice and punishment goals discussed above, the emphasis here is more on how the rest of us, and less on how the parties to torts suits, would respond to the absence of tort law.

Alas, despite a certain theoretical appeal, once again these arguments are unconvincing in the face of modern realities. Apart from a few publicized cases and an amorphous notion of reasonable conduct, tort law transmits few clear signals about what it expects from us.[34] The image of judge and jury somehow collaborating to establish what specific conduct is unacceptable is a poor description of present law. Holmes had hopes for such interaction years ago, but in the United States they have not materialized.[35] Thus, the arguments surrounding the signaling goal largely collapse.

Furthermore, in our society, children are socialized by school and family to act reasonably toward others long before they acquire any conception of tort law. This is not to say that everyone learns and acts on such moral teaching. But it is farfetched to imagine that the socializing mechanisms will break down in a society such as New Zealand that has abandoned tort liability, or that it would in the United States were we to abolish tort claims for accidents. Do people really think that social norms about careful driving have broken down in states with auto no–fault laws? Or that there were no social norms calling for safe conduct by charities toward their beneficiaries, governments toward their citizens, parents toward their children, and physicians toward their patients during an earlier era when all of these actors were largely immune from tort liability?[36]

Because the broad norm of reasonable conduct is already entrenched in our culture, the role for tort as standard setter would be to define that norm for individual circumstances. It should specify exactly what is the appropriate behavior for drivers, doctors, dog owners, deodorant makers, dynamiters, and so on. For many reasons, however, tort fails to impart clear and specific norms. Jury decisions are secretly reached, unexplained, and inconsistent in result. Most claims in any event are settled.[37] Indeed, the worst offenders have the greatest incentives to come to terms. As a result, conduct denounced by actual decisions is typically surrounded in controversy over what really happened, or whether the harm really should have been avoided. Besides, most cases get little publicity. Moreover, tort doctrine is exceedingly complex. Indeed, with the growth of strict liability, much of tort law no longer even purports to set standards of good conduct—rather only standards of when one should pay. Because tort law awards money rather than injunctions, it can be argued that its true lesson is that those who are willing to pay for the harm done are largely free to cause accidents. The upshot is that if people get any message at all from tort law, it is likely to be a cynical one.[38]

Conversely, those who would act reasonably regardless of tort law may well feel better without it. There would then be less room to impugn their integrity. No one could argue that tort law, rather than a moral compass, dictates proper conduct. This satisfaction for many who do "what's right" may overcome any resentment toward the lack of civil consequences attending others who deviate. Finally, contrary to what Professor Steven Smith has argued, tort law is not what is necessary to give people confidence that they can rely on others to conform to social norms about safe conduct.[39] Rather, in most important areas, our society simply does not rely on tort to serve either the signaling or the norm reinforcing function. Instead, the criminal law and regulatory agencies fill this need.

INTERNALIZING COSTS TO WHAT?

There has been much attention paid in recent years to the desirability of *internalizing* accident costs to the activities that cause them. Tort law reputedly serves this social goal. There are a number of difficulties with this line of argument, however. First, considerable confusion exists as to the purpose of such internalization. Some see it as a matter of fairness, quite apart from any behavioral consequences: the cost of the product should reflect "the blood of the worker" and "the blood of the victim." This argument is no more than another way of articulating the corrective justice ideas presented previously.

For example, the contention that an enterprise benefiting from a voluntary activity should bear its accident costs is similar to Epstein's proposition that whoever caused the harm should pay. Of course, people espousing this version of cost internalization will recognize limits to the principle in the same way that Epstein and other fairness devotees do. They do not claim the harm to the victim who uses a chain saw to cut his fingernails should be a cost included in the price of the product. Cost internalization on fairness grounds is only as convincing as arguments in favor of corrective justice generally.

Under a second view, cost internalization is a mechanism providing economic incentives for taking cost-effective safety measures. This, of course, is a restatement of the deterrence theory already discussed at length in Chapter 1.

Yet a third notion of cost internalization is "allocative efficiency," meaning the socially desirable (or efficient) allocation of goods and services. This goal is independent of a specific focus on accident avoidance. Dean Guido Calabresi and others in the law and economics school emphasize this goal. The basic idea is that the price of a good will rise to its "proper" level if it reflects accident costs. Absent such internalization, society in effect subsidizes the good.[40] Such a subsidy, it is argued, entices people to purchase more of those cheaper goods and services than is socially optimal. For example, if driving automobiles, dynamiting new roads, and manufacturing lawn mowers do not include in their prices the full cost of the accidents they generate, then "too many" of these activities will occur. Someone always bears the accident costs. But, according to this argument, when they are externalized, distorted patterns of consumption decrease aggregate social welfare.

Some transportation examples will illustrate this claim in more detail. Assume that ignoring accident costs, truck transport is slightly cheaper than rail transport, but that counting accident costs, trains are cheaper. The point is that unless accident costs are internalized, people will ship by truck when they "should be" using railroads. Put differently, along with labor and materials and speed and reliability of service, a proper basis of interindustry competition between trucks and railroads is safety.

The same considerations apply to interproduct competition. If company A's airplanes are cheaper than those of company B and company C, but on the other hand they pollute more, sales of company A's planes may be less socially desirable. However, externalizing the costs of pollution enables customers to ignore this factor.

At the broadest level, allowing activities to externalize their accident costs yields society-wide misallocations. For example, suppose that previously airlines were not responsible for ground damage in unavoidable crashes, but now those costs attach to air travel by allowing victims to sue in tort. Assuming that, as a result, the price of air travel increases and people would fly less and shift to other activities. Some people would stay at home and work in the garden; others would drive. Some businesses will communicate by other means instead of sending people to meetings. Although the reduction in air travel might result in fewer crashes, the increase in the other activities may yield new accidents. The point, however, is that ripples throughout the economy are supposed to lead to a "better" allocation of resources.[41] Thus, advocates of cost internalization would use tort law to achieve what I call proper or efficient activity levels.

One can criticize this claim in various ways. To the extent that there are accidents that are no one's fault, to which party should costs be assigned? Which is to be discouraged.?[42] This is a considerable problem. If, for example, unexpected lightning hurls an airplane against a farmhouse, is that a cost of farming or air travel? Plainly we need the existence of both for the harm to come about. Returning to the example of the truck and train rivalry, if we allocate the accident costs of road congestion to trucks for the purpose of improving the competition between trucks and trains, these costs will no longer be imposed on cars with which the trucks crash. Does this not then distort the competition between transportation by car and transportation by bicycle? Perhaps assigning accident costs to both (or all) participants would avoid this problem.[43] Whatever the merits of this suggestion, it is not how the tort system functions. That is, while we might administratively charge the defendants' activities and not compensate the plaintiffs, that is hardly what tort law does.

Second, it is not clear that accident cost internalization would actually lead to a more efficient allocation of resources given the great number of market imperfections in our economy. Suppose that without internalizing its accident costs, the amount of airline travel is already at the efficient level because of other offsetting market imperfections, such as excise taxes on air travel or motoring subsidies from the national road-building program. If so, then adding on airline accident costs may upset the balance. Economists call this problem the "theory of the second best." It warns that piecemeal solutions will not necessarily move society toward overall allocative efficiency.[44]

Moreover, besides the general possibility of allocative inefficiency, the theory of the second best shows that to the extent that liability law significantly drives up the price of selected goods and services, people may actually be driven to less safe alternatives to which the liability system does not apply.[45] For example, people may continue to use old, or buy used, machine tools or light aircraft rather than switching to newer, safer products to which strict liability attaches. Or people may engage in more do-it-yourself activity. As Walter Olson puts it, "when liability drives up the price of stepladders, more people climb on boxes and chairs."[46]

Writing in the same vein, Peter Huber emphasizes that modern tort law puts a thumb on the scale against new, generally safer "public risks" and in favor of older, generally more dangerous, "private risks" with the result that our zeal to curb some dangers leads, at least in some important areas, to less overall safety. For example, he says our "safe society" has given us "too many wood stoves, too few central power plants, too many cars, too little public transportation, too many natural toxins, too few mass-produced substitutes."[47] The reason for this imbalance, to reemphasize, is that courts now scrutinize technological change thereby giving old techniques considerable cost advantages over new, and on average, safer ones. And while we, of course, need to prevent excess risk from new technologies, we need, as well, mechanisms for social acquiescence in socially desirable new risks—a function that compensation-minded judges are poorly positioned to perform.

A third problem with the goal of cost internalization is that insurance and insurance-pricing practices once again intercede. Because of actuarial requirements and for administrative reasons, liability insurance classification systems frequently group enterprises in ways that externalize costs to other activities that the tort law would seem to internalize.[48] Moreover, victims too avoid internalization by passing the costs onto collateral sources such as health insurance and Social Security that are not merit rated in the way this view of tort law would imply.

Fourth, even if desirable social consequences would flow from account cost internalizing, given the way damages are determined, as previously discussed, tort law allocates costs arbitrarily and inefficiently. Finally, accident costs are hardly the only "externalities" that allow people to benefit from others without paying for them. My enjoyment of your garden is a common example. Your playing loud music after dark that bothers me is another. These market imperfections riddle our economy. Given our failure to achieve a perfect market economy in so many areas, cost internalization is simply too thin a reed to support tort law's continuation.[49] Besides, society can easily pursue this goal in other ways by adding excise taxes or providing cash subsidies thereby seeking to bring about allocative efficiency directly.

NOTES

1. *See* for example Smith, *The Critics and the "Crisis": A Reassessment of Current Conceptions of Tort Law*, 72 CORN. L. REV. 765 (1987) [hereinafter cited as *Critics*]. *See also* Smith, *Rhetoric and Rationality in the Law of Negligence*, 69 MINN. L. REV. 227, 290–99, 323 (1984) and Little, *Up with Torts*, 24 SAN DIEGO L. REV. 861 (1987). Smith's views have recently been endorsed by Florida's ACADEMIC TASK FORCE FOR REFORM OF THE INSURANCE AND TORT SYSTEMS, FINAL RECOMMENDATIONS 21–26 (1988).

2. Professor Robert Rabin has argued, "I am unpersuaded that there is an intrinsic desire for retribution, in contrast to a need for compensation, that would remain unsatisfied in a system that provided adequate reparation and rehabilitation," Rabin, *Environmental Liability and the Tort System*, 24 HOUSTON L. REV. 27, 43 n. 37 (1987). In a recent British study, only half of accident victims who blamed someone for their loss thought their injurer should provide compensation, *See* Lloyd-Bostock, *Common Sense Morality and Accident Compensation*, in PSYCHOLOGY, LAW AND LEGAL PROCESSES (D. FARRINGTON, K. HAWKINS, and S. LLOYD-BOSTOCK, eds.) 99–100 (1979).

3. In their recent study of tort law in Britain, Harris and his colleagues found that only half the victims filing claims attributed fault to the defendant, HARRIS et al., COMPENSATION AND SUPPORT FOR ILLNESS AND INJURY 321 (1984) [hereinafter cited as COMPENSATION AND SUPPORT]. Two-thirds of

those pursuing a tort claim filed only after being so advised by a third party, *id.* at 318.

4. Henderson, *The New Zealand Accident Compensation Reform* (Book Review), 48 U. CHI. L. REV. 781, 797 (1981) [reviewing G. PALMER, COMPENSATION FOR INCAPACITY (1979)].

5. As Holmes saw it, it would be better for private enterprise or the state to set up an insurance scheme simply to compensate victims, O. W. HOLMES, THE COMMON LAW 94–96 (1881).

6. Fletcher, *Fairness and Utility in Tort Theory*, 85 HARV. L. REV. 537 (1972). Criticism of Fletcher can be found in Englard, *The System Builders: A Critical Appraisal of Modern American Tort Theory*, 9 J. LEGAL STUD. 27, 63–68 (1980); Posner, *Strict Liability: A Comment*, 2 J. LEGAL STUD. 205 (1973); Calabresi and Hirschoff, *Toward a Test for Strict Liability in Torts*, 81 YALE L.J. 1055 (1972); and Schwartz, *The Vitality of Negligence and the Ethics of Strict Liability*, 15 GA. L. REV. 963 (1981). A group of Professor Jules Coleman's articles constitutes an extended critical analysis of Fletcher's views by one who believes in corrective justice. *See* Coleman, *Moral Theories of Torts: Their Scope and Limits: Part II*, 2 LAW AND PHILOS. 5 (1983); Coleman, *Corrective Justice and Wrongful Gain*, 11 J. LEGAL STUD. 421 (1982); Coleman, *The Morality of Strict Tort Liability*, 18 WM. & MARY L. REV. 259 (1976); Coleman, *Justice and Reciprocity in Tort Theory*, 14 W. ONT. L. REV. 105 (1975); Coleman, *On the Moral Argument for the Fault System*, 71 J. PHIL. 473 (1974); and Coleman, *Justice and the Argument for No-Fault*, 3 SOC. THEORY & PRAC. 161 (1974).

7. Presumably, Fletcher's solution to these problems would lead him to the current result through devices such as waiver or assumption of risk. But this, of course, complicates his principle. Moreover, why under this approach does the patient bear the risk of the nonnegligent doctor, but the neighbor does not bear the risk of the nonnegligent dynamiter? There might be a good reason, but Fletcher does not address the problem.

8. Fletcher, *supra* note 6, at 548.

9. *Id.* at 550.

10. *Id.* at 568.

11. *See id.* at 564.

12. A decade later, Fletcher wrote again on the topic, admitting that his original effort was somewhat less satisfactory than he had initially seen it, Fletcher, *The Search for Synthesis in Tort Theory*, 2 LAW AND PHILOS. 63, 81–88 (1983).

13. Epstein, *Nuisance Law: Corrective Justice and Its Utilitarian Constraints*, 8 J. LEGAL STUD. 49 (1979); Epstein, *Defenses and Subsequent Pleas in a System of Strict Liability*, 3 J. LEGAL STUD. 165 (1974); and Epstein, *A Theory of Strict Liability*, 2 J. LEGAL STUD. 151 (1973) [hereinafter cited as Epstein, *Strict Liability*]. For critiques of Epstein, *see* the articles cited *supra* note 6, where Fletcher and Epstein are usually criticized together; Fletcher, *supra* note 12, at 64–72; Borgo, *Causal Paradigms in Tort Law*, 8 J. LEGAL STUD. 419 (1979); and Posner, *Utilitarianism, Economics and Legal Theory*, 8 J. LEGAL STUD. 103 (1979). For a reply, *see* Epstein, *Causation and Corrective Justice: A Reply to Two Critics*, 8 J. LEGAL STUD. 477 (1979) [hereinafter cited as Epstein, *A Reply*].

14. Fletcher, *supra* note 12, at 66–69.

15. Epstein, *Strict Liability*, *supra* note 13 at 168.

16. *Id.* at n. 48.

17. Epstein, *A Reply, supra* note 13, at 479.

18. Weinrib, *Toward a Moral Theory of Negligence Law*, 2 LAW AND PHILOS. 37, 52 (1983).

19. Epstein, *A Reply, supra* note 13, at 488.

20. *Id.* at 499.

21. Fletcher, *supra* note 6, at 549 n. 46.

22. Epstein, *Medical Malpractice: The Case for Contract*, AM. B. FOUND. RE-SEARCH J. 87 (1976).

23. Williams, *The Aims of the Law of Tort*, 4 CURRENT LEGAL PROBS. 140–44 (1951).

24. *Id.* at 141.

25. *See* Coleman's articles, *supra* note 6.

26. Williams also distinguishes unjust enrichment cases, Williams, *supra* note 23, at 170–71.

27. *See* Weinrib, *supra* note 18, at 49–57.

28. Conard, *The Economic Treatment of Automobile Injuries*, 63 MICH. L. REV. 279, 292 (1964).

29. Indeed, an individual's experience in settling an auto-crash case "may harden him in the self-righteous belief that he is a good driver and the 'other fellow' is to blame," Cramton, *Driver Behavior and Legal Sanctions: A Study of Deterrence*, 67 MICH. L. REV. 421, 445 (1969).

30. *See generally* A. EHRENZWEIG, PSYCHOANALYTICAL JURISPRUD-ENCE §§ 205–209 (1971); Ehrenzweig, *A Psychoanalysis of Negligence*, 47 NW. U.L. REV. 855 (1953); and Keeton, *Is There a Place for Negligence in Modern Tort Law?*, 53 VA. L. REV. 886, 888 (1967). Professor Little puts it somewhat differently: "Damaged people . . . want accountability, which in a civilized society means access to a forum and a set of rules by which they may publicly prove themselves right and someone else wrong," Little, *supra* note 1 at 869. Justice Linden defends the "mystery and ritual" of tort law as satisfying psychological needs during a time of declining religious belief. In the same vein, Professor Siciliano, after criticizing tort law as a promoter of efficient conduct, suggests that it "might be more productively analyzed . . . as a tribal device for articulating fears, prejudices and values," Siciliano, *Corporation Behavior and the Social Efficiency of Tort Law*, 85 MICH. L. REV. 1820, 1863 (1987).

31. *See* R. KEETON and J. O'CONNELL, BASIC PROTECTION FOR THE TRAFFIC VICTIM 47 (1965). These reactions can be attributed in part to the anxiety that comes simply from being involved in a lawsuit, part arises from counterclaims or perceived harsh treatment by the other side, and a large part all too often is brought about by plaintiffs' lawyers. Frequent complaints include professional arrogance, endless delays for lawyer convenience, failure to keep clients informed, and inattention to the client's psychological needs, *see* COMPENSATION AND SUPPORT, *supra* note 3, at 320.

32. *See* Smith, *Critics, supra* note 1, at 779; Malone, *Ruminations on the Role of Fault in the History of the Common Law of Torts*, 31 LA. L. REV. 1 (1970); and Williams, *supra* note 23, at 138–40.

33. *See* Smith, *Critics, supra* note 1, at 779–83. *See also* Little, *supra* note 1 at 865, "the true operational goal of the law of torts [is] to serve as a civil law method of

truncating unacceptable extremes of human behavior from the remainder that must be left unfettered in a democratic free society."

34. As John Prather Brown has recently put it, "It is absurd to expect courts to play a regular, effective role in setting standards," Brown, *Comment on Calabresi and Klevorik's "Four Tests for Liability in Torts,"* 14 J. LEGAL STUD. 629, 631 (1985). On the empirical side, Eads and Reuter report that "firms learned little from the results of particular litigation about either specific design decisions or the process of design decisionmaking," G. EADS and P. REUTER, DESIGNING SAFER PRODUCTS: CORPORATE RESPONSE TO PRODUCT LIABILITY LAW AND REGULATION vii–viii (1983) (Rand Corporation Institute for Civil Justice). As a consequence of the tenuous link between good design and liability exposure, "[t]he signal says only: 'Be careful or you will be sued.' Unfortunately, it does not say *how* to be careful, or, more important, *how careful* to be," *id.* at vii–ix (emphasis in original). In a similar vein, Professor Cramton points out that tort law tells people only to "drive safely," noting that this is "advice which is not specific enough to inculcate good driving habits and weed out bad ones," Cramton, *supra* note 29, at 445.

35. *Cf.* Baltimore and Ohio Ry. v. Goodman, 275 U.S. 66, 69 (1927), *with* Pokora v. Wabash Ry., 292 U.S. 98, 102, 104 (1934).

36. *Cf.* Smith, *Critics, supra* note 1, whose support for tort law seems to depend on such assumptions that I find far-fetched. *Cf. also* Bell, *Legislative Intrusions into the Common Law of Medical Malpractice: Thoughts about the Deterrent Effect of Tort Liability,* 35 SYRC. L. REV. 939, 975–90 (1984). I have no doubt that doctors are eager not to get involved with a malpractice action and that they find it a bad experience when they do, and I believe that doctors, as a result, engage in conduct that is not in the best interests of patients. Yet I am highly doubtful that the malpractice liability system in action gives doctors reliable information about what socially undesirable conduct to avoid so that the recent robustness of the malpractice liability system can be credited, because of its psychological impact on doctors as Professor Bell would have it, for significant advances in the quality of care that patients now receive.

37. *See* H. L. ROSS, SETTLED OUT OF COURT: THE SOCIAL PROCESS OF INSURANCE CLAIMS ADJUSTMENTS 237–40 (1970). Ross explains that insurance adjusters use traffic regulations rather than negligence standards in settling cases.

38. Not only does tort law promote cynicism about the law, it also teaches people to be cynical about lawyers. When, in the aftermath of the Union Carbide disaster in Bhopal, India, U.S lawyers flew to India, filed lawsuits, and said they were acting for the benefit of the third world, even other plaintiffs' lawyers reacted negatively. Both the Board of Governors of the California Trial Lawyers Association and the Executive Committee of the American Board of Trial Advocates voted resolutions of condemnation. *See CTLA Board Denounces Tactics of Lawyers in Bhopal Death Suits,* L.A. Daily L.J., Jan. 18, 1985, at 20, col. 5 *But cf. ATLA Board Rejects Bhopal Censure,* Nat'l L.J., Jan. 28, 1985, at 3, col. 1 (Association of Trial Lawyers of America considered but refused to censure lawyers who flew to India to pursue claims).

39. Smith, *Critics, supra* note 1, at 782. *See also* A. LINDEN, CANADIAN TORT LAW 16 (4th ed. 1988).

40. For an interesting discussion of this idea, *see* Atiyah, *Accident Prevention and Variable Rates for Work-Connected Accidents* (pt. 1), 4 INDUS. L.J. 1, 11 (1975).

41. To the extent that accident costs are externalized to product or service buyers and users, they are not really externalized after all, because these costs are then reflected in the total cost. On the other hand, if buyers are not aware of these costs, they will mistakenly underestimate the true cost and continue to buy "too much."

42. *See generally* W. BLUM and H. KALVEN, PUBLIC LAW PERSPECTIVES ON A PRIVATE LAW PROBLEM; AUTO COMPENSATION PLANS 57–61 (1965).

43. *See generally* Shavell, *Strict Liability Versus Negligence*, 9 J. LEGAL STUD. 1 (1980).

44. For example, it has been alleged that the price of cars in the United States has increased by perhaps $600 due to restrictions on Japanese imports. Economists rightfully complain that while the import quotas may increase the jobs available for American autoworkers, the resulting price increase distorts consumer preferences and discourages auto sales. Thus, if we eliminate tort liability and the need for liability insurance, the decreased price of driving might bring us back toward a more efficient level of auto purchases after all.

45. For discussions of the theory of the second best and its application to torts problems, *see* Huber, *Safety and the Second Best: The Hazards of Public Risk Management in the Courts*, 88 COLUM. L. REV. 277 (1985) and Henderson, *Extending the Boundaries of Strict Products Liability: Implications of the Theory of the Second Best*, 128 U. PA. L. REV. 1036 (1980).

46. Olson, *Overdeterrence and the Problem of Comparative Risk*, in NEW DIRECTIONS IN LIABILITY LAW (W. OLSON, ed.) 42, 47 (1988).

47. Huber, *supra* note 45, at 279.

48. The ability of insurers to fine tune premiums is limited by the availability of information regarding the insureds' future conduct as well as the cost of gathering such information. In addition, such information, once collected, cannot be easily protected. Free riders could simply copy the classification systems of others. The result might be industry-wide underinvestment in the acquisition of information. The casualty insurance industry has responded to this latter problem by creating a national cooperative rating bureau, the Insurance Services Office. Still, there is reason to think that present classifications are less exact than information costs would warrant.

49. More than two decades ago Professor Alfred Conard and his colleagues said, "[I]t is tempting to conclude that small departures from optimal resource allocation, and small distortions in the distribution of wealth and income resulting from accidents, might well be ignored on the grounds that their social cost is probably small, and certainly small relative to the costs of a reparation system to determine and offset them," A CONARD, J. MORGAN, R. PRATT, C. VOGAL, and R. BOMBAUCH, AUTOMOBILE ACCIDENT COSTS AND PREMIUMS 127 (1964). Recently, Professor George Priest has called the effect of tort law today on activity levels a "trivial sidelight," Priest, *Modern Tort Law and Its Reform*, 22 VALPARAISO U.L. REV. 1, 9 (1987).

II

CURRENT REFORM IDEAS—FALSE STARTS

There is a widespread social consensus in favor of deterring wrongdoing and compensating accident victims. But in the face of current realities, it is difficult to argue that personal injury law well serves these or other more controversial goals. By trying to do many different things, I have argued, tort law ends up doing none of them well.

This is not to say that tort never deters, never properly punishes, or never properly promotes the efficient allocation of resources. And plainly it does a great deal of compensating—as well as overcompensating. At issue, however, is whether, on balance, a wise form of governmental activity is to continue to give accident victims the right to sue in tort. Of course, maintenance of the status quo and outright repeal are not the only choices.

This part describes and criticizes a variety of current tort reform ideas. There are two chapters: Curtailing Victims' Rights (Chapter 4) and No-Fault Alternatives to Tort (Chapter 5).

Although I see considerable merit in many of the reforms discussed in Chapters 4 and 5, ultimately I find them to be false starts. Rather, I believe, we should build a structure that separates compensation and deterrence goals entirely so that income replacement and medical expense protection, on the one hand, and accident avoidance, on the other, are pursued through different social mechanisms. Discussion of my preferred solutions, however, must await Part III.

4

Curtailing Victims' Rights

INTRODUCTION

The description "crisis" now is regularly attached to the tort law/liability insurance system. Some blame the insurance industry for the rapid upturn of premiums during 1986–1987 in many liability insurance lines, as well as for the sporadic unavailability of liability insurance for certain types of risk. Yet those who lay the primary blame on the law are making more political headway.

Tort Reform Designed to Benefit Defendants

Organized, cooperative lobbying for tort reform by business, professional (mostly doctors), and governmental interests has been triggered by the recent tort and liability insurance "crisis." Having experienced sharp increases in insurance costs and, in some sectors, finding liability insurance unavailable at any price, the defendant side is naturally alarmed.[1] Anxiety has been elevated further when, for many, this is the second major upheaval in insurance markets in a decade,[2] when the newspapers are filled with stories of seemingly outlandish, yet successful, personal injury suits[3] and when some enterprises seem to have been driven into bankruptcy by mass tort claims.[4]

These factors, together with the fact that criticisms of the system have come from influential political, business, insurance, and professional leaders, have persuaded many people that tort law is out of control and needs to be reined in. Blame is placed on liberal judges and on the too effective, professionally questionable conduct of the plaintiffs' bar.

During the past two or three years, a package of tort reform measures has been developed and pushed by the Reagan administration and by defense interests in most states and in Congress. This package of victims' rights rollbacks is meant to return us to the "good old days" when personal injury law was a fairly unthreatening and rather easily digestible cost of doing business. The regime envisioned is one in which, although obvious wrong-doers would be made to make reasonable payments for the consequences of their bad conduct, tort law would largely abandon the instrumental goal of internalizing accident costs either for compensation or deterrence purposes.

Although prompted mainly by liability insurance problems, this per-spective assumes that nothing very helpful can be achieved by trying simply to control the insurance industry itself. Rather, the idea is that the insurance industry now responds to the state of personal injury law, so that altering the latter will change the former. This chapter begins with these proposals and charts their legislative success to date. Their potential impact is assessed at the end of the chapter.

Tort Reform Designed to Benefit Victims

The contrasting view of the plaintiffs' side, given the recent instability in liability insurance markets, is that increased regulation of liability insurers is required. Many trial lawyers and consumer groups blame underwriting and actuarial practices of the insurance industry for the crisis.[5] It has been especially irritating to the plaintiffs' side that availability and affordability problems of the last few years have coincided with an apparently healthy rebound in the profits of the casualty insurance industry.[6]

It is no less important to the plaintiffs' bar than to defendants for the liability insurance system to function smoothly. Not only do unstable in-surance markets create the risk of individually uninsured defendants—who therefore will not generally be worth suing. More important, if private liability insurance cannot cope with tort law over time, this threatens to force a dramatic upheaval in the entire system, leading perhaps to the re-placement of personal injury law with something else—a result that the plaintiffs' bar strongly opposes.

The main proposed insurance reforms include limitations on the ability of insurers to raise premiums and drop customers or even whole lines of coverage, the imposition of antitrust rules on the now-exempt insurance industry, and increased public disclosure requirements regarding insurer accounting and pricing practices, as well as their profitability.

Yet, it is by no means clear that proposals for increased insurance reg-ulation rest on a correct analysis of the underlying situation. Despite charges made in some quarters, thoughtful scholars have argued that market failure explanations for the recent insurance crisis are doubtful.[7] The charges that liability insurers are engaged in improper price fixing, that they are trying to recoup past underwriting losses, that they are making irrational pricing decisions, or that they are being influenced by irrational reinsurer behavior all seem to depend on a belief that the liability insurance market is not a competitive one. Yet part of the complaint from the plaintiffs' side, which seems closer to the truth, is that this industry is an especially competitive one.

Governmental regulation could achieve short-run benefits to at least some classes of insureds. Yet it is by no means clear that it will be healthy for the longer run, given the current personal injury-liability insurance system, for there to be sharp restrictions on the ability of insurers to increase their prices and/or to withdraw coverage from one or more insureds. More attention also needs to be given to the cross-subsidization among insureds that is likely to be brought about were tough controls enacted.

Although the plaintiff side is not now talking about other reforms, there are other changes in the tort-liability insurance system they would probably strongly favor. One would be to require various would-be defendants to carry adequate liability insurance. A clear example concerns auto insurance. In the United States, as compared with most industrialized countries, drivers can easily get away without carrying any liability insurance at all, and even the formal requirement in most states is for only a distressingly low sum. In other countries, liability insurance for motorists usually covers an unlimited amount of damages. While that would be difficult to insist on here, surely U.S. motorists could be required to carry coverage of at least $250,000 per person injured and $500,000 per accident.[8]

Many in the plaintiffs' bar would also like to expand substantive tort liability. In particular, many hope that strict liability in tort will increasingly expand to cover services as well as products. But whether the plaintiffs' lawyers would favor this change by legislation is another matter. Because the courts and common law development have served them so well in recent years, probably the plaintiffs' bar would be content, at least for now, simply to await judicial developments. I will not further discuss these proposals from the plaintiffs' bar.

Tort Tinkering: The ABA and Other Proposals

After sponsoring two important studies carried out over several years, the American Bar Association (ABA) has now endorsed modest tort law reform, most of which would help defendants. However, what the ABA advocates falls far short of what the defense side has proposed and of what a few states have in the meantime enacted. The ABA changes, whether adopted or not, are very unlikely to have an important long-run impact on personal injury law. ABA developments are discussed briefly in this chapter.

Although not otherwise discussed here, I note that much other tinkering with tort law that has been proposed is often designed to single out a specific problem or industry for relief. One example is the effort to lessen some of the very substantial tort burdens now felt by the general aviation industry.[9] Another is reflected in bills introduced in Congress and in California designed to assist in various ways a California manufacturer of allegedly defective heart valves in suits brought against it in California by non-American victims of the malfunctioning valve who seek various advantages of the California forum.[10]

Much of the recent academic literature has focused on doctrinal reform, pitting the forces for strict liability against devotees of negligence. So far as deterrence is concerned, I agree with professors with as diverse outlooks as Richard Epstein and William Whitford that this distinction is of little moment.[11] However, my position is far stronger: I have argued in Part I why I believe that even a rule of no liability will have little negative impact on safety. As for the compensation goal, nearly all of the present problems would remain even after as thoroughgoing a shift to strict liability as is imaginable.

A further shift from negligence to strict liability is also unlikely to satisfy the other goals of tort law. Such a shift would actually undercut the aim of punishment and, in most instances, the idea that liability signals socially unacceptable behavior. Moreover, it is surely inappropriate to support vengeance against a nonnegligent injurer. Similarly, strict liability would, at least sometimes, poorly serve the cost-internalization objective, because it invites the inappropriate allocation of costs away from victims. Furthermore, other problems of cost internalization noted earlier would remain. Finally, sweeping strict liability is calculated to please virtually none of the corrective justice theorists. Semistrict liability might satisfy Professor Epstein if couched one way or Professor George Fletcher if stated another way. But the absence of a consensus theory and the practical realities discussed earlier would continue to rob corrective justice of virtually all its real world relevance.

THE REAGAN ADMINISTRATION'S PROPOSALS

In October 1985, the Reagan administration established a Tort Policy Working Group, chaired by Assistant Attorney General Richard K. Willard, Department of Justice. The Working Group's Report, issued in February 1986, proposed a number of tort reforms[12] that were later endorsed by President Ronald Reagan.[13]

Although the report talks about a desire to "alleviate the crisis in insurance availability and affordability,"[14] and to preserve a tort system that rests on the principle of individual responsibility for fault, its package of victims' rights cutbacks is best seen as seeking to turn the tort law clock back to the 1950s. First, the report repudiates the application of strict liability to many product injuries, a doctrine that only really began in the 1960s.[15] Second, the Working Group objects that de facto strict liability now often occurs in negligence cases when juries are permitted to express their sympathies for victims in cases that traditionally would have resulted in directed verdicts for defendants. Once again, it was the 1960s (importantly reflecting the egalitarianism of the times) that saw appellate courts give more power to juries by increasingly ordering trial courts to take a much more hands-off approach to the negligence issue.[16]

Third, in the 1950s, the plaintiffs' bar was both smaller and less sophisticated in its presentation of individual cases to juries.[17] While there can be no undoing of the increased expertise of trial lawyers, the report's proposals to impose stronger proof requirements on plaintiffs, especially on matters involving scientific uncertainty, and to limit the contingent fees paid to victims' attorneys, both seek to keep from juries cases that are brought in the 1980s but would not have been in the 1950s.

Fourth, the Working Group's call to limit awards for pain and suffering and for punitive damages to an aggregate of $100,000 would reinstate the de facto ceiling of those earlier days.[18] Even in liberal California, for example, it appears that the first reported award of more than $100,000 for pain and suffering damages did not occur until 1961,[19] and, of course, the economy has experienced considerable inflation since then. Fifth, with respect to punitive damages awards, the Working Group envisions a return to the prior era when proof of "actual malice" by the defendant was generally required, effectively precluding such awards in virtually all cases brought against enterprises.

Sixth, the report proposes to reverse the "collateral sources rule" under which juries today are not supposed to learn of or take into account a victim's other means of compensation. As a formal matter, this means overturning, not a recent, but rather, a very long-standing doctrine. Yet, it is important to appreciate that in the 1950s the extent of people's collateral sources was altogether different from what it is today. Collateral sources available then were often paid for by the victims or voluntarily provided by friends, family, or employers who plainly did not intend to benefit the tort-feasor. In the 1950s, many fewer employees routinely obtained job-related medical insurance, sick leave benefits, disability pensions, and the like. Public compensation programs have also exploded since the 1950s. Medicare was enacted in 1965; the disability benefits portion of Social Security was phased in between 1956 and 1960. Given the vast new array of social insurance and employee benefits that the intervening years have brought, abrogating the collateral sources rule would bring us much closer to the practice of the 1950s in which tort damages did not nearly so much duplicate other sources of recovery.

Seventh, more complicated analysis is also required to view the report's proposal to eliminate joint and several liability as a return to the old days.

After all, it is a long-standing American rule that two defendants, even if not acting in concert, are both fully liable for the victim's loss so long as both are the proximate cause of the victim's injury. Because the victim cannot recover twice and because reasonably sensible rules for cost allocation among multiple defendants have long existed, the most important consequence of the principle of joint and several liability has been that the risk of insolvency of one of the defendants is borne entirely by the other and not by the plaintiff.

Serious objections to joint and several liability have been generated by two recent changes. First, the widespread introduction of comparative fault, largely a product of the 1960s and 1970s, has meant that innocent victims are not the only beneficiaries of this doctrine. Rather, a victim may now be considerably more at fault than is the solvent ("deep-pocket") defendant from whom he or she collects. Second, cutbacks in old "no duty" rules, and less aggressive determinations by judges that defendants are either not at fault or not the proximate cause of the victim's harm "as a matter of law,"[20] have meant that little-at-fault, deep-pocket defendants are being required to pay for injuries more frequently than before.

Assuming there is to be no retreat from the legal developments just described, replacing the principle of joint and several liability with the rule that defendants are only liable for damages equal to their share of the fault at least moves some little-at-fault defendants back much closer to where they would have been under 1950s-style tort law.[21]

This description of the Working Group's proposal does not mean either that I think that tort law was in all respects worse in the 1950s than in the 1980s or that I oppose all of the Reagan administration's proposals. Indeed, I endorse several of them as part of a first-step compromise package I will discuss in Part III. The point, however, is that the Working Group and I have quite different ideas about the goals of tort reform.

Fundamentally, the Reagan administration's approach would do nothing to address the needs of otherwise uncompensated victims. It fails to give adequate recognition to the fact that the judicial liberalization of tort law that has occurred in the past twenty-five years has been motivated, in substantial respects, by this concern.[22] Even though, as I have shown, tort law is quite poorly designed to achieve the compensation objective, the remedy simply is not to cut back victims' tort rights. Tort law instead should be replaced with a better compensation mechanism. The judges, perhaps understandably, seized on the one mechanism that was available to them. Legislatures have far more leeway to design and enact an effective program. But the Reagan administration blithely dismissed this objective on the ground that other existing compensation sources are adequate—even when they are not. In short, although the Reagan administration identified a number of important changes that might sensibly be included as part of a package of reforms that also deals with the need for victim compensation, its vision as to what is both necessary and just, was far too truncated.

Put differently, the Reagan administration wanted to go back to when tort law was not very expensive, yet still could be pointed to as a hallowed American process for identifying and punishing clearly bad conduct. I, by contrast, want to move toward the elimination of personal injury law in combination with its replacement by mechanisms that treat the compensation of victims entirely separately from the deterrence and punishment of wrongdoers.

In this connection, it is perhaps useful to say a few words about the recent proposals of Professor George Priest. Although he is probably the most prominent law professor whose recommendations most closely match those of the Reagan administration and the defense coalition, there are critical differences in perspective and detail between him and them that deserve attention.[23] Professor Priest believes that the only sensible social objective for the tort system is accident control. Hence, he rejects all tort doctrines, presumptions such as those used in toxic causation and warning defect cases, procedural features, and so on that might be justified on victim compensation grounds. (He does not discuss "justice" goals.) Looking at current doctrine, especially in the product liability area that is his prime focus, he finds it ill suited to the accident avoidance objective. But for Professor Priest it is not merely a matter of retreating from strict liability and returning to negligence, for he finds traditional negligence law lacking as well. Rather, for him the test of injurer liability should be: "Could this accident have been practicably prevented prior to its occurrence.?"[24] More specifically when applied in the product setting, this test becomes: At the time of manufacture, could the product manufacturer have practicably adopted an alternative design, a production process, or attached an effective warning, that would have prevented the accident?

"Practicability" is ensured by engaging in a "rigorous cost-benefit analysis in every products case."[25] This cost-benefit analysis is to consider the marginal costs and benefits of accident prevention strategies reasonably available to both injurers and victims and to assign responsibility to injurers only when a strategy they failed to follow would have been both effective and more effective than any strategy identified for the victims. While this test sounds something like negligence with a defense of contributory negligence, Professor Priest means its application to be different from, and far more demanding on the plaintiffs than, what has been our actual experience with negligence. Perhaps most striking, but probably realistic in view of the test he proposes, Professor Priest expresses doubt about whether trial by jury (as compared, presumably, with bench trials) could continue to be tolerated.[26] It should also be clear that under this test there would no longer be strict liability for manufacturing defects, a step back to the earlier common law that the Reagan administration and most defense interests have not sought to achieve.

On the issue of damages, Professor Priest has not yet told us precisely what his theory of accident control implies. He appears to oppose punitive damages in tort cases altogether, and to favor both caps on noneconomic damages and the abolishment of joint and several liability.[27] Although he sees some merit in reversing the collateral sources rule, he seems to shy away from outright endorsement of that position, probably because of its seeming inconsistency with his position on the deterrence goal.

In sum, Professor Priest's program, like the Reagan administration's, would mean a one-way rollback in victims' rights (which, however, Priest argues would actually benefit consumers, and especially low-income consumers, as a class). What would be left would be a scaled-down tort doctrine aimed at a single objective—accident reduction—that I continue to doubt it can effectively achieve. Most of my criticisms of tort as deterrent, which Professor Priest largely ignores, would be applicable to his reformed tort law as well. At the same time, unlike what my proposals will offer, nothing new is to be provided for victims in Professor Priest's reforms by way of alternative compensation schemes (except perhaps a public information campaign designed "to inculcate the importance of the private obligation to obtain insurance"[28]).

ACTION BY STATE LEGISLATURES

The Reagan administration's involvement in tort reform was important as a symbol and a catalyst. Although its reform package largely paralleled that promoted by various defense interests from the business, insurance, professional, and municipal communities, the participation of national leaders diffused somewhat the charge that "reform" was merely special pleading by those who had been complaining loudest about the tort law and liability insurance crisis.[29]

And during 1986–1988, a majority of states adopted tort reform measures based on the Working Group's agenda. From the national perspective, however, the pattern one sees is quite ragged.[30] Not only have legislatures generally refused to embrace all of the Reagan administration's wish list, but also those individual items that have been selected often emerged in quite different terms from what had been intended. Therefore, although seeds have been sown that might grow into far-reaching reform, most states so far have acted only in the putting-out-fires mode.

For example, several states have put ceilings on tort recovery for noneconomic losses. Yet, the most important thing to note about the limits is that they are far more generous than the $100,000 ceiling proposed by the Reagan administration. Florida, an important torts jurisdiction, imposed a $450,000 cap;[31] and New Hampshire's ceiling is $875,000.[32] Moreover, in a number of states the limits have exceptions that promise to make the restrictions meaningless. For example, although Minnesota caps "intangible loss" at $400,000, that does not cover "pain, disability or disfigurement."[33]

Research by Professor Patricia Danzon on statutes enacted during the 1970s that significantly limited the amount of damages payable for pain and suffering in medical malpractice cases (such as California's $250,000 cap) suggests that such limits can indeed have an impact on the total amount paid out in medical injury cases.[34] Yet because of their high limits and loopholes, it is doubtful that these more recent across-the-board limits on noneconomic loss will be equally effective.

In other words, whereas many states have made largely symbolic gestures with respect to noneconomic loss that will affect virtually no one, in very sharp contrast the Reagan administration's proposed $100,000 cap would mean that the victim in most serious injury cases would actually net nothing for pain and suffering. This is because the $100,000 (and often more) would be eaten up in legal fees and other costs, even under the Working Group's proposals for curtailing the level of contingent fees.

As advocated by the Reagan administration, a number of states have moved toward reversing the collateral source rule. Going beyond the general principle when actually enacting a statute, legislators usually realize that there are a number of important and complicated details to worry about. Should all other sources count to reduce the defendants' obligation, or should there be a list of exclusions (such as life insurance) and/or inclusions (such as public benefits and employee group benefits)? Should defendants be obligated to repay victim insurance premium costs, if any? What if the collateral source contains provisions for subrogation rights against the defendants? As a result of these questions, there is considerable variation among the statutes that the states have enacted.[35]

Professor Danzon's findings in the medical malpractice field[36] suggest that if tort defendants clearly do not have to pay for things otherwise covered by the victims' social insurance benefits, sick leave benefits, and health insurance benefits, that should reduce considerably the amount of tort damages paid out. How well these new statutes will do on that score is uncertain.

Although California imposed a fairly restrictive sliding scale limit on contingent fees in medical malpractice cases during the 1970s, there has been little willingness by states, as yet, to adopt this approach for all personal injury cases.[37] Most state reforms in this area have tended to give judges power to review fees for reasonableness and to provide for attorney's fees sanctions as a way of seeking to deter frivolous complaints (or defenses).[38] Given Danzon's findings in the medical malpractice area,[39] it is rather doubtful whether either sort of change concerning fee arrangements will have a significant impact on the aggregate amount of tort awards. Apparently, such limits are more likely to affect how the victim and his or her lawyer share the awards than the amount the defendant pays.

Regarding the principle of joint and several liability, some states have, as the Working Group favored, abolished the rule outright;[40] yet a number of others have only limited its application with respect to noneconomic losses and rather-less-at-fault defendants.[41] It is dubious that any of these efforts to protect deep-pockets from what is perceived to be unfair picking will by themselves have any noticeable impact either on the ability of certain notorious deep-pockets (e.g., municipal governments) to obtain insurance, or on the level of premiums they pay. What does seem quite clear, however, is that individual victims whose injury unluckily involves an insolvent defendant as well as a deep-pocket are going to be left in a worse position.

Although no state seems to have adopted the Working Group's idea that a single dollar ceiling should limit both pain and suffering damages and punitive damages, some states have sought to curtail the amount of punitive damages by restricting them, in most cases, to the amount of compensatory damages awarded or some multiple thereof.[42] Other solutions have also been adopted, such as imposing a high standard of fault or a high standard of proof before punitive damages are awarded and establishing mechanisms under which a share of any punitive damages award is paid over to a special fund to be used for public purposes.[43]

Even if punitive damages were completely abolished, it is unlikely that this would have an obvious and substantial impact on the financial costs of the tort system. Recent studies have shown that a very small percentage of cases actually attract punitive damages.[44] Indeed, the biggest impact of the recent liberalization in the award of such damages may well be in promoting the settlement of cases for more generous amounts of compensatory damages. If that leverage were removed, compensatory awards might be lowered; but measuring changes in negotiated settlements and determining whether they are attributable to changes in the law of punitive damages would be extremely difficult work.

Still, defendants might derive some security from these new laws on punitive damages in that they are far less likely to be hit with multimillion dollar exemplary damage awards for what they believe is either a minor mistake or even faultless behavior, where the jury decides, as the defendants see it, that they are to be punished for failing to know the unknowable. Although that security may mean little in advance of being sued, it could mean a lot once the parties are locked in litigation combat.

Several states have imposed new restrictions—of quite uncertain impact— on the liability insurance industry. It is just possible that this seemingly unanticipated legislative response will lead the industry to conclude that its complaints about the civil justice system are backfiring and that it is getting more trouble than relief.

A few states have addressed defendant and Reagan administration complaints about strict liability by enacting modest reforms. Most important, in New Jersey, where the courts have embraced what is perhaps the most proplaintiff tort doctrine in the product injury area, the legislature adopted a complex set of rules for product cases, which have the effect of cutting back on some of the most far-reaching court decisions, essentially by eliminating strict liability for what have been termed unknowable or unpreventable dangers.[45] In California, the legislature has, in effect, adopted comment i of Section 402A of the *Restatement (Second) of Torts* by providing that manufacturers are not liable for injuries caused by inherently unsafe common consumer products, such as butter, sugar, alcohol, and tobacco, where the danger is known by the consumer.[46] It is by no means clear that this changes California law, however. Other states have exempted providers (such as blood banks) of specific items (such as blood, human tissue, and body parts) from the application of strict liability doctrines.[47]

But the Reagan administration's pleas for clear fault-finding before liability is imposed has not yielded much. Perhaps this is explained by the view that ending de facto strict liability in what are nominally negligence cases really requires action by judges, not legislatures.

In sum, the movement for victims' rights cutback, as played out from 1986 to 1988, has so far failed to move tort law back to the 1950s in the sweeping way envisioned by the Working Group. And it now looks unlikely to achieve a great deal of significant tort relief for defendants. The simple political explanation of why only modest change has occurred turns on the fact that the Reagan administration's defense-minded proposals do nothing for victims. This has permitted the plaintiffs' bar and consumer groups to characterize these reforms as unfair bailouts of business and insurance interests, who allegedly have manufactured the crisis atmosphere in the first place.[48] Combining the political power of the plaintiffs' bar and these arguments about the one-sidedness of the proposed changes means that only a few states have been willing to make substantial reforms. Elsewhere, defense pressures seem to have been diffused by measures such as the establishment of study commissions and, in many key states, the enactment of primarily symbolic relief for the defense.

THE CONGRESSIONAL IMPASSE

Congress has been considering product liability law reform for a decade, and on a number of occasions something fairly dramatic has almost passed. This ongoing attention to the issue dates from the product liability insurance crisis of the 1970s. At that time, a federal interagency task force, formed to study the problem, made a series of recommendations for change.[49] Further work and a new administration led to the Model Uniform Product Liability Act that reduced general recommendations for reform to specific statutory form.[50] Aimed at states, it was also designed so that Congress could adopt its provisions as well.[51] Although product liability bills have engaged Washington's attention nearly every year since the task force's report,[52] Congress has not yet enacted anything (apart from a special childhood vaccine injury program discussed in the next chapter).

The main theme of the proposed reform in the product liability area has been a search for uniform national standards. Defendants and insurers have consistently complained that, although many products are distributed nationwide, enterprises are subjected to a bewildering variety of local rules. Although many have thought this to be a powerful reason for federal action in this area, it is by no means clear what is supposed to be wrong with the lack of uniform national legal standards. One possible outcome of uneven tort law is that companies find that some states demand more safety than do others. Because of uniform production and marketing requirements, these states may in turn set the standard for the nation. Although creating safer products is hardly objectionable by itself, if the consequence were that products became more expensive, less convenient to use, and/or less attractive than consumers in states with more lenient standards wanted, or that certain products became unavailable everywhere, that would be a basis for saying that consumer interests in less-demanding states were being ill served. One problem with this line of argument, however, is that the advocates for change have not been consumer groups from states with less-demanding tort laws.

Moreover, the call for uniform national standards, like most calls for equality, leaves open the possibility for equality at radically different levels. Yet is is perfectly clear that those asking Congress to enact uniform national standards would not want to nationalize the law of California, which is widely seen as having among the most proplaintiff products liability laws. Rather, advocates for substantive law change by Congress mainly want to be free from the rulings of the highest courts of states such as California and apparently believe that their chances of obtaining such relief are greater in Congress than with the legislatures of those states.

Specifically, most bills seeking to set uniform national standards want to eliminate strict liability in all but the run–of–the–mill manufacturing defect cases. These bills insist on proof of defendant fault in what now are typically called both design defect and warning defect cases. In effect, the defendants are seeking to have Congress insulate them from liability for dangers that were not reasonably knowable or avoidable at the time their product was made.[53]

Traditionally, tolerating state differences in tort law has not only been a matter of loyalty to our federal system generally, but it also reflected the notion that the negligence concept itself depends on community standards. Yet, some claim that certain states are now using their tort law as a vehicle for turning the drug manufacturers, automakers, and others who do business in that state into insurers of injured victims. Perhaps it is appropriate to ask Congress to decide whether individual states ought to be able to force such enterprises to take on that role, especially if it is thought that out-of-state consumers end up paying for the benefits provided to tort victims in the most liberal states.[54] Whether Congress should preempt the states in this way is, of course, quite a different matter.

A second congressional strategy starts from an entirely different premise. It seeks primarily to control the amount of tort damages that are payable in product cases, leaving it to the states to continue to decide when liability is appropriate. This approach, simply put, urges congressional enactment for cases concerning product injuries of the Reagan administration's Working Group recommendations on issues such as pain and suffering damages, the collateral sources rule, punitive damages, joint and several liability, and attorneys' fees.[55]

A third approach to product injuries surfaced in Congress in 1986. This strategy creates incentives meant to achieve settlements of tort claims in which victims quickly obtain compensation for their net out-of-pocket economic loses. The idea is to specify certain offers that plaintiffs and defendants can make to each other that, if not accepted, will lead to penalties if the party refusing settlement continues to litigate, especially if the result of that litigation is less favorable than the settlement offer. For example, simplifying somewhat, if a defendant refuses a product injury claimant's offer to accept payment for only net economic loss, the claimant might then be entitled to payment of his or her attorneys' fees on top of whatever full tort recovery is obtained at trial. Alternatively, if the defendant offers to pay net economic loss and the claimant refuses, the plaintiff might then be restricted in the amount of pain and suffering he or she can obtain through litigation, or might be penalized by having to pay defense attorneys' fees if less than the settlement offer is obtained at trial.[56]

Good things can be said in favor of financial incentives that promote reasonable settlements. But it seems very odd to have Congress select for national treatment an area of litigation administration that is usually considered especially within the province of states and their courts. Such proposals certainly are a far cry from the idea of uniform national substantive law standards that has been at the heart of the congressional deliberations in this field.

Promoting settlement is even further afield from a related concern that is clearly a matter of congressional responsibility. Rather than worrying so much about defining what duties manufacturers ought to have toward people hurt by their products, Congress should pay more attention to the inadequacies in the way the Social Security and Medicare systems now treat the seriously disabled as a whole. If those plans better served the compensation needs of that group, both state court judges and state legislatures could be counted on to see tort law in quite a different light. In any event, as of this writing, congressional reform of product liability law remains at an impasse.

THE TIMID AMERICAN BAR ASSOCIATION

Some leaders in the American Bar Association have seen trouble brewing on the torts front for a while. In 1979, a special committee created by the Board of Governors was charged with the broad duty to examine "the present day validity of the tort liability system in dealing with claims for physical injury."[57] Chaired by former Attorney General Griffin Bell, this committee issued an enormous report in November 1984 that is largely the work product of the committee's reporter, Professor Marshall Shapo.

The committee's charge included giving consideration to "appropriate modification or alternatives to the current system aimed at curing identifiable defects *while preserving the recognized strengths*."[58] Given this mandate, coupled with Professor Shapo's past published enthusiasm for tort law,[59] and the ABA's history of avoiding radical reforms, one should not have expected a report calling for dramatic change. Nor did we get one. The committee's report is, most importantly, a work that extols the virtues of tort law.

Although the committee endorsed the existing workers' compensation system and "cautiously" supported modest auto no-fault schemes of the sort now in place in some states, it firmly opposed what it called the "importation of full-scale legislative compensation schemes for all tort-like injuries."[60] The use of the word *importation*, while clearly referring to New Zealand's solution (of which more later), also captures the lawyers' xenophobia toward legislative encroachment on the common law turf. In short, the committee's essential message was that existing tort law is a tremendous American achievement that ought to be largely left alone. To the extent that modest problems may exist, the committee's view was that they can largely be taken care of by judges and lawyers of goodwill working together on behalf of the public interest.

The Bell Committee's report is a perfectly understandable example of professional solidarity in support of a system in which the profession has made an important psychological investment, wholly apart from any question of financial livelihood that would be hard to give up. After all, a rather small proportion of the ABA membership critically relies on torts cases, let alone accidental personal injury cases, for a living. On the other hand, what tort law is meant to represent—precise, individualized justice meted out through the full-scale adversary system—is an idea that an overwhelming percentage of lawyers has probably long ago embraced and internalized as a way of importantly justifying to themselves their professional role in our society.

Faced with criticism of the Bell Committee's unduly rosy picture,[61] the ABA promptly appointed yet another committee. The Action Commission to Improve the Tort Liability System was announced in November 1985, with Professor Robert McKay as its chair and Professor Robert Rabin as its reporter.[62]

Although the Action Commission was broadly charged with examining all aspects of the tort liability system, it did not take advantage of that broad mandate. Rather, as judged by the recommendations contained in its February 1987 report, the Action Commission seems largely to have allowed the Reagan administration's proposals to set its agenda. That is, just as the Working Group took a stand on pain and suffering damages, punitive damages, joint and several liability, attorneys' fees, the collateral sources rule, and improved dispute resolution processes, so did the Action Commission; its positions on these matters comprise the bulk of its report. On the whole, however, the Action Commission's stands, although largely prodefendant, are far less sweeping.

The Action Commission's report raised the question of "whether fairness and efficiency suggest the need for replacement rather than incremental efforts to improve the existing system of tort liability," noting that "much of the recent academic criticism of tort law attacks the major foundations upon which the system is built."[63] It then sought to justify why it failed to undertake "a comprehensive analysis of the case for universal social insurance or broad-ranging no-fault schemes replacing the tort system" even though some members of the Action Commission favored such solutions.[64] First, this was too big a job in view of the commission's limited time frame. Second, in view of the deliberately selected diversity of its membership, the Action Commission believed it could never achieve a consensus favoring a "substantial dismantling of the tort system."[65] Hence, the Action Commission adopted an incremental approach to reform, assuming consensus would be more likely, because even those members favoring dramatic change would prefer some change to merely retaining the status quo.

The Action Commission's justifications for the narrowness of its reach do not convince me. Substantial first steps in the direction of "replacement" are already well enough worked out for the Action Commission to have taken a stand on them, even within its time frame. Furthermore, the consensus strategy failed anyway, as four of the fourteen members dissented.[66] In February 1987, amid feeling that the bar had to support some tort reform proposals, the ABA's House of Delegates approved virtually all of the commission recommendations.[67] By this time, however, the Action Commission was too late to catch the main wave of crisis-inspired legislation that, where enacted, frequently went further in a prodefendant direction than the Action Commission's more carefully crafted proposals envisioned.

HOW IMPORTANT ARE VICTIMS' RIGHTS ROLLBACKS TO DEFENSE INTERESTS?

Although there has been a great deal of public hand wringing and passionate talk about the recent troubles, what is not often discussed is just how important it is to the defense side to achieve the sorts of changes proposed by the Reagan administration, and just what will be the negative social consequences if they are not made.

One issue is whether the costs of liability insurance premiums (or self-insurance) plus the costs of cooperating in the defense of claims are seriously impairing the competitiveness of American enterprises, or are likely to do so in the future. While it is no doubt true that American enterprises on the whole now face higher personal injury liability costs than do their competitors from other countries, the relative significance of these burdens should not be exaggerated. For example, a 1986 survey by the Conference Board of a sample of more than 200 major U.S. corporations found that, even with recent increases, liability insurance was still 1 percent or less of sales for two-thirds of the enterprises, and 3 percent or less for nearly 80 percent of firms.[68] Hence, even with the liability insurance premium increases of the past two years, most manufacturing firms are still probably no more (and often less) burdened by their personal injury liability costs than by, say, their workers' compensation costs.[69] Similarly, enterprises generally face considerably higher costs for employee sick leave than for personal injury liability.[70] Broadly speaking, therefore, in terms of international comparisons, both wage differentials and overall employee benefit package differentials are far more significant than are personal injury liability differentials.

This is not to say that even 1 percent of a firm's revenue is an irrelevant sum or that enterprises in certain industries are not considerably worse off. Still, industries have long lived, for example, with variations in their workers' compensation and unemployment compensation burdens amounting to several percent of payroll costs. In short, the direct costs of personal injury law are probably most bothersome, not so much because they are larger than before, but because they are unstable and, as a consequence, are more difficult to pass on to consumers.

The future burden of personal injury law on American enterprises is, of course, another matter. Clearly, liability insurance costs have lately been increasing far faster than the cost of living, and based on price increases of 1986–1987, one could project a curve out to, say, the year 2010 that would be menacing indeed. On the other hand, given the frantic price competition in the product liability insurance industry in the late 1970s and and early 1980s, it is likely that, in those years, enterprises' other cost increases significantly outstripped their personal-injury-law-driven cost increases. This instability makes predicting the future very difficult. One recent study found that tort law cost increases over the past couple of decades have broadly paralleled increases in workers' compensation costs and medical costs generally;[71] and the growth in the past decade in the burdens on the Social Security disability insurance trust fund are well known. These points suggest that if our economy is going to have a long-term problem of paying for disability in general, personal injury law is likely to be but a small part of the problem.[72]

Moreover, even if one were to view the current or projected financial burden of personal injury law on American enterprises as more significant than suggested here, the next question is what impact the Working Group package of defense-minded reforms is likely to have on that burden. While there is little doubt that insurers' payouts would be significantly reduced were the defense side's wish list fully enacted, the size of premium reductions that would follow remains uncertain. Because a significant share of insurers' costs are largely unrelated to the level of payouts, even a reduction in overall personal injury awards by 33 percent is not likely to achieve dramatic across-the-board financial relief for U.S. enterprises. Of course, putting strict limits on damages and on substantive liability could dramatically reduce payouts for certain industries, but the results would be both unpredictable and overall still rather trivial when compared to the larger economic picture.

In terms of financial burden, it appears that physicians and hospitals are now far more affected by personal injury law than are enterprises in general. Recent General Accounting Office (GAO) studies have put the average cost of medical malpractice insurance nationally at 9 percent of total physician expenses and 4 percent of physician gross income in 1984—up from 7 percent and 3 percent, respectively, since 1982.[73] Many doctors paid even higher proportions. Additional increases since 1984 mean that many physicians paid more than $25,000 for malpractice insurance in 1986, which for some specialties, meant that many doctors were paying more than 10 percent of their gross income for tort protection. Indeed, obstetricians and gynecologists recently surveyed said that their malpractice insurance costs for 1986–1987 accounted for 23 percent of their gross income.[74] This financial burden might be significantly reducing physicians' incomes, or, more likely, increasing patient health care costs. Yet, once again, malpractice insurance for physicians and hospitals remains a very small share of total health care costs—less than 1 percent according to the GAO.[75]

Moreover, to the extent that personal injury law is currently a serious burden for doctors, it is doubtful in many states that the basic package of defense proposals now being circulated (or recently enacted) would do very much for them. This is mainly because in many states, doctors have already had most of those protections since the mid–1970s. Indeed, the main defense-oriented proposals essentially seek to extend those protections earlier given to doctors to other defendants. To be sure, these earlier reforms may well have served to restrain what would otherwise have been even larger increases medical malpractice. Nonetheless, according to the GAO nearly all specialties in California (a state with such protections for doctors) have experienced premium increases since 1980 that substantially exceeded the increase in the cost of living during that period.[76] All of this suggests that, at least for the medium term, the defense proposals should not be counted on to achieve direct, broad-scale financial relief of a significant amount.

It is also by no means clear just how the defense package is supposed to solve the insurance availability problem—assuming that it remains an important problem, which it may well not. Short of much sharper changes in substantive law than those typically proposed at present, it is hard to see how insurers still will not be afraid of potential lawsuits against, say, child-care providers on grounds of child molestation, against midwives where babies are born in trouble, or against sports equipment manufacturers by injured athletes. There is little reason to believe that the fears that underwriters have of such suits are not genuine if no other underwriters can be found to write that insurance except at a very high price—whether or not the past record of the potential insureds, or the insureds' whole industry or line of work, justifies the current fears. Eliminating liability for even negligence might make a great difference, but that is not what the defense side is proposing.

The defense proposals are better seen, therefore, as an attempt to change the ambience surrounding tort law. If that were achieved, it might lead to fewer negative behavioral responses, to fewer would-be defendants going without liability insurance, to fewer local governments, enterprises, and professionals ceasing to provide services, to less excess caution by those who should be innovators, and so on. These could be very important changes for the future of the United States' economy and the quality of life of Americans. It is important to avoid having a reputation as a place where doctors are disgruntled and where firms feel under siege.

Whether the defense package, even if fully enacted, would actually succeed in changing the tort ambience is, however, uncertain. Doctors, for example, still appear to resent the tort system despite the reforms they achieved more than ten years ago. In sum, if (contrary to my views) the defense package were thought to make personal injury law a good deal fairer, that would be a good reason to favor its enactment. But its critical importance to the long-run health of the U.S. economy has by no means been proven.

NOTES

1. General liability insurance net premiums increased from $6.5 to $20 billion between 1984 and 1986. *See* Harrington, *Prices and Profits in the Liability Insurance Market* in LIABILITY: PERSPECTIVES AND POLICY (R. LITAN and C. WINSTON, eds.) 42 (1988). On the other hand, the availability problem should not be overblown. A 1986 Conference Board survey of major U.S. corporations found few without liability insurance—10 percent, up from 7 percent in 1982 when the liability insurance market was soft and availability was not thought a problem, N.

WEBER, PRODUCT LIABILITY: THE CORPORATE RESPONSE 3 (1987) (Conference Board Rept. No. 893).

2. Similar problems plagued medical malpractice insurance and product liability insurance in the mid–1970s. *See* Robinson, *The Medical Malpractice Crisis of the 1970s: A Retrospective*, 49 LAW & CONTEMP. PROBS. 5 (1986) and *Executive Summary of the Final Report of the Federal Interagency Task Force on Product Liability*, INS. L. J. 686 (1977).

3. One widely circulated story concerns a jury award of $1 million to someone who claimed to have lost her psychic powers from a CAT scan. In fact the trial court set aside this award. *See* Strasser, *Tort Tales: Old Stories Never Die*, Nat'l L.J., Feb. 16, 1987, at 39, col. 1.

4. Both A. H. Robins, maker of the much-sued IUD the Dalkon Shield, and Johns-Manville, the major defendant in the asbestos litigation, have sought reorganization and protection through the bankruptcy system.

5. *See generally* Moskal and Berge, *Tort "Reform": Minnesota Does Not Need Legislation That Makes Victims Pay for the Negligence of Others*, 13 WM. MITCHELL L. REV. 347 (1987).

6. *See* U.S. ATTY. GEN., TORT POLICY WORKING GROUP, AN UPDATE ON THE LIABILITY CRISIS 22–31 (1987) [herinafter cited as UPDATE].

7. *See* for example Harrington, *supra* note 1, at 89–91; Trebilcock, *The Social Insurance-Deterrence Problems of Modern North American Tort Law: A Canadian Perspective on the Liability Insurance Crisis*, 24 SAN DIEGO L. REV. 929 (1987); and Priest, *The Current Insurance Crisis and Modern Tort Law*, 96 YALE L.J. 1521 (1987). *See also* Abraham, *Making Sense of the Liability Insurance Crisis*, 48 OHIO ST. L.J. 399 (1987).

8. Low auto insurance ceilings and ineffective policing of the required coverage rules are importantly responsible for the deep-pocket complaints of cities and counties. For example, when someone is injured by the combined major negligence of a reckless driver and minor negligence of the local authority (say, in not properly maintaining the road), were the driver to have been adequately insured, the city's ultimate share of the liability would be modest even under a regime of joint and several liability.

9. *See* for example Aviation Accident Liability Standards Act, H.R. 2238, S.473 100th Cong. 2nd Sess. (1988).

10. *See* Berkman, "Shiley Seeks Law to Limit Damage Suits by Foreign Litigants Over Heart Valves," Los Angeles Times, May 3, 1988, Part IV, at R, col.3.

11. Whitford, *Strict Products Liability and the Automobile Industry: Much Ado about Nothing*, WIS. L. REV. 83, 160 (1968) and Epstein, *The Social Consequences of Common Law Rules*, 95 HARV. L. REV. 1717, 1724 (1982).

12. U.S. ATTY. GEN., TORT POLICY WORKING GROUP, REPORT ON THE CAUSES, EXTENT AND IMPLICATIONS OF THE CURRENT CRISIS IN INSURANCE AVAILABILITY AND AFFORDABILITY (1986) [hereinafter cited as REPORT]. *See also Hearings Before the House Subcomm. on Econ. Stabilization of the House Comm. on Banking, Fin. and Urban Affairs*, 99th Cong., 2nd Sess. (Aug. 6, 1986) (testimony of Richard Willard, Assistant Attorney General, U.S. Dep't. of Just.). Mr. Willard and then Attorney General Meese were the main Reagan administration spokesmen on tort reform. For reports of remarks by Mr. Willard attributing the liability insurance crisis to improper expansions of tort liability by liberal

judges, *see* Carlsen, *Liability Crisis Is Blamed on Liberal Judges*, San Francisco Chron., Aug. 27, 1987, at 17, col. 1 and L.A. Daily J., Nov. 20, 1985, at 1, col. 2. For the comments of the attorney general, *see* Meese, *Address on Tort Reform Given Before the National Legal Center for the Public Interest*, 23 IDAHO L. REV. 343 (1986/87).

13. *See State of the Union Address Delivered Before a Joint Session of Congress*, 24 WEEKLY COMP. PRES. DOC. 59 (Feb. 2, 1987); *see also* 616 CCH PROD. LIAB. REP. 6 (1987) (referring to fact sheets released with the president's State of the Union Address, describing the administration's proposed tort law reforms). For earlier comments by President Reagan, *see* his *Remarks to Members of the American Tort Reform Ass'n, May 30, 1986*, 22 WEEKLY COMP. PRES. DOC. 720 (June 2, 1986). The Working Group largely reaffirmed its initial proposals in March 1987, *see* UPDATE, *supra* note 6, at 75–87 (1987).

14. REPORT, *supra* note 12, at 4.

15. Two seminal cases embracing strict liability for product injuries were decided in the early 1960s: Henningsen v. Bloomfield Motors, Inc., 32 N.J. 358, 161 A.2d 69 (1960), and Greenman v. Yuba Power Products, Inc., 59 Cal. 2d 57, 377 P.2d 897, 27 Cal. Rptr.1 697 (1963). Section 402A of the RESTATEMENT (SECOND) OF TORTS, embracing strict products liability, was adopted in 1964.

16. This is well illustrated by Rowland v. Christian, 69 Cal. 2d 108, 443 P.2d 561, 70 Cal. Rptr. 97 (1968).

17. Although there clearly were talented and legendary trial lawyers in earlier years, it is only in the last couple of decades that so many personal injury specialists have emerged (e.g., in medical malpractice or aviation law, and even in highly specific kinds of cases, such as asbestos litigation specialists). The growth in continuing education programs and other outreach efforts presented by a great variety of lawyers' groups, such as the Association of Trial Lawyers of America, has also importantly contributed to a more widely trained and talented plaintiffs' bar.

18. In view of the political realities of what states were doing, the Working Group later increased its proposed ceiling on pain and suffering to $200,000. This figure would also no longer include payments for punitive damages, which would be separately controlled. *See* UPDATE, *supra* note 6, at 78–83.

19. Seffert v. Los Angeles Transit Lines, 56 Cal. 2d 498, 364 P.2d 337, 15 Cal. Rptr. 161 (1961).

20. Expanding duties of care have occurred, for example, in the areas of landowner and occupier liability, liability for emotional harm, and liability for injuries to or injuries by persons with whom the defendant has a preexisting relationship.

21. Full ending joint and several liability, however, would probably lead to undesirable overkill, even from the Working Group's perspective. Suppose two independent and equally negligent motorists simultaneously crash into each other and in the process an innocent pedestrian on a nearby sidewalk is hurt. Should that pedestrian only recover half of his or her damages if one of the drivers is uninsured? Or suppose a doctor treating the victim of a negligent motorist commits malpractice. The usual rule is that both the motorist and the doctor are the proximate cause of the harm caused by the malpractice. Should the patient only recover a portion of those damages if the motorist is uninsured? Or suppose a landlord's negligence with respect to building security allows a rapist to attack and injure a tenant. Should the tenant only recover a presumably small portion of her damages, assuming the rapist is not found or cannot pay? These examples are a far cry from those cases usually

considered when the elimination of joint and several liability is proposed—such as municipal liability for the insolvent, drunk driver on the ground that the highway was improperly maintained. Yet a simple elimination of joint and several liability and its replacement with liability based on the proportion that the individual defendant's fault bears to the total fault would seemingly relieve not just the city, but also the solvent landlord, doctor, and motorist in the examples given above. I would be surprised, however, if even the Working Group would endorse those results.

22. *See* Priest, *The Invention of Enterprise Liability: A Critical History of the Intellectual Foundations of Modern Tort Law*, 14 J. LEGAL STUD. 461 (1985). Priest identifies Professor Fleming James as the key intellectual figure behind bringing into common law discourse beginning in the 1960s the loss-spreading notion of enterprise liability. As Priest summarizes it, "James believed in absolute liability; his academic program was designed to achieve it," *id.* at 527.

23. I draw here on Priest, *Products Liability Law and the Accident Rate*, in LIABILITY: PERSPECTIVES AND POLICY (R. LITAN and C. WINSTON, eds.) (1988); Priest, *Modern Tort Law and Its Reform*, 22 VALPARAISO U.L. REV. 1 (1987); and Priest, *The Current Insurance Crisis and Modern Tort Law*, 96 YALE L.J. 1521 (1987).

24. Priest, 22 VALPARAISO U.L. REV., *supra* note 23, at 21.

25. Priest, LIABILITY, *supra* note 23, at 221.

26. Priest, 22 VALPARAISO U.L. REV., *supra* note 23, at 36.

27. Priest, 96 YALE L.J. *supra* note 23, at 1588–89.

28. Priest, 22 VALPARAISO U.L. REV., *supra* note 23, at 37.

29. *See* for example THE DEFENSE TRIAL LAWYERS' TASK FORCE ON LITIGATION COST CONTAINMENT, STATEMENT AND REPORT (1985). Many of the task force's proposals parallel those of the Working Group that have already been discussed. For example, the task force favored limiting or eliminating punitive damages, limiting or eliminating joint and several liability, eliminating the collateral source rule, and controlling contingent fee arrangements between plaintiffs and their lawyers. The task force also favored various changes in the administration of civil justice, including limiting discovery abuse, promoting more active case management by trial judges, and encouraging the use of alternative dispute resolution techniques. Published in September 1985, this report announced the formation of the National Coalition on Litigation Cost Containment, whose stated goal is to work to enact reforms of the sort proposed by the task force.

See also INSURANCE INFORMATION INSTITUTE, THE CIVIL JUSTICE CRISIS (1984). Published by a nonprofit action and information center of the insurance industry, this pamphlet emphasizes public opinion poll surveys that suggest widespread public unhappiness with the civil justice system and proposes reforms that are broadly similar to those supported by the Working Group and the task force. Another important national interest group on the defendant side has been the American Tort Reform Association (ATRA) a business, trade, and professional coalition formed in January 1986 and headed by former Congressman James K. Coyne.

30. Resitrup, *The Final Frontiers*, Nat'l L.J., Dec. 7, 1987, at 13, col 1.

31. FLA. STAT. ANN. §768.80 (West Supp. 1987). The Florida Supreme Court has held that this cap is inconsistent with the Florida Constitution. Smith v. Department of Ins., 55 U.S.L.W. 2608 (Fla. Sup. Ct. May 12, 1987). In late 1988,

Florida voters rejected an initiative petition that would have limited damages for pain and suffering to $100,000.

32. N.H. REV. STAT. ANN. § 508:4–3 (Supp. 1987). By contrast, Maryland has capped noneconomic losses at $350,000, MARYLAND CH. 639, § 11–108 (1986). Washington has adopted a novel limit on noneconomic damages which is determined by multiplying the life expectancy of the victim by 43 percent of Washington's average annual wage; the idea is to allow a higher cap for younger people who have longer to suffer from their injuries, *see* Washington Tort Reform Act of 1986, ch. 305, § 301, 1986 Wash. Laws.

33. MINN. STAT. ANN. § 549.23 (WEST SUPP. 1987). *See also* ALASKA STAT. § 09.17.010 (1986), which imposes a $500,000 cap that does not apply to "disfigurement or severe physical impairment."

34. Danzon, *The Frequency and Severity of Medical Malpractice Claims: New Evidence*, 49 LAW & CONTEMP. PROBS. 57, 76 (1986).

35. *See* for example ALASKA STAT. § 09.17.070 (1986): FLA. STAT. ANN. § 768.76 (West Supp. 1987); ILL. ANN. STAT. ch. 110, § 2–1205 (Smith-Hurd Supp. 1986); MINN. STAT. ANN. § 548.36 (West Supp. 1987).

36. *See* Danzon, *supra* note 34, at 72, 77.

37. Connecticut is the only state I have found, CONN. GEN. STAT. ANN. § 52–251c (West Supp. 1987). California voters in November 1988 rejected such a proposal put to them in the form of a citizens' initiative—proposition 106.

38. For court reviews, *see* for example HAW. REV. STAT. § 607–14.5 (1985); N.H. REV. STAT. ANN. § 507.15 (Supp. 1987); and WASH. REV. CODE ANN. § 4.24–005 (Supp. 1987). For sanctions for frivolous litigation, *see* for example MICH. COMP. LAWS ANN. § 600.2421–.2421C (West 1986) and OKLA. STAT. tit. 23, § 103 (West 1987).

39. *See* Danzon, *supra* note 34, at 78.

40. *See* for example UTAH CODE ANN. § 78–27–38 (Supp. 1986); WYO. STAT. § 1–1–109 (1987).

41. For noneconomic damages, *see* for example California Proposition 51, Civil Code § 1431.2 (West Supp. 1987). For low-fault defendants, *see* for example ALASKA STAT. § 09.17.080 (1986). For a combination, *see* for example HAW. REV. STAT. §§ 663–1 to 663–1.8 (1985).

42. *See* for example FLA. STAT. ANN. § 768–73 (West Supp. 1987); OKLA. STAT. tit. 23, § 9 (West 1987). Although New Hampshire has enacted a statute abolishing punitive damages, it is not clear that such damages were actually available previously, N.H. REV. STAT. ANN. § 507.16 (Supp. 1987).

43. *See* for example ALASKA STAT. § 09.17.020 (1986) (clear and convincing evidence) and FLA. STAT. ANN. § 768.73 (West Supp. 1987) (portion to be paid to Public Medical Assistance Trust Fund or General Revenue Fund).

44. *See* M. PETERSON, S. SARMA, and M. SHANLEY, PUNITIVE DAMAGES: EMPIRICAL FINDINGS (1987). The authors find, however, that the frequency and incidence of total dollars awarded as punitive damages are on the upswing.

45. 632 CCH PROD. LIAB. RPTS. ¶ 93,150 (1987). Ohio had adopted a fairly similar set of rules for products cases, 635 CCH PROD. LIAB. REPTS. ¶ 93,610 (1987).

46. 638 CCH PROD. LIAB. RPTS. ¶ 90,578 (1987).

47. For example, South Dakota, 632 CCH PROD. LIAB. RPTS. ¶ 94,350 (1987) and Texas 638 CCH PROD. LIAB. RPTS. ¶ 94,552 (1987). Texas also limited the rights of victims in product injury cases where victims are primarily at fault, 628 CCH PROD. LIAB. RPTS. ¶ 94,510 (1987).

48. For some charges and countercharges *see* for example *Availability and Cost of Liability Insurance, Hearings Before the Senate Comm. on Commerce, Science, and Transportation*, 99th Cong., 2nd Sess. (Feb. 19 and Mar. 4, 1986) and *Availability and Affordability Problems in Liability Insurance, Hearings Before the Subcomm. on Business, Trade and Tourism of the Senate Comm. on Commerce, Science and Transportation*, 99th Cong., lst Sess. (1985). For the argument that insurance regulation, rather than tort reform, is needed to protect consumer interests, *see* Hunter and Brozilleri, *The Liability Insurance Crisis*, 22 TRIAL 42 (Apr. 1986). *See generally* Nader, *The Corporate Drive to Restrict Their Victims' Rights*, 22 GONZ. L. REV. 15 (1986–1987).

49. REPORT OF THE INTERAGENCY TASK FORCE ON PRODUCT LIABILITY (1977).

50. The act was published at 44 Fed. Reg. 62,714 (1979).

51. Victor Schwartz, a key man in the task force's efforts and the drafting of the model act, has become an important lobbyist for congressional action. A former law professor, the author of a leading treatise on comparative negligence, and a coauthor of the Prosser-Wade casebook on torts, Schwartz has, from his new base as a Washington lawyer, continued to publish widely on the need for tort reform. *See* for example Schwartz, *Tort Law Reform: Strict Liability and the Collateral Source Rule Do Not Mix*, 39 VAND. L. REV. 569 (1986) and Schwartz and Mashigian, *Failure to Identify the Defendant in Tort Law: Towards a Legislative Solution*, 73 CALIF. L. REV. 941 (1985).

52. *See generally* Twerski, *A Moderate and Restrained Federal Product Liability Bill: Targeting the Crisis Areas for Resolution*, 18 J.L. REFORM 575 (1985).

53. This is essentially the approach of the model act and of S. 2631, 97th Cong. 2d Sess., 128 CONG. REC. S. 6878 (daily ed. June 8, 1982) and its near twin S. 44, 98th Cong., lst Sess., 129 CONG. REC. S. 90 (daily ed. Jan. 26, 1983), which together have gained considerable legislative attention. The 1985 version was numbered S. 100, 99th Cong. lst Sess. (1985). *See* XLI CONG. Q. ALMANAC 278 (1985). A plan seeking to set uniform national standards was again taken up in 1988 as H.R. 1115, Uniform Product Safety Act, 100th Cong. 2nd Sess. (1988).

54. *See* R. NEELY, THE PRODUCT LIABILITY MESS (1988) and Sugarman, *Holding Down the Tort* 74 A.B.A.J. 115 (Sept. 1, 1988) (book review of Neely). On the role of the federal government in tort reform generally, *see* Kitch, *Can Washington Repair the Tort System?*, in NEW DIRECTIONS IN LIABILITY LAW (W. OLSON, ed.) 102 (1988).

55. In 1986, this package was introduced by Senator Kasten as Amendment No. 1814 to Senate Bill 100, 99th Cong., 2d Sess. (1986). *See* Starobin, *Senate Panel to Tackle Three Insurance Plans*, 44 CONG. Q. 1219–22 (May 31, 1986). It is, of course, possible to combine both national substantive standards with national limitations on damages, as did Kasten's proposal.

56. For discussions tracking the politics of these proposals, contained in a bill by Senator Danforth, S. 1999, 100th Cong., lst Sess. (1986) and comprehensive amendments proposed by senators Gorton, Kasten, and Dodd, *see* 44 CONG. Q. 1219–22 (May 31, 1986); 1268 (June 7, 1986); 1362 (June 14, 1986); 1511–12 (June 28,

1986); and 2316 (Sept. 27, 1986). For further discussion of the legislative history, political wrangling, and the settlement incentive proposal eventually included in S. 2760, 99th Cong., 2d Sess. (1986) and passed by the Senate Commerce Committee, *see* Gordon, *Federal Product Liability Reform: A Comparison of S. 2760 and the System in the United Kingdom*, 9 U. PA. J. INT'L BUS. L. 265, 275.95 (1987). For a further discussion of the settlement incentive idea of S. 2760, *see* Perlman, *Products Liability Reform in Congress: An Issue of Federalism*, 48 OHIO ST. L.J. 503 (1987).

For a federal settlement incentive proposal designed for the medical malpractice area and meant to encourage states to design their own plans in order to avoid having a congressional solution imposed, *see* congressmen Moore and Gephardt's *Medical Offer and Recovery Bill*, H.R. 3084, 99th Cong., 1st Sess. (1988). This plan draws on Moore and O'Connell, *Foreclosing Medical Malpractice Claims by Prompt Tender of Economic Loss*, 44 LA. L. REV. 1267 (1984). For a settlement incentive proposal aimed at toxic torts cases, *see* Feinberg, *The Toxic Tort Litigation Crisis: Conceptual Problems and Proposed Solutions*, 24 HOUS. L. REV. 155 (1987).

57. *See* the committee's preface to TOWARDS A JURISPRUDENCE OF IN-JURY; THE CONTINUING CREATION OF A SYSTEM OF SUBSTANTIVE JUSTICE IN AMERICAN TORT LAW (Report to the American Bar Ass'n of The Special Committee on the Tort Liability System, 1984) [hereinafter cited as TOWARDS A JURISPRUDENCE OF INJURY].

58. *Id.* (emphasis added).

59. *See generally* M. SHAPO, PRODUCTS LIABILITY; CASES AND MA-TERIALS (1980); M. SHAPO, CASES AND MATERIALS: TORT AND COM-PENSATION LAW (1976); and Shapo, *A Representational Theory of Consumer Protection*, 60 VA. L. REV. 1109 (1974).

60. TOWARDS A JURISPRUDENCE OF INJURY, *supra* note 57, at 14–10.

61. This was first evident at a conference I attended that the ABA sponsored in Lexington, Kentucky, in 1985 on the unveiling of the report.

62. The product of this group's work is contained in REPORT OF THE AC-TION COMMISSION TO IMPROVE THE TORT LIABILITY SYSTEM (1987) [hereinafter cited as ACTION COMMISSION REPORT].

63. *Id.* at 5.

64. *Id.*

65. *Id.*

66. *Id.*

67. *See* American Bar Association Mid-Year Meeting, 55 U.S.L.W. 2450 (Feb. 24, 1987) and Coyle, *ABA Takes a Stand on Tort Reform—Finally*, Nat'l L.J., Mar. 2, 1987, at 8, col. 1.

68. N. WEBER, *supra* note 1, at 13.

69. In 1984 workers' compensation nationally cost on average 1.66 percent of covered payroll, *see* 50 SOCIAL SEC. BULL. 32, table 6 (April 1987).

70. CHAMBER OF COMMERCE OF THE U.S. SURVEY RESEARCH CENTER, EMPLOYEE BENEFITS, 1985 reports, at table 4, that paid sick leave on average cost those companies surveyed that provided such benefits 1.3 percent of payroll.

71. *See* R. STURGIS, THE COST OF THE U.S. TORT SYSTEM: AN AD-DRESS TO THE AMERICAN INSURANCE ASSOCIATION (Nov. 1985).

72. *See* Pedrick, *Perspectives on Personal Injury Law*, 26 WASHBURN L.J. 399 (1987).

73. GENERAL ACCOUNTING OFFICE, MEDICAL MALPRACTICE: IN-SURANCE COSTS INCREASED BUT VARIED AMONG PHYSICIANS AND HOSPITALS 28–29 (1986).

74. Nye, Gifford, Webb, and Dewar, *The Causes of the Medical Malpractice Crisis: An Analysis of Claims Data and Insurance Company Finances*, 76 GEO L.J. 1495, 1506–07 (1988).

75. GAO, *supra* note 73, at 25.

76. GENERAL ACCOUNTING OFFICE, MEDICAL MALPRACTICE: CASE STUDY ON CALIFORNIA (1986).

5

No-Fault Alternatives to Tort

Many academics have long favored dramatic changes in the tort law/liability insurance system. They have proposed a great variety of schemes, broadly modeled after the workers' compensation system, for replacing pieces of the tort system with no-fault compensation plans covering all sorts of accidents. Some academics have also been attracted to even bolder comprehensive accident compensation schemes, such as that enacted in the early 1970s in New Zealand, which has supplanted virtually the whole of personal injury law.

TRADITIONAL STRATEGIES: TAILORED COMPENSATION PLANS

Compulsory Plans

In the United States workers' compensation and automobile no-fault plans are the major tailored compensation schemes. Workers' compensation is the oldest and most important. Widely enacted at the beginning of this century, it is now a feature of every state's accident-compensation program. Workers' compensation (income loss, medical expenses, and rehabilitation costs) formally provided by the employer as part of the employment relationship, covers injuries on a no-fault basis that arise out of and occur in the course of the job. In principle, workers' compensation was meant to replace a worker's tort right with assured compensation for basic economic loss.

No-fault automobile insurance was enacted in about two dozen states during the late 1960s and 1970s. Although varied in design, the general goal of these plans is to ensure compensation for basic economic loss to moderately injured victims of road accidents. Unlike workers' compensation, auto no-fault plans extinguish tort rights, if at all, for less-serious injuries only. Although at one time auto no-fault seemed likely to sweep the nation, by 1980 its momentum appeared to have dissipated. With the recent surge in auto insurance costs, however, it is receiving revived attention. For example, although an insurance industry sponsored auto no-fault plan, it was soundly defeated by California voters in November 1988; the idea has now become a legislative issue.

A wide range of other tailored accident-compensation schemes has been proposed, and a few have been enacted. These schemes target categories such as nuclear accidents,[1] drug injuries,[2] toxic chemical injuries and diseases,[3] accidents occurring during medical treatment,[4] public transportation accidents,[5] dangerous product injuries,[6] victims of human experimentation,[7] injured school children,[8] and victims of violent crimes.[9]

Advocates of tailored compensation plans seem primarily motivated by a concern for uncompensated victims—those people for whom tort law fails to provide a satisfactory remedy. Sometimes tort law's shortfall arises for clear doctrinal reasons, such as when the injurer is not at fault and strict liability is unavailable. Many medical accidents are in this category. Other times the problem is the insolvency of defendants, as with crime victims. Still other times, the connection between the victims and their injurers may be overly speculative, as in toxic tort claims. In any case, the public typically will consider most of the victims for whom these compensation plans are tailored to be needy and deserving.

Many reformers further conclude that tort law now pays some victims too generously. Thus, reformers propose that benefits paid through compensation schemes be lower in some respects than what tort law provides. Lower compensation benefits conserve funds to allow coverage of more claimants. Also they may promote timelier payments. The four main sources of reduction are (1) sharply curtailing damages for pain and suffering, (2) eliminating payment for losses covered by other sources, (3) imposing ceilings on recovery of economic loss, for example, by limiting the percentage of monthly earnings to be replaced, and (4) introducing waiting periods or other deductibles that shift the cost of small injuries onto victims.

The administrative inefficiencies and high costs attending the tort apparatus often appall reformers. Their proposed compensation alternatives are meant to be simpler, faster, and far cheaper to administer. They strive for administrative efficiency by reducing the need for lawyers, obviating proof of fault, and, in some cases, eliminating high marketing costs such as sales commissions on private insurance policies. No-fault plans also typically strive (crime victims' plans aside) to internalize accident costs to activities responsible for them. I later return to this feature.

The expertise of the reformers is one reason why tailored compensation plans are proposed. Reformers interested in the problem of plane crashes, for example, and dismayed by their treatment under current tort law would understandably propose a plan specifically tailored to that subject.[10] Such single-issue proponents would not attempt to solve related problems about which they may know and care little. The result, however, could be an overall pattern that looks like a crazy quilt.

Political considerations also play a role in determining which sorts of accidents are addressed by compensation schemes. During the Progressive Era, for example, when workplace reforms were generally a matter of high priority (e.g., child labor laws were also enacted then), the political climate was ripe for passage of workers' compensation rather than plans aimed at other or all injuries. Similarly, around 1970 when, with consumer-protection measures and auto regulation generally in vogue, the time seemed right for the enactment of auto no-fault plans. Moreover, auto insurance companies were then suffering losses despite rapidly escalating premiums. Thus, reformers could emphasize the unhappiness of both insureds and insurers.

Interest in compensation plans for victims of crimes ebbs and flows with political concern over the "crime problem." Likewise, because toxic chemicals are currently in the public eye, compensation proposals for these victims are now fashionable. By contrast, most Americans probably do not now think in terms of accidents in general.[11] This fragmented approach can create considerable problems, however. A whole series of independent and costly bureaucracies managing uncoordinated schemes filled with gaps and overlaps, can come into being in this way.

Some argue that major accident-compensation reform will emerge only as the final product of a series of smaller steps that bring many tailored plans on line. But because state legislative agendas have not significantly advanced beyond automobile no-fault plans and workers' compensation, it remains unclear whether tailored plans as stepping-stones are the right politics.

The adoption of a tailored compensation plan does not ensure the end of tort law even for the subject of the plans. For example, when professors Robert Keeton and Jeffrey O'Connell effectively campaigned for auto no-fault in the late 1960s, although they well demonstrated that the tort system inadequately compensates many seriously injured motoring victims, their scheme limited no-fault damages to $10,000. Even in New York and Michigan, the states that have since adopted the broadest auto no-fault plans,[12] the most seriously hurt still must resort to the tort system and no doubt are still undercompensated. In addition, having made a strong case against general damages, Keeton and O'Connell advocated their elimination in only run-of-the-mill auto accident cases. Plainly, they might have proposed a more drastic curtailment of pain and suffering awards for those left in the tort system so as to free up more funds to pay no-fault benefits for the economic losses suffered by the more seriously injured. So, too, they might have favored deductibles in the no-fault plan's coverage of economic losses in order to shift funds from the less seriously injured to the more so. However, Keeton and O'Connell's proposals served to placate both lawyers, who could continue to look forward to handling the big cases, and potential plaintiffs in the mass of little cases, who would retain their ability to recover all their economic losses.

Keeton and O'Connell were apparently astute. About twenty states now have in place at least halfway no-fault measures. By contrast, although one portion of the insurance industry and the Uniform Law Commissioners did finally support far more sweeping auto no-fault plans,[13] no American jurisdication has yet taken such a bold step. That the reason is politics, not feasibility, has since been demonstrated by the action of the Canadian province of Quebec, which has fully replaced tort law in the auto accident area with a government-run, no-fault scheme.[14]

Elective Plans

Over the years, out of a frustration over stalled auto no-fault reform, legislative failure to impose no-fault solutions on various other accidents, as well as the perceived impracticality of a mandated, legislative no-fault solution in some areas, Professor O'Connell has advanced a series of inventive proposals that contemplate the substitution of no-fault plans for tort benefits through some kind of election process.[15] In return for giving up their tort claims, victims would be promptly paid for their out-of-pocket losses. In most versions, O'Connell imagines that the "election" will occur before any injury occurs; in others, however, the election comes afterward. In some of his proposals, the election is effectively to be made by the injurers and is binding on victims; other times the power to elect is in the hands of victims.

The major example of O'Connell's elective no-fault idea being put into place so far is in the area of high school athletics. There, nationwide, schools have arranged for generous disability insurance benefits to be offered to students who are injured while playing school sports—on the condition that they give up their tort claims. In short, victims have the choice, after the accident, to accept the no-fault benefits or to sue. O'Connell claims that this arrangement is working quite well, and it is estimated that by the end of 1987, forty-eight of fifty-one victims to whom offers were made elected the no-fault benefits.[16]

A quite different approach to substituting no-fault for fault is illustrated by O'Connell's recent, creative proposal for elective auto no-fault.[17] Motorists would choose to be covered by either the fault or the no-fault scheme. If two motorists were involved in an accident and both were in the fault system, their possible claims against each other would be governed by the existing tort rules. If two no-fault–electing motorists were in an accident, they would each turn exclusively to their own insurers and would have prompt access to generous compensation for net economic loss. What if a fault-covered motorist and a no-fault–covered motorist were in an accident? The no-fault motorist would claim solely against his own insurance no-fault policy. The problem comes with fault-covered victims. To allow them to sue the other motorist undermines the principle that the no-fault–electing motorist is to be free from tort suits. O'Connell's inventive solution is to have a fault-covered victim claim against the uninsured motorist coverage of his own insurance policy, a standard insurance contract feature in fault states today that is used to deal with the problem of the large number of motorists who drive without insurance. To the objection that his solution forces those in the fault system to pay for accidents that should be the responsibility of those in the no-fault system, O'Connell correctly responds that under his plan those in the fault system will have reciprocally escaped from liability to those in the no-fault system whom the fault-electing motorists negligently injure. As O'Connell figures it, as more people choose the no-fault alternative, those in the fault system should see both a decline in their premiums for liability insurance and an increase in their uninsured motorist premiums. Faced with the option his plan would offer, O'Connell confidently predicts that, over time, the no-fault choice would capture most of the market.

A still different O'Connell idea for an elective no-fault approach is illustrated by a plan that briefly gained attention in Congress in 1986 during debates on product liability law reform.[18] The basic idea is to create a two-tier system for product injuries. Those victims handled by one tier would obtain prompt payment for their out-of-pocket losses on a no-fault basis. Those on the other tier would receive full-scale tort law recovery, but would face full-scale traditional tort burdens, most likely including proof of defendant fault. Such plans aspire to move to the no-fault tier both a significant share of cases that now eventually lead to tort recovery and a significant number of cases that now generate no recovery at all.

If one tries to adapt auto no-fault and workers' compensation schemes to product injuries as a class, it quickly becomes apparent that there is no convenient and acceptable boundary line that would define when no-fault compensation is due that is analogous to the auto accident or the workplace injury. "But for" causation simply will not do. If that were used, knife makers (and their consumers) and whiskey makers (and their consumers) would have to pay for injuries to those who were injured through deliberate, reckless, and negligent use of these products, even if there were no defect in the product itself. Most people would find this result unfair. What is troubling is not the sense that such victims should be denied compensation, even for self-caused injuries from such products. Rather, the objection is that the maker and other buyers of the product would be singled out to pay. Moreover, in a cause-based system it would very often be uncertain which product to charge; if I am slicing a lime to put in my gin and tonic and cut my finger, do I claim from the knife maker, the lime grower, or the gin distiller?

Professor O'Connell's elective solution is meant to resolve the problem of deciding when no-fault is appropriately applied to product injuries. In such a system, the parties themselves define the triggering compensatory event. Of course, because the parties cannot really be expected to negotiate individually before the event over what events will generate no-fault benefits, the power to elect must generally be lodged with either victims or injurers.

As O'Connell recognizes, problems are created whether it is the plaintiff or the defendant who determines on which tier a case is to fall. The defendant would have an incentive to opt for lower no-fault recovery only in those cases where it would otherwise be found liable in tort. That is true whether the enterprise is permitted to elect for individual cases after the accident or for classes of cases beforehand. Under these circumstances, what would have been sold as a scheme to give benefits, albeit lower benefits, to more victims would mainly be a rollback of victim rights.

On the other hand, if victims have the option of electing no-fault recovery, one must be concerned that those who will do so are only those who would not otherwise recover in tort. While this may be good from the narrow perspective of expanding victim benefits, it no longer looks like a compromise reform that would be attractive to defendants.[19]

Still, over the years, O'Connell has invented various clever variations on this main theme that cope reasonably well with these incentive problems and promise to put on the no-fault tier, not only a considerable number of cases that would have led to full tort recovery if litigated, but also at least a fair number that would not have led to recovery if litigated.[20]

Yet, in the end, even if an elective no-fault scheme would work as well as O'Connell hopes, it simply could not serve accident victim compensation needs in a comprehensive manner. Masses of disabled people, surely as equally deserving as many who would be served by O'Connell's plan, will not be covered. Thus, for me, elective no-fault can only be supported as a step on the way to some other arrangement.[21] My own more sweeping elective plan, intended as just such a stepping stone, is described in chapter 9.

No-Fault Benefits for Vaccine-Damaged Children

Although Professor O'Connell was pushed toward elective no-fault in the product area at least in part because of the difficulty in determining legislatively what injuries to cover, it turns out that in some important situations the problem of deciding which product injuries are appropriate for tailored no-fault treatment is not so difficult after all. One nice illustration of this point involves the reasonably well understood and occasionally very serious side effects of the anti-*pertussis* (whooping cough) vaccine routinely administered to nearly all American children. This also brings us to the United States' most important, actually enacted, no-fault development in nearly twenty years.

It is now well established that a rather small but uncertain proportion of children who receive immunization injections against *pertussis* suffer serious injuries from the vaccine. This immunization is nearly universally required before children can attend school. Some have argued that it makes sense today on narrow cost-benefit grounds for an individual family to seek to avoid having its child immunized, in effect free riding on the decisions of others to use the vaccine. But, from the overall societal perspective, the public health community still strongly believes that, notwithstanding the occasional unfortunate consequences, mass immunization should continue in order to keep at bay a disease that killed thousands of children annually in the 1930s and kills nearly no one today.[22]

What to do about the victims of this public health campaign is another matter. By the fall of 1986, tort suits for enormous sums had been filed on behalf of many of them.[23] In the closing weeks of the 99th Congress, a no-fault plan to deal with such victims was enacted. The National Childhood Vaccine Injury Act of 1986[24] is designed to provide compensation to an estimated seventy seriously disabled or killed victims a year of the anti-*pertussis* vaccine as well as victims of some other designated vaccines. No-fault damages are to be paid merely upon a showing that the victim had been vaccinated and soon thereafter suffered one of the statutorily recognized side-effects. No demonstration is required of the defectiveness of the vaccine, regardless of state law.[25] As compared with a tort remedy, relief from this burden is an especially important benefit in states that protect a manufacturer from liability if it had reasonably warned doctors of risks that the vaccine maker had reason to know about. In those states where such warning was given, in order to win in tort, the plaintiffs have to show that the manufacturer was negligent in failing to discover or market a safer vaccine. While some victims might be able to prove that to the satisfaction of a jury, it would probably be an extremely heavy burden for most.[26]

Under the Vaccine Injury Act, unlike in the usual no-fault proposal, victims are entitled not only to their otherwise uncovered medical expenses, incidental expenses, and lost earnings (here set for children in terms of the state average wage once the child reaches age eighteen), but also to pain and suffering damages of up to $250,000.[27] Of course, if a seriously harmed child were ever to get to the jury on the question of damages in a torts case, far more than $250,000 might be awarded.

Although this scheme is designed to be elective for victims, this is not because of the typical O'Connell concerns in product injury cases. After all, once the triggering compensatory event has been identified, as it has been here, why not impose this no-fault solution on victims and vaccine makers alike? The elective feature here was meant to appease the trial bar. Whether many victims will choose to litigate, however, is uncertain. Under the Vaccine Injury Act, in order to bring a tort claim the claimants must first file for and then forfeit whatever no-fault benefits would otherwise be available. In this respect it is like the high school sports injury plan, described above, that O'Connell helped develop. (That, of course, is a private plan where only an elective solution is possible.) Moreover, under the Vaccine Injury Act, those who choose the tort route are, regardless of current state law, to be subjected to legal hurdles that make such a path highly treacherous.[28] Therefore, unless strong evidence of manufacturer wrongdoing comes to light, the Vaccine Injury Act presents victims with an offer they probably cannot refuse.

Although the Vaccine Injury Act was passed by Congress and signed by the president in the fall of 1986, at that time no funding mechanism for the no-fault benefits was included.[29] The original idea was to have the plan fully funded by an excise tax on each vaccine dose. Because the vaccine manufacturers have, in response to tort liability fears, boosted their price per dose by far more than the proposed tax and because there have been serious fears of vaccine unavailability from time to time during the past couple of years, one might have imagined that this no-fault solution, together with its funding mechanism, would be fairly attractive all around.[30] Yet in the face of strong White House opposition to the tax mechanism, the plan was initially passed with the funding arrangement for the benefits to be worked out later.

That finally occurred at the end of 1987. Direct federal appropriations of $80 million per year for fiscal years 1988–1991 were authorized. These are intended to cover injuries and deaths that occurred before October 1, 1988. An excise tax is set starting in 1988 at $4.56 per dose of anti-*pertussis* vaccine that is meant to cover injuries occurring after October 1, 1988. The amendments also permit those with pre–October 1, 1988 injuries to sue in tort, not only without going through the no-fault scheme, but also without being subject to the new restrictions on tort recovery.[31]

There is, of course, a great deal to be said in favor of providing generous no-fault benefits to children who have been injured while performing what may be termed a public service. Therefore, I find it difficult to object to the Vaccine Injury Act as a short-run solution. Yet from a broader perspective, this example well illustrates my general objection to tailored compensation plans. There are, after all, enormous numbers of children, who are born with birth defects or contract serious childhood diseases, and who, in my view, are as deserving as vaccine-damaged children. But there is little prospect of reaching their compensation needs through plans that depend on identifying enterprises that have somehow caused their condition. To be sure, some of these "defective" children will be compensated through successful suits brought on their behalf against their mothers' obstetricians, whether truly at fault or not. That, of course, is part of what is driving many doctors from the baby-delivery business. But many disabled children will simply have no access to either tort recovery or a special compensation fund. What is required instead are new ways of thinking about disabled children in general.

In the same vein as the Vaccine Injury Act, Virginia has recently adopted innovative legislation that attempts to take some of the so-called bad baby cases out of the medical malpractice system.[32] As already indicated, it is widely believed within the medical profession that obstetricians have been successfully sued of late in cases where babies have been born with birth defects or have suffered injuries during or immediately after birth, even though the doctors were not negligent. Such cases are thought to play a major role in the soaring costs of malpractice insurance for obstetricians and in driving many doctors from that line of practice.

The Virginia plan is designed to provide reasonable no-fault compensation for net economic loss to eligible babies in lieu of their tort claims, thereby curtailing huge pain and suffering awards, removing the high legal costs from the system, providing psychological relief for doctors, and ensuring adequate medical services in connection with childbirth. Effective starting in 1988, the program is funded by assessments on hospitals ($50 per delivery), those doctors doing obstetrics work ($5000 per year), and all other physicians ($250 per year). A claim against the program is meant to be the exclusive remedy of eligible children whose physicians participate in the plan, unless willful bad conduct is shown. On the one hand, a doctor can elect not to participate in the plan (by not paying the obstetrician's fee); in return, the child is ineligible for the plan's benefits, but may still sue the doctor for malpractice. The same goes for hospitals. By May 1988, however, about 80 percent (more than 500) of Virginia obstetricians had signed up. At the same time, malpractice insurance had become easier to obtain and doctors in the plan were typically given a 10 percent cut in their rates.

The law defines eligible children as those who suffer injury to brain and spinal cord as a result of "the deprivation of oxygen or mechanical injury occurring in the course of labor, delivery, or resuscitation in the immediate post-delivery period" and as a result are rendered "permanently nonambulatory, aphasic, incontinent and in need of assistance in all phases of daily living." Plainly, this definition is meant to capture a narrowly defined class of severely neurologically injured babies. It is estimated that there will be up to forty valid claims per year at an average cost of $500,000 per claim, for a total annual cost of $20 million. (Of those, an estimated two to five would sue and win in tort under the traditional system.) How well this definition of eligible claimants will work as an administrative matter remains to be seen. It is to be anticipated that some parents will seek coverage and will be denied for failing to meet some part of the definition, whereas others, believing themselves otherwise to have a good tort claim, will seek to escape coverage and thereby retain their right to sue by alleging that their child's injury is not quite covered. As of October 1988 there had been no claims under the plan. What is clear is that this plan leaves out, not only other cases where obstetricians are sued, but far more important, a much larger number of innocent and needy newborns with severe disabilities arising from quite different causes.

BROADER STRATEGIES: ACCIDENT-COMPENSATION PLANS

Tailored compensation schemes fail to resolve the inadequacies of tort law as a compensation system. As already indicated, the primary defect lies in the lack of a principled explanation for picking out separate classes of accident victims for compensation on a no-fault basis. Victim need is independent of cause or type of injury. For example, are the heirs of someone killed when an airplane unavoidably crashed after being hit by lightning more deserving of compensation than are the heirs of someone killed directly by lightning? As Professor Marc Franklin has said in attacking tailored plans, "I see little reason to single out automobile victims for special treatment. I do not see why, as an initial proposition, today's law should care *how* a limb was broken, whether by an intentional wrongdoer, a negligent automobile driver, a nonnegligent driver, a wall toppled by an earthquake or a fall in the bathtub."[33] Reform-minded scholars who find tailored compensation schemes too narrow usually conceptualize the problem as one of accidents taken as a whole. These politically bold advocates propose general accident-compensation plans to replace tort law.

General plans have been advocated by many, including Professor Franklin, Professor Richard Pierce,[34] Professor Roger Henderson,[35] and Mr. Eli Bernzweig.[36] Perhaps most significant, New Zealand enacted a plan of this sort in the 1970s. The New Zealand plan is indebted to a Royal Commission, which issued the Woodhouse Report of 1967, and to the singular efforts of Geoffrey Palmer, then professor, later member of Parliament and deputy prime minister.[37]

These comprehensive compensation plans all replace tort damages with guaranteed compensation for lost income, medical expenses, and rehabilitation costs without regard to type of accident or fault. The plans differ somewhat along basic dimensions such as (1) legal mechanisms,[38] (2) administration,[39] (3) level of benefits provided, such as the proportion of income to be replaced,[40] and (4) integration with other compensation schemes such as social insurance and employee benefits, including health insurance. I will not evaluate these policy choices here.

I will focus on financing, however, which is an important and controversial dimension of these proposals. Some, like me, argue that a compensation plan's funding mechanism is not the place to pursue either the deterrence or cost-internalizing goal. Professor Palmer is now in this camp, despite earlier views to the contrary. Under this approach, the most attractive financial source would probably be a progressive general tax, like the national income tax. An alternative might be another broad-based mechanism like the payroll, sales, or value-added tax.

At the opposite extreme are those advocates of comprehensive no-fault plans who would use the funding arrangements to serve the deterrence and cost-internalization goals. Like many advocates of tailored plans, they generally agree that tort law does not well serve these goals. Nonetheless, they believe that a well-structured, general-accident compensation scheme will effectively and efficiently further them. The Franklin and Pierce plans, which would impose differential charges at the firm level so as to emphasize strongly accident-avoidance incentives, are good examples of this approach.

In Professor Franklin's proposal, the compensation fund would initially receive revenue from general taxes and license fees paid by automobile drivers. But in cases of entrepreneurial activity *every* accident leading to a payout would be charged back to the cause of the harm. Franklin is confident that over the long run this financing method would be fair; but he recognizes that a run of bad luck could unfairly drive some firms out of business. Therefore, firms would be permitted to insure against the charges the fund would impose.

Very plainly, for Franklin, the main point of the reimbursement funding strategy is deterrence. However, he is also interested in having industries pay their way, even where no safer behavior can efficiently be achieved. On the other hand, beyond business activity, Franklin finds the costs of individualizing contributions to outweigh the benefits of possible behavior change or social cost accounting. He is also concerned that nonbusiness activities may face unfairly large charges that they could not then pass on. Motorist payments, therefore, would be based not on individual driving records, but rather on the sort of criteria that liability insurance uses today, such as age, miles driven, and car location. The aggregate sum collected from these license fees would equal approximately half of the benefits paid out to victims of private motoring accidents. Under Franklin's plan, the same agency that disperses benefits would also levy charges on the specific enterprises that reimburse the fund. However, this agency would not have other safety-promoting functions.

In contrast, Professor Pierce advocates the creation of a "Safety Enhancement and Compensation Agency" that would compensate accident victims and regulate safety "in all areas of the economy."[41] Although this agency would regulate directly, its major technique of behavioral control would be to impose accident costs on those "entities in the best position to control those costs."[42] More precisely, Pierce envisions that this agency would "accumulate data on accident costs by type of activity and, when possible, by the firms whose products or services were involved in accidents."[43] Payments to accident victims would not be the only source of data; the agency would also use statistics to determine the relationships of activities to injuries and to identify the cheapest cost avoider.

Unlike Franklin, Pierce proposes that when assigning costs to accidents, the agency use standardized damage amounts rather than the figures used for compensation. For example, death would carry a fixed cost no matter who was killed, and wage losses would be treated the same regardless of prior wage of the victim. Using these data, the agency would then assess costs to the relevant activity and industry. Pierce would allocate costs to individual firms when firm-level data were reliable and the firms could spread accident costs over time. The central purpose in assigning costs would be to provide market incentives for optimal investment in safety. Pierce is optimistic about changing injurer conduct through such cost-allocation strategies. However, he remains skeptical whether denying compensation for certain behavior would modify victim conduct.

In an important sense, the Pierce and Franklin plans approximate a series of separately funded tailored compensation schemes that use merit-rating and cost-allocation principles wherever feasible. Compared to a series of tailored plans, however, their proposals have the decided advantage of uniform benefits across different types of accidents. Furthermore, the compensation-administering agency would be the same. These plans also avoid large gaps and overlaps in compensation that would likely occur were equivalent tailored plans adopted serially.

Falling in between the fine-tuned approaches of Franklin and Pierce and the broad-based financing plans now favored by Palmer is an approach illustrated by Professor Terrence Ison's proposal for Great Britain. This plan would vary costs at the industry or activity level, but not at the individual firm or act level. Employers' rates would vary according to the severity and frequency of accidents and industrial disease occurring in each industry. The charge on motoring would vary for different categories of vehicles based on "varying degrees of the risk created."[44] Presumably this means that trucks, buses, and taxis would pay more than private cars. Other activities might also have to pay into the fund because of claims they generate. Ison suggests cigarette smoking as an example. Finally, general taxes would make up the difference.[45]

New Zealand's compensation system, in practice, employs a funding strategy similar to what Ison proposes. At first the New Zealand Royal Commission advocated a broad-based financing mechanism. It envisioned a flat levy on all employers of 1 percent of wages and salaries because "[a]ll industrial activity is interdependent and there should be a general pooling of all the risks of accidents to workers."[46] There was, however, concern that "insufficient attention had been given to the economic implications of allocating accident costs under the scheme."[47] As enacted, therefore, the legislation provided, à la Franklin and Pierce, for both "classifications and rates of levy" that vary by occupation or industry as well as individual, firm-level penalties and rebates.[48]

What actually happened was that in 1973 a number of industrial classifications were established; in 1976, more were added, and they have been further subdivided in the years following.[49] Contribution levels are then based on the prior claims history of the various industry classes. However, neither the firm-level penalty nor the rebate provision had been used at all through 1979[50] and only to a tiny extent since then. For example, in 1985 a little more than $1 million was awarded to about 175 employers as safety-incentive bonuses; this compares with claims paid that year of more then $300 million.[51] In regard to motor vehicles, the scheme from the start set different levies for cars, trucks, taxis, and buses. The rates do not depend, however, on one's driving record, the miles one drives, or the kind of driving one does.

EVEN BROADER HORIZONS: COMPREHENSIVE DISABLIITY COMPENSATION PLANS

The next step in the development of compensation systems may be to expand the New Zealand approach by erasing the line between victims of accident and victims of illness. In 1967 Professor Ison advanced a scheme for Great Britain that would cover both of these classes of the disabled.[52] The Woodhouse Report for New Zealand, probably influenced by Ison, discussed the idea that same year.[53] Indeed, a Woodhouse Report for Australia endorsed just such a broadened scheme in 1974, as has Professor Palmer.[54] None of these recommendations has yet been adopted.

If compensation is the central purpose of the plan, there seems no principled reason to single out accident victims when victims of disease or birth defects are equally deserving.[55] For example, is someone who is disabled because of the unexpected side effects of a drug designed to relieve the pain of arthritis more deserving of compensation that someone who is directly disabled by arthritis? Or is a child who accidentally breaks his leg while bicycling or who accidentally burns his arm on a stove more deserving of compensation than is a child born without an arm or a leg? Both sorts of disabilities can come without warning and be equally disruptive. Both accidents and illness can incite their victims to anger, with the world in general and with specific individuals. Indeed, many might think the ill or the congentially disabled are a more innocent group than the injured.

In addition, as New Zealand has learned, administering a general-accident compensation plan creates awkward boundary-drawing problems. Defining an accident raises the same sort of difficulties as workers' compensation has continually faced determining whether the workers' harm arose "out of and in the course of" the job. While there will be some boundary-line problems in any scheme, the ones created by a general-accident compensation plan can be very thorny.[56]

Where a plan compensates only accident victims, the ill might receive highly unequal treatment. New Zealand does have social welfare provisions for victims of disease, but they are less generous. Because the United States guarantees the sick even less protection than does New Zealand, the problem would be greater if the United States were to adopt an accident-compensation plan.

At a less lofty level, a general-accident compensation plan must cover occupational diseases, if workers are not to be left worse off than they are today under workers' compensation. This creates another horizontal inequity problem. Failing to have a comprehensive disability plan means that workers' off-the-job accidents would be covered, but their nonoccupational sickness would not be. It also creates a practical problem, because many diseases have ambiguous origins or appear to be the result of mixed work and nonwork causes.

In order to avoid duplication of benefits, any no-fault accident-compensation plan must deal with the difficult and often costly problem of coordination with our vast, underlying social insurance and employee benefit system. This is illustrated by automobile no-fault plans. Although these plans are a decided improvement over the tort system, automobile accident victims with good employee benefits have at least two potential sources of compensation for their medical bills and lost income. If an automobile plan is set up to pay only for otherwise uncompensated losses, then it is not a very good buy for people with other sources of protection—unless the no-fault plan also includes a complicated pricing arrangement that permits motorists to opt for large deductibles so that their no-fault benefits can be meshed with their other benefits. On the other hand, if automobile no-fault is set up to be primarily responsible for accident losses, complicated reimbursement arrangements with employee health plans, sick leave plans, disability insurance plans, Social Security, and so on must be established. And besides, when no-fault is primary, motorists with good basic benefits are being forced to buy first-party auto no-fault protection for which they have little or no need. This point about coordination is particularly relevant to American workers in progressive employment who are already well protected against income losses and medical expenses from almost any accident.

Donald Harris and his colleagues at the Centre for Socio-Legal Studies, in Oxford, England, have responded to objections to both tailored and general-accident compensation plans with even more sweeping proposals. Their plan would bring all the disabled together for common treatment in a single social welfare scheme.[57] This plan would include the victims of accidents, illness, and birth defects. These proposals bear a closer resemblance to proposed income maintenance reforms than to traditional tort reforms. For example, some aspects of Harris's plan parallel recent Thatcher government legislation on mandatory sick leave.[58] Others resemble the agenda of Britain's Disability Alliance, which arose in the context of welfare reform and call for cash payments to all the disabled regardless of their means.[59]

Altering an accident-compensation plan to include the disabled entails a dramatic expansion of the scheme, however. Illnesses are a considerably larger economic problem than accidents, costing more workdays and greater medical expenses. Illnesses not only disable more people, but also lead on average to more debilitating medical consequences.

Yet, from a national budgetary perspective, the proposed changes may not be as sweeping as might be imagined. Countries such as Great Britain, Australia, and New Zealand already have strong social welfare programs in place. These deal with both income losses and medical expenses associated with sickness. As Ison recognized nearly twenty years ago, such proposals contemplate the sensible integration of accident coverage into the basic social welfare fabric of the country. The United States, of course, must start from a more modest baseline of governmentally provided protection. In my judgment, therefore, our vast private employee benefit system must play an important role in any parallel proposals here.

Harris and his colleagues are to be commended for rethinking these problems from the ground up. They have focused their income-replacement proposals on the duration of need—envisioning distinct treatment for short-term, temporary, and permanent disabilities.[60] This focus is similar to my own strategy, which I will discuss later. At that time, I will also criticize the Harris approach for still thinking too narrowly about the income maintenance task.

NOTES

1. *See* Estep, *Radiation Injuries and Statistics: The Need for a New Approach to Injury Litigation*, 59 MICH. L. REV. 259 (1960). For a proposal to internalize catastrophic losses arising from nuclear power plants and liquid natural gas terminals, *see* Meyer, *Regulating Catastrophes through Financial Requirements: A Model State Statute*, 20 HARV. J. ON LEGIS. 441 (1983).

2. *See* Fleming, *Drug Injury Compensation Plans*, 30 AM. J. COMP. L. 297 (1982) and Merrill, *Compensation for Prescription Drug Injuries*, 59 VA. L. REV. 1 (1973). For proposals restricted to DES injuries, *see* Note, *Bearing the Burden of DES Exposure*, 60 OR. L. REV. 309, 317–24 (1981) and Comment, *Industry-Wide Liability*, 13 SUFFOLK U.L. REV. 980, 1015–22 (1979).

3. *See* Soble, *A Proposal for the Administrative Compensation of Victims of Toxic Substance Pollution: A Model Act*, 14 HARV. J. ON LEGIS. 683 (1977); Trauberman, *Statutory Reform of "Toxic Torts": Relieving Legal, Scientific, and Economic Burdens on the Chemical Victim*, 7 HARV. ENVTL. L. REV. 177 (1983); Treiger, *Relief for Asbestos Victims: A Legislative Analysis*, 20 HARV. J. ON LEGIS. 179 (1983); Note,

The Inapplicability of Traditional Tort Analysis to Environmental Risks: The Example of Toxic Waste Pollution Victims Compensation, 35 STAN. L. REV. 575 (1983); and Note, *Mass Tort Claims and the Corporate Tortfeasor: Bankruptcy, Reorganization and Legislative Compensation Versus the Common-Law Tort System*, 61 TEX. L. REV. 1297, 1344–56 (1983). For a proposed no-fault solution to losses caused by hazardous waste, *see* INJURIES AND DAMAGES FROM HAZARDOUS WASTES— ANALYSIS AND IMPROVEMENT OF LEGAL REMEDIES, A REPORT TO CONGRESS BY THE "SUPERFUND SECTION 301(E) STUDY GROUP," 97th Cong. 2nd Sess. (Sept. 1982). For comments on the Superfund Study Group's proposals, *see* Freeman, *Toxic Torts, Hazardous Waste and the Superfund*, 2 J. PROD. LIAB. 149 (1983) and Grad, *Injuries from Exposure to Hazardous Waste: Can the Victim Recover?*, 2 J. PROD. LIAB. 133 (1983).

For discussion of proposals for federally funded occupational disease compensation schemes, *see* Schroeder, *Legislative and Judicial Responses to the Inadequacy of Compensation for Occupational Disease*, 49 LAW & CONTEMP. PROBS. 151, 163–73 (1986).

For doubts as to whether so-called toxic torts (including drug injuries) "can be equitably disaggregated from the undifferentiated mass of accidental harms" to be given special treatment in a compensation scheme, *see* Rabin, *Indeterminate Risk and Tort Reform: Comment on Calabresi and Klevorik*, 14 J. LEGAL. STUD. 633, 641 (1985). For criticisms of both focused no-fault solutions and *ad hoc ex post* solutions to selected mass tort problems, *see* Rabin, *Environmental Liability and the Tort System*, 24 HOUSTON L. REV. 27, 44–50 (1987).

Because of causation uncertainties and the likely retroactive imposition of liability, Professor Kenneth Abraham opposes the adoption of no-fault compensation funds for mass toxic tort problems. Abraham, *Individual Action and Collective Responsibility: The Dilemma of Mass Tort Reform*, 73 VA. L. REV. 845, 885–98 (1987).

4. Carlson, *A Conceptualization of a No-Fault Compensation System for Medical Injuries*, 7 LAW & SOC'Y REV. 329 (1973); Havighurst, *"Medical Adversity Insurance"—Has Its Time Come?*, 1975 DUKE L.J. 1233; and Havighurst and Tancredi, *"Medical Adversity Insurance"—A No-Fault Approach to Medical Malpractice and Quality Assurance*, 51 MILBANK MEMORIAL FUND Q. 125 (1973). *See also* Henderson, *The Boundary Problems of Enterprise Liability*, 41 MD. L. REV. 659 (1982) and Keeton, *Compensation for Medical Accidents*, 121 U. PA. L. REV. 590 (1973). For an important earlier treatment, *see* Ehrenzweig, *Compulsory "Hospital-Accident" Insurance: A Needed First Step Toward the Displacement of Liability for "Medical Malpractice,"* 31 U. CHI. L. REV. 279 (1964). For a comparative perspective, *see* Cohen and Lorper, *The Swedish No-Fault Patient Compensation Program: Provisions and Preliminary Findings*, INS. L.J. 70 (1976). For a recent innovative solution, *see* Pollack, *Medical Maloccurrence Insurance (MMI): A First-Party, No Fault Insurance Proposal for Resolving the Medical Malpractice Controversy*, 23 TORT & INS. L.J. 552 (1988).

5. Ballantine, *A Compensation Plan for Railway Accident Claims*, 29 HARV. L. REV. 705 (1916); Baxter, *The SST: From Watts to Harlem in Two Hours*, 21 STAN. L. REV. 1 (1968); and Milford, *A No-Fault Aviation Insurance Plan*, 41 J. AIR. L. & COM. 211 (1975).

6. *See generally* J. O'CONNELL, ENDING INSULT TO INJURY: NO-FAULT INSURANCE FOR PRODUCTS AND SERVICES (1975). *See also* O'Connell, *Expanding No-Fault Beyond Auto Insurance: Some Proposals*, 59 VA. L.

REV. 749 (1973) (where Professor O'Connell first published his sweeping proposals to replace tort law with no-fault enterprise liability).

7. *See* 1 PRESIDENT'S COMM'N FOR THE STUDY OF ETHICAL PROB-LEMS IN MEDICINE AND BIOMEDICAL AND BEHAVIORAL RESEARCH, COMPENSATING FOR RESEARCH INJURIES (1982).

8. *See* Kimball, *Compulsion without Protection or Recourse: The Case for No-Fault Accident Insurance for School Children*, UTAH L. REV. 925 (1975).

9. *See* for example Geis and Edelhertz, *California's New Crime Victim Compensation Statute*, 11 SAN DIEGO L. REV. 880 (1974) and Rothstein, *How the Uniform Crime Victims Reparation Act Works*, 60 A.B.A.J. 1531 (1974).

10. *See* Sugarman, *Right and Wrong Ways of Doing Away with Commercial Air Crash Litigation*, 52 J. AIR L. & COM. 681 (1987).

11. Keeton and O'Connell first tried to justify their focus on auto accidents on the ground that, unlike bathtubs, autos are a social problem. I am baffled by this argument unless it merely restates their observation that auto problems are "in the public eye." More realistically, Keeton and O'Connell contended that "a narrower focus than concern about all misfortune is the only hope for marshaling public opinion to support reform," R. KEETON and J. O'CONNELL, BASIC PRO-TECTION FOR THE TRAFFIC VICTIM 4 (1965). In short, they made a strategic decision to attempt the reform of only a large piece of the problem. Of course, the piece they chose is well understood by the legal profession and poorly managed by tort law. Otherwise, one would think that people hurt in bathtub falls actually need more protection because tort law ignores them. Nevertheless, auto accidents are a more inviting target in view of the resources they already command, whereas compensation for bathtub accidents implies new costs.

12. *See* O'Connell and Beck, *An Update of the Surveys on the Operation of No-Fault Auto Laws*, INS. L.J. 129, 131–32 (1979); and DEP'T OF TRANSPORTATION, COMPENSATING AUTO ACCIDENT VICTIMS: A FOLLOW-UP REPORT ON NO-FAULT AUTO INSURANCE EXPERIENCES (1985).

13. *See Uniform Motor Vehicle Accident Reparations Act*, 14 U.L.A. 41 (1980).

14. For a discussion of the Quebec system, *see* O'Connell and Tenser, *North America's Most Ambitious No-fault Law: Quebec's Auto Insurance Act*, 24 SAN DIEGO L. REV. 917 (1987).

15. O'Connell's 1973 proposals for expanding no-fault coverage beyond auto insurance, *supra* note 6, envisioned both mandatory no-fault in extrahazardous activity settings and elective no-fault in other settings. Interestingly enough, O'Connell's ideas for both mandatory no-fault enterprise liability and elective auto no-fault draw on earlier proposals of Professor Ehrenzweig. *See* Ehrenzweig, *"Full Aid" Insurance for the Traffic Victim—A Voluntary Compensation Plan*, 43 CALIF. L. REV. 1 (1955) and A. EHRENZWEIG, NEGLIGENCE WITHOUT FAULT; TRENDS TOWARD AN ENTERPRISE LIABILITY FOR INSURABLE LOSS (1951). Soon O'Connell began to concentrate on the elective strategy. *See* for example O'Connell, *Harnessing the Liability Lottery: Elective First-Party No-Fault Insurance Financed by Third-Party Tort Claims*, WASH. U.L.Q. 693 (1978); O'Connell, *An Alternative to Abandoning Tort Liability: Elective No-Fault Insurance for Many Kinds of Injuries*, 60 MINN. L. REV. 501 (1978); O'Connell, *Elective No-Fault Liability by Contract—With or Without an Enabling Statute*, U. ILL. L.F. 59 (1975); O'Connell, *No-Fault Liability by Contract for Doctors, Manufacturers, Retailers and Others*, INS.

L.J. 531 (1975); O'Connell, *An Elective No-Fault Liability Statute*, INS. L.J. 261 (1975); and O'Connell, *No-Fault Insurance for Injuries Arising from Medical Treatment: A Proposal for Elective Coverage*, 24 EMORY L.J. 21 (1975). *See generally* J. O'CON-NELL, THE LAWSUIT LOTTERY: ONLY THE LAWYERS WIN (1979). For his most recent salvo against the tort system, *see* J. O'CONNELL and C. B. KELLY, THE BLAME GAME: INJURIES, INSURANCE, & INJUSTICE (1987).

For comments on O'Connell's proposals, *see* for example Ford, *The Fault with "No-Fault,"* 61 A.B.A.J. 1071 (1975); Freedman, *No-Fault and Products Liability: Can One Live without the Other?*, 12 FORUM 100 (1976); Freedman, *No-Fault and Products Liability: An Answer to a Maiden's Prayer*, INS. L.J. 199 (1975); Schwartz, *Products Liability and No-Fault Insurance: Can One Live without the Other?*, 12 FORUM 130 (1976); Schwartz, *Professor O'Connell's No-Fault Plan for Products and Services: Have New Problems Been Substituted for Old?*, 70 NW. U.L. REV. 639 (1975); and Keeton, *Book Review*, 13 HARV. J. ON LEGIS. 429 (1976) [reviewing J. O'CONNELL, ENDING INSULT TO INJURY (1975)].

Professor Franklin also ventured into the elective no-fault arena in connection with a specific problem in *Tort Liability for Hepatitis: An Analysis and a Proposal*, 24 STAN. L. REV. 439 (1972).

16. *See* O'Connell, *A "Neo No-Fault" Contract in Lieu of Tort: Preaccident Guarantees of Postaccident Settlement Offers*, 73 CALIF. L. REV. 898 (1985).

17. O'Connell and Joost, *Giving Motorists a Choice Between Fault and No-Fault Insurance*, 72 VA. L. REV. 61 (1986).

18. *See* Senator Danforth's original Senate Bill 1999, 99th Cong., 2d Sess. (1988), developed by the Senate Commerce Committee staff and described in a floor statement by Danforth, 131 CONG. REC. S. 18, 321–22 (daily ed. Dec. 20, 1985).

19. A scheme with victim election also raises the difficult problem of deciding to whom to make the election available; plainly, the wider the circle beyond those who would otherwise recover in tort, the less attractive the plan to defendants.

20. In a recent discussion, the similarities and differences between O'Connell's elective proposal and the settlement incentive proposals I discussed in Chapter 4 are made clear. O'Connell, *Balanced Proposals for Product Liability Reform*, 78 OHIO ST. L.J. 317 (1987). For his latest version, *see* O'Connell, *Neo No-Fault: A Fair-Exchange Proposal for Tort Reform*, in NEW DIRECTIONS IN LIABILITY LAW (W. OLSON, ed.) 186 (1988). For earlier discussions, *see* for example O'Connell, *A "Neo No-Fault" Contract in Lieu of Tort*, supra note 16; O'Connell, *Offers That Can't Be Refused: Foreclosure of Personal Liability Injury Claims by Defendants' Prompt Tender of Claimants' Net Economic Losses*, 77 NW. U.L. REV. 589 (1982); and O'Connell, *Harnessing the Liability Lottery: Elective First-Party No-Fault Insurance Financed by Third-Party Tort Claims*, WASH. U.L.Q. 693 (1978).

Kenneth Feinberg, the special settlement master in the Agent Orange litigation, has proposed a voluntary settlement incentive proposal for toxic torts cases that, because it would limit the rights of those claimants who would otherwise wish to go the tort route, could become, in practice, a one-way defendant election scheme, *see* Feinberg, *The Toxic Tort Litigation Crisis: Conceptual Problems and Proposed Solutions*, 24 HOUS. L. REV. 155 (1987) and Rosenberg, *Toxic Tort Litigation: Crisis or Chrysalis? A Comment on Feinberg's Conceptual Problems and Proposed Solutions*, 24 HOUS. L. REV. 183 (1987).

21. More than ten years ago O'Connell argued that "given the relatively worthless

nature of tort liability insurance as an insurance mechanism, one forced to choose between retaining the present system and simply abolishing it (at least as applied to personal injury for products liability and medical malpractice), would probably more sensibly abolish it than retain it," O'Connell, *An Alternative to Abandoning Tort Liability*, *supra* note 15, at 517. But for "political, practical, and constitutional reasons," *id.* at 519, he instead proposed "elective no-fault."

As for the constitutional issue, while it is quite unpredictable just what individual state courts would do under their own constitutions, I have long been unimpressed with the claim that states cannot simply repeal tort law for personal injuries without thereby depriving people of federal constitutional rights. Such thinking reflects a long-past era of judicial intrusion into legislative policy-making in the area of economics and social welfare on substantive due process grounds. From this perspective, I fail to see why the enormous destruction of defendant rights in recent years, through the expansion of tort liability, would not also be violative of due process. I side with former Harvard Dean Erwin N. Griswold who has said that even Congress could abolish tort law, *id.* at 515.

22. *See generally* REPORT OF THE WORKING GROUP ON VACCINE SUPPLY AND LIABILITY, REPORT OF THE CABINET COUNCIL ON HUMAN RESOURCES, reprinted in National Childhood Vaccine Injury Compensation Act of 1988, before the Sen. Comm. on Labor and Human Resources, 99th Cong. lst Sess. (1985), at 120–53.

23. *See* Tarr, *DTP Vaccine Injuries: Who Should Pay?* Nat'l L.J., Apr. 1, 1985, at p. 1, col. 1. For a selection of these cases, *see* Toner v. Lederle Laboratories, 779 F.2d 1429 (9th Cir. 1986); 732 P.2d 297, 112 Idaho 328 (1987) (on questions certified to the Idaho Supreme Court); CCH PROD. LIAB. RPTS. ¶ 11,965 (9th Cir. 1987); Hurley v. Lederle Labs., 651 F. Supp. 993 (E. D. Tex. 1986); Flood v. Wyeth Labs., 183 Cal. App. 3d 1272, 228 Cal. Rptr. 700 (1988); Martinkovic v. Wyeth Labs., CCH PROD. LIAB. RPTS. ¶ 11,564 (N. D. Ill. 1987); Patten v. Lederle Labs., CCH PROD. LIAB. RPTS. ¶ 11,727 (D. Utah 1987); Shaucil v. Lederle Labs., CCH PROD. LIAB. RPTS. ¶ 11,578 (N. J. 1987); Senn v. Merrell-Dow Pharmaceuticals, CCH PROD. LIAB. RPTS. ¶ 11,729 (Ore. 1988); and Wack v. Lederle, CCH PROD. LIAB. RPTS. ¶ 11,739 (N. D. Ohio 1987).

24. P. L. 99–660. This act was part of an Omnibus Health Bill, S. 1744, signed by President Reagan on November 14, 1986. *See* 44 CONG. Q. 2920 (Nov. 15, 1986). For the original report of the act, *see* HOUSE COMM. ON ENERGY AND COMMERCE, NATIONAL CHILDHOOD VACCINE INJURY ACT OF 1986, H.R. REP. No. 908, 99th Cong., 2d Sess. (1986). For a discussion of the act, *see* Schwartz and Mashigian, *National Childhood Vaccine Injury Act of 1986: An Ad Hoc Remedy or a Window for the Future?*, 48 OHIO ST. L.J. 387 (1987). For a discussion of the problem *see* David, *DTP: Drug Manufacturers' Liability in Vaccine-Related Injuries*, 9 J. PROD. LIAB. 361 (1986); Sturges, *Vaccine-Related Injuries: Alternatives to the Tort Compensation System*, 30 ST. LOUIS U.L.J. 919 (1986); and Mariner, *Compensation Programs for Vaccine-Related Injuries Abroad: A Comparative Analysis*, 31 ST. LOUIS U.L.J. 599 (1981).

25. *See* HOUSE COMM. ON ENERGY AND COMMERCE, NATIONAL CHILDHOOD VACCINE INJURY ACT OF 1986, H.R. REP. No. 908, 99th Cong., 2d Sess. §§ 2113–14 (1986).

26. Even when strict liability would apply, many DTP plaintiffs would have

problems. Whether the harm was caused by the vaccine or something else is one problem. Another is showing which vaccine manufacturer made the vaccine that they received.

27. HOUSE COMM. ON ENERGY AND COMMERCE, NATIONAL CHILDHOOD VACCINE INJURY ACT OF 1986, H.R. REP. No. 908, 99th Cong. 2d Sess. § 2115 Cal (1986). In case of death, a fixed award of $250,000 is also provided, *id.*

28. Id. at § 2122.

29. *See* Statement by the president, Office of the Press Secretary, Nov. 14, 1986 on the occasion of President Reagan's signing of S. 1744.

30. *See* HOUSE COMM. ON ENERGY AND COMMERCE, NATIONAL CHILDHOOD VACCINE INJURY ACT OF 1986, H.R. REP. No. 908. 99th Cong.,2d Sess. Title II § 211 (1986) (Addition to the Internal Revenue Code) and the REPORT OF THE WORKING GROUP ON VACCINE SUPPLY AND LIABILITY, *supra*, note 22 at 132, 149.

31. The Vaccine Compensation Amendments of 1987 were passed by Congress as part of the Budget Reconciliation Act of 1988 (P. L. 100–203) and approved by the president on December 12, 1987.

32. *Virginia Birth-Related Neurologial Injury Compensation Act*, VA. Code § 32.2.5000 *et seq* (1987). For a description, *see* American College of Obstetricians and Gynocologists, 6 LEGIS-LETTER (May 1987). Some of the information that follows is based on telephone interviews on October 7, 1988 with Penny Rutledge, staff attorney with the American College of Obstetricians and Gynecologists, Del Chip Woodrum, the Virginia legislator who introduced the plan, and Bob Miller from the Virginia Bureau of Insurance.

33. Franklin, *Replacing the Negligence Lottery: Compensation and Selective Reimbursement*, 53 VA. L. REV. 774, 777 (1967) (emphasis in original).

34. Pierce, *Encouraging Safety: The Limits of Tort Law and Government Regulation*, 33 VAND. L. REV. 1281 (1980).

35. Henderson, *Should Workmen's Compensation Be Extended to Nonoccupational Injuries?*, 48 TEX. L. REV. 117 (1969).

36. E. BERNZWEIG, BY ACCIDENT NOT DESIGN (1980).

37. For early discussions of the New Zealand plan, *see* Franklin,*Personal Injury Accidents in New Zealand and the United States: Some Striking Similarities*, 27 STAN. L. REV. 653 (1975); Harris, *Accident Compensation in New Zealand: A Comprehensive Insurance System*, 37 MOD. L. REV. 361 (1974); Palmer, *Compensation for Personal Injury: A Requiem for the Common Law in New Zealand*, 21 AM. J. COMP. L. 1 (1973) [hereinafter cited as Palmer, *A Requiem*]; Palmer, *Abolishing the Personal Injury Tort System: The New Zealand Experience*, 9 ALTA. L. REV. 169 (1971); Palmer and Lemons, *Toward the Disappearance of Tort Law—New Zealand's New Compensation Plan*, U. ILL. L.F. 693 (1972); Szakats, *Community Responsibility for Accident Injuries: The New Zealand Accident Compensation Act*, 8 U.B.C.L. REV. 1 (1973); and Vennell, *The Scope of National No-Fault Accident Compensation in Australia and New Zealand*, 49 AUSTL. L.J. 22 (1975).

For appraisals of the New Zealand scheme after several years of operation, *see* T. ISON, ACCIDENT COMPENSATION (1980); G. PALMER, COMPENSATION FOR INCAPACITY (1979); Hodge, *No-Fault in New Zealand: It Works*, 50 INS. COUNS. J. 222 (1983); Palmer, *What Happened to the Woodhouse Report?*,

N.Z.L.J. 561 (1981) [hereinafter cited as Palmer, *What Happened*]; and Pfenningstorf, *Accident Compensation in New Zealand: How Does It Work?*, AM. B. FOUND. RESEARCH J. 1153 (1981). *See also* Henderson, *The New Zealand Accident Compensation Reform* (Book Review), 48 U. CHI. L. REV. 781 (1981). For a current description of the scheme, *see* Accident Compensation Corp., ANNUAL REVIEW (1988).

38. Henderson would broaden workers' compensation to cover nonwork injuries of both employees and their dependents. By contrast, the others would create new regimes as New Zealand did.

39. An important set of choices is whether to use regular public agencies, independent public corporations, or private claims handlers. There is also the delicate matter of whether the plan should be administered on the national or state level.

40. New Zealand's plan generously replaces income and, to a limited extent, compensates for serious disfigurement and long-term pain and suffering. Benefits under Franklin's plan would include all reasonable medical expenses and 85 percent of wage loss above a modest deductible. There would be a moderate weekly ceiling, however, above which high earners would provide their own protection, Franklin, *supra* note 33, at 799–800. No pain and suffering benefits would be paid, and victims guilty of serious misconduct would be limited to 75 percent of wage loss, *id.* at 800–01. These benefits would be the first and primary source of compensation for an accidental loss, *id.* at 802.

41. Pierce, *supra* note 34, at 1320.

42. *Id.* at 1321.

43. *Id.* at 1322.

44. T. ISON, THE FORENSIC LOTTERY 57 (1967).

45. Somewhat analogously, in the context of a discussion of injuries arising from toxic substances with uncertain causal correlation, Judge Jack Weinstein, who handled the Agent Orange litigation, has recently endorsed the idea of a very broad-based compensation remedy, with the costs of the plan charged back, where sensibly attributable to the industry that is the source of the loss, Weinstein, *Preliminary Reflections on the Law's Reaction to Disasters*, 11 COL. J. ENVTL. L. 1, 43–44 (1986).

46. WOODHOUSE REPORT, ROYAL COMM'N OF INQUIRY, COMPENSATION FOR PERSONAL INJURY IN NEW ZEALAND ¶ 467, at 172 (1967).

47. Palmer, *A Requiem, supra* note 37, at 30.

48. G. PALMER, *supra* note 37, at 367–68.

49. *Id.* at 367.

50. For the situation as of 1977, *see id.* at 368. As of 1979 it was reported that although the Accident Compensation Commission had not yet levied extra costs on employers with "exceptionally poor accident records" the reason was that it was awaiting more detailed and reliable statistics before doing so, Holyoak, *Accident Compensation in New Zealand Today*, in ACCIDENT COMPENSATION AFTER PEARSON (D. Allen, C. Bourn, and J. Holyoak, eds.) 191 (1979).

51. ACCIDENT COMPENSATION CORP., ANNUAL REPORT 20 (1986).

52. T. ISON, *supra* note 44, at 54–67. Professor Ison's Canadian version of his proposal can be found in Ison, *Tort Liability and Social Insurance*, 19 U. TORONTO L.J. 614 (1969).

53. WOODHOUSE REPORT, *supra* note 46, ¶ 17, at 26. For pragmatic reasons,

the Woodhouse Report adopted the first step only, hoping to solve at the outset problems associated with the existing tort and workers' compensation plans, *id.* As for his 1967 plan, Franklin noted, "disease presents a similar social problem to the extent it disables and causes serious medical expense and income loss. Disease is omitted for ease of discussion," Franklin, *supra* note 33, at 777 n. 10. Nevertheless, Franklin offers no specifics on how a scheme covering disease would meet his concerns about resource allocation, nor does he confront the complicated collateral source issues raised by such an extension.

54. *See* for example Palmer, *What Happened, supra* note 37, at 568–69. Tempered by current sensitivities to our limited national wealth, Professor David Owen has also endorsed the adoption of a disability compensation plan in the United States— when we can afford it. *See* Owen, *Rethinking the Policies of Strict Liability*, 33 VAND. L. REV. 681, 705 (1980).

55. *See* P. S. ATIYAH, ACCIDENTS, COMPENSATION AND THE LAW 498–508 (3d. ed. 1980); T. ISON, *supra* note 37, at 18–32; and Palmer, *What Happened, supra* note 37, at 568–69. For a criticism in the British context of the favored treatment of victims of industrially caused disabilities as compared with others, *see* Lewis, *Tort and Social Security; The Importance Attached to the Cause of Disability with Special Reference to the Industrial Injuries Scheme*, 43 MOD. L. REV. 514 (1980). And for the argument that road accident victims should not receive better treatment than others of the disabled, *see* Lewis, *No-Fault Compensation for Victims of Road Accidents: Can It Be Justified?*, 10 J. SOC. POL. 161 (1981). *See generally* J. STAPLETON, DISEASE AND THE COMPENSATION DEBATE (1986).

56. Henderson says,

[t]he distinctions that must be drawn under the Act sometimes border on the ridiculous. If a person drinks contaminated water and becomes ill, presumably he will not recover compensation; but if the same person contracts malaria from having been bitten by a mosquito that came into contact with the water, he can recover because the bite was an "accidental" injury, Henderson, *supra* note 37, at 783 n. 10.

Similar problems plagued early U.S. workers' compensation programs, which covered accidents but not occupational disease.

Professor Craig Brown describes some of the difficulties New Zealand has had in determining what is a "medical misadventure," and hence compensable, and what is merely a failure of treatment or an expected adverse consequence, and not compensable, *see* C. BROWN, NO-FAULT FOR MEDICAL ACCIDENTS (1988).

57. *See* D. HARRIS et al., COMPENSATION AND SUPPORT FOR ILLNESS AND INJURY 329–49 (1984). For reviews of the Oxford study *see* Conard, 35 AM. J. COMP. L. 431 (1987); Abel, *£'s of Cure, Ounces of Prevention*, 73 CALIF. L. REV. 1003 (1985); and Kornhauser, *Theory and Fact in the Law of Accidents*, 73 CALIF. L. REV. 1024 (1985).

58. *See* Sugarman, *Personal Injury Law Reform: A Proposed First Step*, 61 INDUSTRIAL L.J. 30 (1987).

59. *See generally* DISABILITY ALLIANCE, POVERTY AND DISABILITY: BREAKING THE LINK (1987); DISABILITY ALLIANCE, DISABILITY RIGHTS HANDBOOK FOR 1980 (L. LOACH, P. TOWNSEND, and A. WALKER, eds.), 48 (1980); and DISABILITY ALLIANCE, MEMORANDUM TO THE DHSS ABOUT THE RECOMMENDATIONS OF THE ROYAL

COMMISSION ON CIVIL LIABILITY AND COMPENSATION FOR PER-
SONAL INJURY 1 (1978).

60. In supporting the extension of New Zealand's plan to cover disease, Ison also distinguishes between long- and short-term problems. He proposes that the employer be responsible for the first month of coverage through mandatory minimum sick leave benefits. The national plan would take over after the first month, T. ISON, *supra* note 37, at 188. In his original plan, Ison too had divided responsibility between different mechanisms depending on duration, *see* T. ISON, *supra* note 44, at 59–65. For another endorsement of the policy of providing separate treatment for short and long term injuries, *see* Atiyah, *What Now?*, in ACCIDENT COMPENSATION AFTER PEARSON (D. ALLEN, C. BOURN, and J. HOLYOAK, eds.) 227, 247 (1979).

III

BETTER IDEAS

In this Part, I offer my approach to personal injury law reform that rests on the idea that, in the long run, the compensation and behavior control objectives of tort law should largely be pursued with entirely separate social mechanisms. Chapter 6 advances my broad solution to the compensation goal. In Chapter 7, I consider various deterrence strategies on the assumption that ordinary personal injury law will basically be repealed and that the compensation plan that takes its place will not have a cost-internalizing funding mechanism. Chapter 8 details a substantial first step—serious personal injury law reform that state legislatures should enact now. Failing that, Chapter 9 considers whether individuals, employers, would-be defendants, and insurers could together achieve much of my first-step proposal by contract.

Americans working today for what I call progressive employers are well protected against out-of-pocket losses (income replacement and medical expenses), whether they are the victim of a tort or some other disabling cause. They also enjoy generous paid public holidays, paid vacations, good private pensions as well as Social Security, and adequate unemployment compensation. Unfortunately, not all employment provides such benefits, and many people have no employment at all (or are not part of a household with a related employed worker) that would give them access to job-related benefit schemes. If we could put nearly everyone in a broadly equivalent position to those with good employee benefits, our need to use tort law to compensate for economic loss would essentially disappear. This is one helpful way of envisioning the goal toward which we should work.

6

A Comprehensive Compensation Strategy

THE BASIC PRINCIPLE: COMPENSATION OF PERSONAL INJURY VICTIMS THROUGH REGULAR LOSS-PROTECTION MECHANISMS

A new regime of social insurance and employee benefits should eventually take care of the income replacement and medical and other expense problems that tort victims face. The long-run arrangement I propose involves a division of responsibility between employers, employees, and society at large. Employers would cover short-term needs; government would assume basic obligations for long-term problems. Individuals would have both rights and responsibilities. The divisions I favor are primarily based on administrative convenience, but fairness and a desire to provide proper incentives are also considerations.

Under the proposed substantial first step discussed in Chapter 8, income needs arising from short-term disabilities are the focus of employer duties, but under the long-run proposal described here, short-term income needs of all sorts are addressed by a single employment-based plan. Under the substantial first step, long-term needs of incapacitated people would still be partly addressed by the tort system, albeit sharply altered; but under the long-run proposal, personal injury law, apart from the limited availability of punitive damages, is fully supplanted by new arrangements for the disabled that are part of our broad social insurance system.

In short, I agree with advocates of comprehensive disability plans, such as the Oxford group described in the last chapter, who reject the accident victim as the proper focus of attention. But, I believe they are wrong to assume that it follows that the proper long-term focus of policy ought therefore be on the disabled. In other words, although the Oxford group argues that "we should move towards the abolition of every compensation scheme which is based on a particular category of causation,"[1] it has failed to adhere to that very dictum.

Americans who suffer personal injuries in circumstances now entitling them to tort damages incur two basic sorts of pecuniary loss: lost earnings and medical-related expenses (including rehabilitation costs). My position is that, to the extent possible, we should address these needs for income and medical care as such, and therefore, as part of comprehensive approaches to those needs.

As for income, the basic social concern is that people have a continued flow of cash during periods when they are not working. Under current nontort compensation schemes, those who are temporarily incapacitated obtain income replacement through state temporary disability schemes, employee sick leave plans, and sickness and accident insurance; those who are injured at work are protected by workers' compensation, veterans' disability benefits, and similar programs; and those who become totally disabled at or away from work are eligible for Social Security disability insurance and, sometimes, employment-based, long-term disability benefit plans.

But our social insurance-employee benefit system is by no means restricted to the disabled. We also provide income protection to the unemployed through unemployment insurance and to both the retired and dependent survivors of deceased workers through Social Security, life insurance, and private pension plans. Moreover, most employers ensure a continued flow of income to their workers by proving paid public holidays and paid vacations. Once we understand that the basic problem is continued income during periods of nonwork, then we see that the focus adopted by the Oxford group is too narrow.

Thus, while I would prefer either the New Zealand plan or the Oxford proposal to the United States' present arrangements, I find neither ideal. Many reformers have cogently argued that accident victims should not be treated better than the sick. But, in the same vein, how can income-support mechanisms for the disabled be fairly evaluated until all provisions for periods of nonwork are considered? I do not claim that the disabled, the unemployed, and the retired must all be placed on exactly the same footing. Rather, I argue that the claims of other groups count in determining what the disabled should get. These claims all compete for society's resources. In sum, policymakers must address our collective responsibility toward all people who do not have income because they are not at work.

Policymakers might think it proper to provide more support to those who have worked recently. Similarly, they might prefer to provide more dollars to those who have worked more and earned more in the past. In addition, they may perceive varying levels of collective responsibility for different problems. These levels might depend on the problem's time frame, judgments about ability to work, concerns about incentives for rehabilitation and job searches, and ideas about the roles of the private and public sectors. These considerations underlie rational social insurance and employee benefit policy. But the point is that any differential treatment we might adopt should be based on overarching considerations that are applied to the general problem of people's need for income when not working.

Our existing Social Security program reflects my point of view in significant respects in that it covers, in one broad design, retired workers, workers' survivors, and totally disabled former workers. Alhough there are somewhat different past work requirements for each of the benefits, there is a common formula for determining benefits, as well as a common financing mechanism. This program also reflects the policy view that the three groups have the same general need for long-term income replacement.

In the United States, our existing social insurance and employee benefit arrangements need reform in their own right. This need stands apart from any impetus to do away with personal injury law and the attendant concern that tort victims would thereby lose a necessary source of compensation. Indeed, tort victims are only a small proportion of our society's income-support claimants. This state of affairs leaves me in a potentially difficult position. Because of inadequacies in our existing income support regimes, many, including me, think it harsh simply to take away tort rights as the Reagan administration favored. Does this mean I must advance a politically plausible comprehensive scheme for the reform of our social insurance-employee benefit system before I dare argue for doing away with tort law?

My solution is the two-step approach that I will soon lay out. My long-run reform proposal is indeed comprehensive; my first step moves substantially in that direction. Although the interim package would only do away with the personal injury law system in less-serious injury cases, it is economically and politically feasible now. Moreover, its enactment would focus tort law on the relatively few remaining cases involving serious injury. This first step, once enacted, would then promote discussion of the desirability of the further elimination of tort law and the need for my proposed comprehensive compensation package.

THE CURRENT AND POSSIBLE FUTURE STATUS OF COLLATERAL SOURCES FOR TORT VICTIMS

Although I concede that current social insurance and employee benefit arrangements do not adequately provide for the out-of-pocket losses of tort victims, it is important not to overplay their shortcomings. Recent studies by Professor Jeffrey O'Connell provide one useful perspective on the relative roles of tort law and other sources of compensation for the disabled. O'Connell estimates that tort payouts for personal injury in 1984 reached almost

$40 billion, up from $2 billion in 1960.[2] Although $40 billion is a large number, it represented in 1984 only 9.8 percent of the total payments estimated to have been made that year for injury and illness by all of the United States' principal loss-shifting systems. And at 9.8 percent of the total in 1984, tort had moved up but 2 percent from 7.9 percent of the total in 1960; for just as tort payouts were expanding considerably faster than the cost of living, so were the other compensation mechanisms—most importantly private health insurance schemes, public medical care programs, and public income-transfer programs such as Social Security. The next few paragraphs describe in more detail current injury and illness compensation arrangements so as to set the stage for the specific long-run reforms I favor.[3]

Income Replacement

As noted earlier, most tort victims are not seriously hurt;[4] the great bulk miss few or no days of work. In short, most tort victims do not suffer substantial income loss. However, a sizable proportion of modestly injured tort victims are disabled for periods lasting as long as many weeks. The most important existing nontort, income-replacement mechanism in such circumstances is sick leave. Unlike many other nations, such benefits in the United States are neither publicly provided nor mandated of all employers. Nevertheless, the voluntary development of private employee benefit plans has created a substantial sick leave scheme nationwide. Formal plans cover around two-thirds of the work force; and a sizable number are protected informally.[5] Still, there are gaps: some workers remain unprotected while others have protection of inadequate duration. Appreciating this problem, five states (California, New York, New Jersey, Rhode Island, and Hawaii) have adopted temporary disability insurance schemes (TDI) to help close the gaps in private voluntary arrangements. These TDI plans ensure average- and lower-paid workers fairly substantial income-replacement benefits for periods of up to six months (following a brief waiting period of typically one week). For better-paid workers, supplemental employee benefits or private arrangements must take over. If, however, all states had generous TDI plans or mandated that employers provide equivalent coverage, the income-loss problems of temporarily disabled tort victims would be well solved. This insight forms the basis for a critical feature of my first-step proposal set out in Chapter 8.

A small proportion of tort victims, though by no means a small number, suffer permanent and total disability or are killed.[6] For those in the work force at the time of their accident, existing collateral sources can and often do fairly adequately replace lost wages. As for totally disabled former workers, Social Security benefits are generally available after a five-month waiting period. They replace between 45 and 80 percent of the earners' Social Security-covered wages, depending on the victims' past wage level and the number of dependents the victims have.[7] Lower wage earners have a higher wage-replacement rate; higher earners have a lower rate. These benefits continue so long as the individuals are disabled and traditionally increase each year to reflect cost-of-living increases. In addition to Social Security, some workers have employment-based, long-term total disability benefits, typically funded either through their employers' pension funds or through separate insurance. Such benefits are especially available to those with fairly high wages or those who work for large private employers, for the government, or in jobs with strong unions. Private total disability insurance is also available in the marketplace and is purchased by a modest proportion of Americans.[8]

Comparable sources exist for death benefits. Social Security again provides for workers' dependents, as do employer-provided life insurance and pension plans. Life insurance is also widely available for private purchase, especially through group insurance plans offered at the workplace. Thus, for employees who are fully disabled or killed by torts, existing collateral sources, although they rarely completely replace lost income, are suitably generous in a significant proportion of cases. If such coverage could be broadened and deepened a bit, tort would have no important income-replacement role to play with respect to such workers' lost earnings.

There is an important group of incapacitated workers that our society typically treats poorly: the permanently, but only partially disabled. Workers disabled on the job in this way obtain more than half of all the benefits paid out by the workers' compensation system and, even so, it is widely agreed that the workers' compensation system for treating such claims has its problems.[9] Worse, if a person is partially and permanently disabled off the job, unlike many other countries, compensation in the United States, apart from tort, is quite limited.

The basic problem in such cases is determining what wage loss, if any, partially disabled workers suffer. Although not totally disabled, many will be unable to earn wages equal to those paid by their former job. Because of employer preferences or prejudices, many partly disabled people will be unable to find any decent work at all, despite their residual functional capacity for work. On the other hand, many people with permanent partial disabilities return to their former job or an equivalent job, or obtain even a better one. An intuitive way to approach dealing with such people's income needs is simply to seek to replace lost wages on an individual basis. Yet this turns out to be very complicated. First, it is often extremely difficult to determine how much the claimant would have been earning but for the disability. In addition, this approach, which decreases benefits as postdisability wages increase, creates disincentives to rehabilitation and reemployment. On the other hand, a one-time estimate of future wage loss (the torts approach) is almost surely to result in an inaccurate payment, because the future is very likely to unfold in individual cases differently from that predicted.

Most existing private disability arrangements do not help long-term, partially disabled workers, because they require total disability. Yet some disability insurance policies and disability plans for some public employees (such as police and fire fighters) contain generous definitions of total disability, and pay full benefits to people who clearly can still hold (and often hold) a lesser job. This is probably not a viable, universal public program approach, however. Private accident insurance is a device designed to provide compensation for certain partially disabling injuries such as loss of an eye or a dismemberment. However, this solution is not well aimed at income replacement.

Despite these problems, our workers' compensation systems and the disability compensation schemes of other countries have nevertheless adopted various tolerable compromise solutions to the dilemma of compensating the partially disabled. Some emphasize individual wage-loss replacement and utilize other mechanisms to deal with behavioral disincentives. Others base financial awards on the extent of the victims' medically determined impairment (although sometimes such awards wind up constituting payments for the impairment more than as a sensible proxy for wage loss). Surely we could duplicate the more sensible of these approaches in a broad scheme for partial disabilities. The Netherlands appears to be a particularly good example of a nation that has dealt satisfactorily with this problem.[10]

Existing collateral sources in the United States also treat would-be earners inadequately. Tort, by contrast, when compensating disabled children, students, homemakers, and other potential wage earners, at least considers, even if inaccurately, the probable future earnings they would have had. The lack of protection for would-be earners is not a significant problem for those who are merely temporarily disabled; after all, they were not likely to have earned much, if anything, in the short run anyway. But when one's disability is permanent, the lack of coverage can be very serious.

For example, our existing social insurance system provides no income protection for current homemakers (typically women) who become disabled. This seems to rest on the assumption that they will indefinitely depend on the earnings of another breadwinner, even though the large number of women who move in and out of the labor force undermines this assumption.[11] Students in higher education epitomize the poorly protected. Their earning prospects, though excellent, currently go unprotected against permanent impairment. Similarly, Social Security now expects disabled children to be supported indefinitely by their parents, providing benefits only on the parents' death or retirement. Moreover, the benefits actually paid in such cases may fall well below the victims' probable earnings without the disability.

Because of the difficulties of constructing a workable scheme to cover nonearners and because of the problems noted with partial permanent disabilities generally, my first-step proposal set out in Chapter 8 leaves the long-term disabled in the tort system, albeit within a reformed personal injury law, as I will detail there. But in the long run, the needs of all the long-term disabled should be addressed by better social insurance mechanisms, and I offer my solution later in this chapter.[12]

Medical and Other Expenses

About 80–85 percent of the American population are reasonably well protected against the risk of incurring substantial medical expenses, including the medical expenses resulting from torts.[13] Most people obtain group health insurance benefits for themselves and their families through their jobs; some of those plans provide inadequate protection, however. Individual plans are also available, although they tend to be more expensive and are often less generous in their coverage. The elderly and the disabled on Social Security are reasonably well protected by Medicare, and most of the poor are eligible for Medicaid, which, to be sure, too often provides access to only second-class service.

Approximately 15 percent of the population who are left unprotected in advance against the risk they will incur health care costs include many self-employed people, employed people who do not obtain health insurance as an employee benefit, and many of the unemployed and their families. Under recent legal changes, a laid-off worker must be permitted to transfer his group coverage to an individual plan; however, the shock of a job loss and its concomitant income reduction may of necessity make health insurance a low spending priority.

In sum, although the inadequacy of heath insurance hits only a small proportion of tort victims, it is clearly an important national problem.[14] Thus, ensuring access for all to good health care is part of my long-term plan, and providing wider health care coverage for those with lesser disabilities is part of my first-step proposal.

Three further concerns are rehabilitation expenses, the costs of household services that must be purchased when you can no longer do-it-yourself, and the high costs of certain situations that the disabled face (such as for mobility or special diets). Although these are, in principle at least, compensated by tort law, they are of course, by no means confined to tort victims alone. Apart from tort law, various programs now exist to provide rehabilitation services to the disabled in general, although some, no doubt, receive inadequate assistance. Clearly, however, too few in-home services for the disabled or members of the family are provided, and coverage of the extra expenses of disability is spotty. Plainly, all these needs must be addressed by a comprehensive plan.

Finally, I come to pain and suffering. Pain and suffering is generally not compensable by social insurance, employee benefit, or private insurance schemes. The main exceptions, as noted earlier, are some workers' compensation and private disability or accident insurance plans that pay compensation to partially disabled victims for the impairment itself.

The failure generally to provide compensation for pain and suffering is best explained by the fact that most people would not (and do not) voluntarily choose to insure against such losses regardless of their seriousness. The apparent reason for that is that, because money really is not a substitute for the freedom from pain and suffering, giving up money now (in insurance premiums) is typically less attractive to people than is having lump sum of money later in case you are in pain. Still, many people do believe that, as a solace for being seriously disabled, a person should receive something from the rest of society that symbolizes society's concern. Again, a comprehensive plan must address this issue. As noted earlier, New Zealand, for example, does provide compensation for pain and suffering in its accident-compensation scheme, and at present about 20 percent of the benefits go for such purposes, remembering that medical costs are generally not borne by the plan.

Like sensible auto no-fault plans, my first-step plan eliminates recovery for pain and suffering for not very serious injuries. I also propose restricting its availability through tort law for serious injuries. For the long run, I want to eliminate such recovery through tort. I would not, however, object to moderate payments, in serious injury cases through other mechanisms, as New Zealand, for example, provides. Yet, such benefits would not be a high priority for me. I definitely think that money should not be devoted to pain and suffering compensation until disabled people's needs are reasonably met on an individual basis for identifiable things such as personal assistants and other arrangements that permit the disabled to enjoy as much of an independent life as is feasible for them. And the more that such needs are generally satisfied, the less important pain and suffering awards, as a means for buying alternate forms of pleasure, become. Payments for pain and suffering, as so far discussed, should be distinguished from the matter of financial payments sought in compensation for the outrage of having been wronged and injured as a result. That is an issue I address in Chapter 7 when I consider the extent to which tort should play a residual role in providing a punitive damage remedy for especially bad conduct.

SPECIFIC LONG-RUN COMPENSATION PROPOSALS

In general, all Americans should be ensured reasonable levels of income for periods of nonwork and should have generous protection against the risk they will incur medical and other expenses. There are many ways to reach this goal. The government could play an exclusive or minor role, depending on the extent of mandated employee benefits. An enormous range of program design decisions are inevitable; the possible alternatives are far too numerous to discuss here. Instead I emphasize the long-run solution I prefer.

Income Support

Under my plan, the government and employers would divide responsibility for replacing workers' income according to the duration of the need. Employers would take responsibility for short-term income needs through a simple, uniform regime of compulsory employee benefits. Long-term needs would be a collective national responsibility. A single social insurance plan would provide for them.

Short-Term Income Protection

Temporary income protection benefits would come in a new, simple form and would not separately focus on disability (as would be true under my first-step plan set out in Chapter 8). Rather, based on past work, employees would accrue earned and generally unrestricted days of paid leave. These days could be used at the employees' discretion. The philosophy of employee freedom and self-sufficiency underpinning this plan contrasts sharply with the existing system's reliance on categorical eligibility and insurance. The new regime would replace benefits now provided by vacation leave, public holiday leave, sick leave, temporary disability insurance, unemployment insurance, and severance pay, as well as the temporary disability benefits currently provided by workers' compensation and tort damages.

More precisely, the basic rule would allot one paid leave day for every five days of work. A full-time worker would thereby earn more than forty paid leave days per year to be used for short-term needs and desires.

As they earn their paid leave days, workers would be required to set aside some of them each year in a "reserve account" until they had nearly six months worth. The reserve would become available to workers after a fortnight's worth of disability or unemployment. Where people have need but their reserve account is empty, they could obtain some more paid leave days in the form of modest advances against their long-term Social Security accounts. These would have to be repaid as the people return to work.

So, if an earner were injured in a transportation accident, or by a product, or by a slip and fall on someone else's premises, or whatever, and needed to miss work, he or she, just like someone who was laid off, became ill, or wanted to go on vacation, would simply draw down on his or her paid leave account. Usually this would mean staying in full-pay status and using up earned days of credit held on the books of the person's employer. Were a person to have no more current credit on his or her employer's books, he or she would turn to the designated financial institution where funds representing unused days of earned paid leave from prior years would be held. Moreover, as indicated above, access to one's reserve account days (also held at one's financial institution) would be triggered once two weeks or more of unemployment or incapacity to work were incurred.

For nearly all people who are significantly attached to the work force, this plan would generously provide income protection for up to even six months of disability, although the need to claim for so long is, of course, quite rare. The beauty of such a plan is that, generally speaking, it would mean that in most instances in which paid leave days were used, no explanation or justification to an employer, agency, or court for claiming such compensation would be required of employees—as is now generally necessary. As a result, workers would have expanded liberty and less intrusion into their private lives, to say nothing of the benefits this plan would bring in terms of eliminating separate bureaucracies needed for today's many programs and of saving costs by doing away with the need for most eligibility determinations. Finally, as compared with today, there would be much less cheating by and public antipathy toward claimants of short-term income support, because, under my proposal, the benefits workers claim would truly be theirs.

Even in this abbreviated form, it should be clear that an income-replacement scheme can provide for the temporarily disabled as part of a larger group, rather than through a separate benefit as tort reformers usually imagine. Because I have a book in process that centers on this proposal, and because I have already published a law journal article that provides far more details than are offered here, the reader seeking more information should look elsewhere.[15]

Long-Term Income Protection

The income-protection scheme I favor for longer periods of nonwork would be an expanded version of our existing wage-related Social Security system. Minimum benefits would be increased for the totally disabled, the retired, and workers' survivors. Additional benefits would go to the permanently partially disabled, the long-term unemployed, and those who are disabled but who have no history of substantial prior earnings. This latter category would include children over 18, homemakers, students, and others with work records inadequate to qualify for the earnings-related portion of the plan. Other existing long-term disability schemes, such as workers' compensation and the "black lung" program as well as tort law, would be replaced by this single national program.

There are several possible mechanisms that might be employed to deliver the income-protection package I favor for other than temporary periods of nonwork. For example, this program, like my short-term paid leave proposal, could be tied to the employment relationship. Indeed, one could seek to structure benefits around an expanded workers' compensation system. This is the sort of approach proposed two decades ago by Professor Roger Henderson.[16] His idea was to extend workers' compensation in two directions: first, employees would be covered for nonwork injuries and second, this broadened package would be made available to the families of workers. While this strategy is the very one I favor for medical and other expense protection, as I will shortly detail, I have concluded that it is not the proper long-run solution for the permanent income-protection plan.

This is not to say that the workers' compensation solution does not have several attractions. First, it provides potential beneficiaries with instant protection; like private insurance generally, workers are covered by their job-based plan as soon as they start employment. Moreover, income-replacement rights are based on their earnings at the time of their disability and not some, often lower, earlier average. And, as I have previously explained, the workers' compensation system already contains protection for the partially permanently disabled (even if this part of the program is problematic in many states). Finally, the state-based nature of workers' compensation would readily permit experimentation if that were desirable.

In the end, however, I favor the mechanism of an expanded Social Security system. Social Security has the advantage of a broad national funding base and can provide what ultimately is most desirable—a uniform national solution. Its benefits are paid periodically and increased over time for inflation; by contrast, the workers' compensation tradition is not to have inflation adjustments and all too many seriously injured workers take lump-sum settlements, which private insurers tend to prefer (although I admit, of course, that these aspects of workers' compensation could be changed).

Besides, as a practical matter, if workers' compensation were to become the basic program, what would happen to Social Security's existing disability benefits? Because the coordination between the two systems today is awkward at best, it would be desirable to eliminate the overlap. Yet simply to cut out Social Security disability benefits and to rely instead on the vagaries of state programs obviously would generate significant concerns in states with histories of ungenerous treatment of the disabled. In addition, it would be very awkward to cover, through workers' compensation, those nonearners who are not a part of families with covered workers, thus requiring a separate plan anyway for such people.

Finally, and for me probably most important, by dealing with the income needs of all the disabled as part of the Social Security system, policy decisions concerning them are inevitably influenced by the way society decides to treat others who need income replacement—for example, the retired and the survivors of deceased workers. As I have argued before, because the need addressed here is that for long-term income support, a unified policy toward those with such need is desirable.

But to say that the long-term, permanent, income-replacement strategy is to be built around Social Security is not to say that the existing Social Security should remain without significant change. First, as indicated already, additional benefits need to be added for the partially permanently disabled. In the Netherlands, for example, a partial pension is available to former workers with as little as a 15 percent loss of earnings capacity. Benefits increase with increased partial disability until a full pension is available to those who are deemed 80 percent or more disabled. A disabled claimant's loss of earnings capacity in the Netherlands is determined by an independent body, the Joint Medical Service. Other countries have similar approaches, although the minimum amount of earning capacity loss necessary to receive any pension is often greater, for example, 40 percent in Finland and 50 percent in Israel and Sweden.[17] From an income-replacement perspective, the trick is to avoid spending money on those who can well return to the labor force at the same or an equivalent job despite some disability, while at the same time not insisting on such a significant disability so as to exclude from protection those who, in practice, are either not going to get back into the work force, or must do so at a considerably lower pay. An assessment of impairment and its consequent connection to loss of earnings capacity is bound to be inaccurate in a significant share of cases. The Netherlands approach minimizes the risk of exclusion, but is probably more frequently overgenerous than are the plans of the other countries noted. Of course, to the extent that the pension sum is reduced as the disability percentage is smaller, this minimizes the amount spent too generously.

Second, I would favor improved income-replacement rates for people with income up to twice the national average wage. Because private disability income insurance planners generally agree that between 60 and 67 percent is a suitable income-replacement rate, that should be the Social Security goal as well, at least up to the level of Social Security covered wages, which is now set at about twice the national average wage. Workers with dependents and quite low income, however, need more than a two-thirds replacement rate to maintain a decent standard of income—as reflected in the current system's higher replacement ratios for such claimants. However, instead of extra benefits for dependent spouses and children that are a percentage of the workers' benefit, as provided in the present scheme, I would favor instead either uniform additions for dependents or, perhaps even better, a high family minimum benefit.[18]

Our Social Security disability plan now provides no benefits for nonearners, except to the extent they are dependent on disabled former workers. But a long-term universal approach should include as well those who are not attached to the paid labor force at the time of their disability. The retired who become disabled can be separately taken care of, so far as income support is concerned, by the retirement component of the social insurance plan. But other current nonearners who become disabled need protection from the disability component of the plan. These include the currently unemployed without sufficient recent labor force attachment to qualify, homemakers, students, and children. My long-run proposal, therefore, which parallels the current arrangements of several other nations,[19] would include these categories of disabled people in an expanded Social Security plan.

For current (or recent) workers, I would continue, as noted above, to have the plan's benefits be wage related. Indeed, as there suggested, I would make its benefits more generous for some workers. I would also base the benefits more so than does the present formula on the average of fairly recent earnings, and I would liberalize somewhat the duration of past labor force attachment necessary to qualify for earnings-related benefits at all. But, in addition, I would include at least a basic income-support benefit for disabled adults who do not otherwise qualify for earnings-related benefits, regardless of their past paid labor force record. This would exclude disabled children, until they are eighteen. But at that point, and for homemakers, adult students, and the unemployed, Social Security disability benefits would be provided.

The level of benefits provided to such people and the degree of disability necessary for eligibility are difficult questions. Surely those who are totally disabled within Social Security's current definitions would be covered in my plan, and perhaps it would be best to start simply with them. Moreover, surely some minimum or basic income-support benefit would be available to all in this group. A harder issue is whether to provide more than basic benefits for those, such as students in higher education, whose earning potential is plainly greater than average. On the one hand, such people have, in one sense, only good luck to thank that they had the talent to pursue higher education and the prospects of higher earnings to follow and now only the offsetting bad luck to become unable to realize such potential. Moreover, they, unlike current workers, typically have not yet contributed their labor to the society as a whole. On the other hand, they plainly have expectations of higher earnings that become disappointed by their disability. Perhaps one solution would be to insist on contributions to the system on their behalf during their period of higher education and then to treat them as having earned, say, at 150 percent of the average wage if they are disabled while studying.

Homemakers represent an even more difficult problem because what their future entry into the paid labor force would have been, absent their disability, is often highly unpredictable. Hence, perhaps there is no good solution for most of them other than to provide only a basic benefit—although perhaps those who were once in work could be allowed, voluntarily, to continue to make contributions while temporarily at home so as to preserve disability income protection based on their previous earnings level. Another justification for providing benefits to homemakers (that is, other than replacing possible future earnings) is to provide funds to permit the purchase of replacement services that the homemaker can no longer perform.

The amount of the basic or minimum benefit in this expanded Social Security system should surely be set above the poverty level for a single person. Just how generous it should be I leave for later debate. But the important consequence to note now would be that disabled people would be able to rely on this benefit without having to turn to means tested programs as the disabled poor must do today. That is, by blanketing into the Social Security system all of the disabled, we would do away with the need to provide for such people through the current Supplemental Security Income (SSI) plan. The poor would benefit from avoiding whatever stigma now attaches to SSI as well as from escaping SSI's narrow limits on the assets they may have. The disabled near poor and those disabled living in families with another earner who are disqualified from SSI today would be treated as individuals and obtain income support in their own right.

In the design of a social insurance scheme with universal coverage of the disabled, I do not mean to suggest that conduct variables are not to be considered, at least on the benefit side.[20] Concerns about malingering, for example, do justify both requiring cooperation with rehabilitation and job placement efforts and a less than 100 percent net disposable income-replacement benefit formula.

I would also favor including a long-term unemployment benefit in the revised Social Security system. This is a serious shortcoming of our current system. Such people now must turn to means tested programs, and often, beyond food stamps, even they are not available. I mention this point mainly to show how the new social insurance plan I envision would apply to the full range of those people in need of income replacement. I will not otherwise discuss this unemployment benefit except to note its connection with the proposed disability benefit. First, it is sometimes difficult to tell if a person's lack of work is really a disability problem or an unemployment problem. The fact that the United States has no long-term unemployment benefit surely causes many to seek disability benefits and puts considerable pressure on the disability determination process, especially in times of high unemployment. This would be substantially relieved if a person could claim an unemployment benefit instead, even if at a lower dollar level. Second, it would be fair for society if it wanted to, to set the benefits, as just noted, lower for the unemployed than for the disabled on the ground, say, that the work disincentive problem with the unemployed is greater. Third, the anguishing problem of what to do with the disabled who can work but who cannot find employment would be reduced. At present, Social Security has a harsh stance toward such claimants and intends to deny them benefits; this is perhaps understandable because other unemployed people have no comparable benefit. But under my proposal, the partially disabled could be treated as fully disabled if no suitable work could actually be found for them (as is the case in some other countries today); at the same time, and as in some other places, more efforts might be made to insist that employers (at least large employers) take a reasonable number of disabled but capable people into their work force.

Medical and Other Expenses

As noted, the United States today has an inadequate health care system. Although certain patients may receive the best health care in the world, others are treated badly. Moreover, over the past two decades health care costs have been undesirably rising to an alarmingly increasing share of Gross National Product (GNP). It is widely agreed that reforms are in order. Many have written extensively on this issue, and a number of plausible solutions to the problem of inequality of access are routinely put before Congress. Most recently, interest has centered on Senator Edward Kennedy's proposal to require employers to provide health care benefits, an approach that I favor.[21]

More generally, I believe that all those attached to the work force (and their families) should obtain through their employment reasonably comprehensive medical and hospital expense protection by having either good health insurance or membership rights in a good health maintenance organization (HMO) or its equivalent. Employers could, of course, provide deluxe packages, but they would have to provide a generous minimum package. Employees could be required to contribute to the cost of such benefits, but no more than, say, half. This, it seems to me, is primarily a symbolic matter. Over time, employees, broadly speaking, pay for their own employee benefits with lower wages so that employer-paid benefits are more a matter of psychology than economics. Still, symbolism and psychology have their values. On the other hand, to impose generous plans that are fully employer-paid might impose serious short-run disruption costs on employers currently without health care plans. Hence I would permit as much as, say, a fifty-fifty shared funding arrangement, which is the split used by Social Security today. Moreover, a rule allowing some employee contributions could permit those employers so wishing to adopt plans in which the cost of covering the employees' family members (spouse and/or children) could be assigned, all or in part, to the employees. But coverage of such persons, except where they are already covered through another plan, should be mandatory. Moreover, health care benefits for employees with longer than, say, three months of service should automatically extend for, say, at least three months after the cessation of work (or until they are otherwise covered by another plan, if earlier). This would better plug the gap that now occurs when people lose health care protection by becoming unemployed and find themselves unable to afford to continue coverage for which they are eligible.

These arrangements would ensure the bulk of the American population access to good-quality health care. The remainder, including most importantly the elderly retired and the poor, would, as today, be the target of governmental programs.

Those people now eligible for Medicare or Medicaid, should, in addition to current options, be ensured a range of HMO choices broadly equivalent to what workers and their families would have. Finally, the Medicaid program should be expanded to include those remaining poor Americans (generously defined) who would still fall outside of the package described above.

These proposals would put virtually all Americans in a prefunded health care plan. Of course, even the minimally acceptable plans would have to include sufficiently generous benefit levels for the purpose of this network of protection to be achieved. I will not discuss here the extent to which deductibles and copayment requirements should be allowed in a minimum package, except to agree that, in modest amounts, these would be acceptable. Nor will I attempt to detail the sorts of traditional medical services that would have to be covered, other than to note with favor the recent expansion of Medicare to cover the small risk of far longer term hospitalization than has been covered before.

I will, however, comment on a few types of expense that the disabled face that have been typically excluded from health insurance programs and that need attention in a comprehensive long-run solution. For example, I believe that health care plans should cover the cost of rehabilitation programs in addition to traditional medical needs. Such plans should also be the funding source for other special needs of the disabled that arise from their incapacities, such as wheelchairs, personal attendants, and unusually expensive diets. Finally, gravely disabled people may need institutional care, not so much so as to receive traditional medical treatment, but rather to obtain custodial care when they are no longer able to care for themselves. (Some of the less seriously disabled may do far better with in-home services, which also should be provided.) Long-term care insurance is a new product now coming strongly onto the market to deal with this risk.[22] While this need is primarily associated with the elderly, it is by no means restricted to them. People who are very badly injured in accidents and those born with grave disabilities are other candidates. As with the need for rehabilitation programs, personal assistants, special diets, etc., again my point here is that the health care package of the future should not so narrowly focus on hospital and medical services as has traditionally been the case, but rather should cover the whole battery of goods and services that incapacitated people need to deal reasonably with their disability.

Some have suggested that the extra costs (or at least some of those costs) that go along with being disabled be handled with a formula-based disablement allowance that connects the amount of the benefit to the degree of disability.[23] The advantage of this approach is that it gives the disabled person an ensured sum and the freedom to spend the allowance as he or she sees fit; put differently, it does not require the person to demonstrate to another the need for any specific extra-cost item. On the other hand, it is bound to be a quite inaccurate measure of need in a large number of cases. One possible compromise would be to have such a formula-based benefit serve as a proxy for most extra-cost needs (the more typical and less costly things), reserving for individual determination and award those benefits that cover, say, personal attendants, housing accessibility remodeling, and mobility needs such as auto modifications and wheelchairs. Were this two-part solution employed, then perhaps the formula portion should be attached to the income-replacement scheme and only the individualized need portion would be attached to the broadened health care scheme discussed here.

As earlier indicated, I would not oppose arrangements such as New Zealand's that also provide the disabled with modest cash compensation as a solace for their incapacity—i.e., for pain and suffering. Consistent with my first-step proposal set out in Chapter 8, however, I would limit any such sums to those who are either permanently and seriously disfigured or impaired, or unable to return to their normal activities for more than six months. The key point for me is that in the long run, if they are made available, such benefits should be provided independently of tort law. As will be seen in Chapter 8, in my first-step plan tort damages for pain and suffering would be restricted to the seriously disabled as defined above, and they would be limited in amount to $150,000. With tort general damages so limited, we could better focus on the serious and, I believe, essentially equal suffering of people with equivalent disabilities but who have no tort claim or who cannot find a solvent tort-feasor to sue. With that relatively small group of the disabled before us, I think most would agree to the fairness of treating all within it alike, that is, ignoring whether or not they can in fact recover under today's tort rules. And if the solution were to expand coverage to include all such people, that would be fine with me.

The details of such awards I generally leave for another time. I would continue to favor, however, a maximum (in today's dollars) of $150,000 or less with benefits possibly age adjusted so as to account for the longer suffering that the younger disabled are likely to face. As for the mechanism by which these benefits would be provided, it seems to me that while they could be attached to the long-term income-replacement scheme, a more likely source would be the health care scheme.

FINANCING OF THE COMPREHENSIVE PLAN

Employers would finance short-term paid leave from current revenues. Employers and employees would share of the cost of the health care program as described above. The social insurance system for long-term income support and the health care needs of those not covered by a job-based plan would depend on the broad employer and employee-paid payroll taxes now used to finance Social Security and, in the case of Medicaid, general public revenues. In short, the system would not aim to allocate costs in a carefully tailored way to those people or activities thought responsible for causing the claims on the system.

My proposal, therefore, is to be contrasted with financing mechanisms for compensation plans that seek to incorporate sophisticated social cost accounting features. In taking this position, I recognize that I differ from many reformers who believe that any substitute for tort (whether a tailored accident compensation plan, a general-accident compensation plan, or even a comprehensive disability compensation plan) should, in principle, be funded in a way that attempts to allocate accident (and illness) costs to their sources.

Indeed, many advocates of compensation plans often appear to care as much about who pays as who benefits. For example, advocates of tailored proposals such as professors Richard Merrill (drug injuries) and Clark Havighurst (medical injuries) seem to think it crucial to link victim costs to charges imposed on their injurers.[24] Professor O'Connell, too, despite his vehement and unrelenting attacks on tort law, has endorsed the cost-internalizing approach in his no-fault proposals—including his auto no-fault plans, his enterprise liability programs, and his elective no-fault schemes.

I agree, however, with Professor Izhak Englard who, in his review of Dean Guido Calabresi's work and the idea of cost internalizarion, said "[i]t is highly probable that accident law will eventually become a combination of social insurance (the extreme distributional method) and criminal sanction (the extreme method of deterrence). In the face of these expected developments, the tenacious attachment to the notion of market deterrence appears to be a desperate attempt to maintain an ideal of a free-market system in a strongly socializing world".[25]

I divide this discussion of cost internalization into three familiar parts. I deal with individual deterrence or accident prevention first, then activity-level deterrence or allocative efficiency, and finally fairness.

First, at the accident-prevention level I see little likelihood that either the existing New Zealand plan or the proposals from professors Terrence Ison and Donald Harris will stimulate safer individual conduct. Under these plans, as we saw in Chapter 5, although costs are allocated to industries and other activities, they are not (or virtually not) individualized to people or to firms. Thus, personal efforts at accident avoidance go largely unrewarded. Any accident-prevention programs generated by compensation agencies that are supposed to go along with these schemes could, of course, be adopted independently of the scheme's financing mechanism as part of the strategy of relevant regulatory bodies.

Proposals I earlier described, such as those of professors Marc Franklin and Richard Pierce, do envision firm-level cost adjustments. Thus, they do, in theory, offer the promise of individual behavior control. However, these plans create offsetting problems that undermine the value of their individual deterrence strategy. First, the administrative costs of fine tuning the financing arrangements would clearly be significant. For example, I assume that some mechanism would have to exist to allow parties to appeal from any assignment of costs to them by a single governmental agency. Moreover, as both Franklin and Pierce seem to recognize, enterprises too small to self-insure would be at the mercy of bad luck unless the scheme were to permit some kind of insurance. But the result for most firms would be that the introduction of insurance would undo the initial fine tuning in a way similar to the way that liability insurance today undoes tort law's cost allocations. Thus, at the level of individual incentives, these proposals differ little in their promise from today's tort system.[26] Besides, even though there is potential for positive behavioral responses from large enterprises, as with the present tort system, the factors of ignorance, incompetence, discounting, high stakes, small penalties, and perverse incentives will impede even this limited opportunity. In sum, I find the model of individual deterrence that underlies the cost-internalizing proposals of various compensation schemes as theoretically unsatisfying and as empirically unproven as the model underlying tort law.[27]

We now come to the activity-level argument. As we have seen, most of the accident-compensation plans seek to have broad categories of activities, goods, and services bear their accident costs. I conclude, however, that it is doubtful whether society would benefit from such an investment in allocative efficiency. Second-best problems will continue to plague these strategies. The determination of where to allocate costs remains problematic. Moreover, identifying and computing these costs are extremely difficult, as Pierce and Ison have conceded.

Other practical problems also get in the way. A sensible cost-internalization strategy would make the benefits paid by a compensation scheme primary. Yet for quite understandable administrative reasons, neither the New Zealand plan nor the Australian and British proposals do so for medical care or for lost wages during the waiting period. Likewise, on cost-internalizing grounds, New Zealand is wrong to allocate, as it does, the costs of nonwork-related injuries to the work place; these costs should be allocated to the activities that cause the harm.

Furthermore, it still seems odd to me to pay close attention to accident cost externalities while ignoring others such as dislocations caused by plant shutdowns. It also seems ill-advised to establish one centralized (compensation-minded) agency to pursue safety through efforts at social cost allocation while leaving other regulatory agencies to implement different strategies to control the same accidents.[28]

Finally, it makes no sense to tie the amount of compensation paid out to the cost-internalizing charges that are levied. For one thing, a comprehensive plan will pay out some benefits not sensibly allocable to any specific human activity. For another, just because a compensation program may limit victim benefits, say, to some monthly maximum, the principles of cost internalization should not limit the charges imposed on the accident source. Given these sorts of considerations, it is highly unlikely that a scheme's outgo and its source-based charges would be equal. Hence, in any broad scheme that envisions financing through cost internalization, this leaves the problem of where the extra money will come from (or where it will go). Because more (or less) charges to specific causes of claims on the system would upset the allocative efficiency balance so dearly sought, general revenues from (or contributions to) the Treasury is the obvious answer, as many have recognized. But once this is admitted, and the two sides of the equation are disengaged, one can see that it is no longer necessary to fund the compensation side at all with a charge system. That is, people can obtain benefits from traditional income-maintenance sources, and independently, regulatory agencies could experiment with new charge, fine, or tax strategies to supplement more direct regulation. Therefore, even if imposing externalities on disability-causing activities could increase allocative efficiency, this strategy, I believe, should be part of a regulatory apparatus that is divorced from the provisions for compensation.

One might argue that a complete separation of the compensation and regulatory schemes makes it more difficult politically to achieve either goal. Yet, this is a complex issue. For example, Ison observes that those who control high-risk industries often hold considerable political power. Therefore, these industries might support a compensation scheme dependent on flat-rate financing because it would be cheaper for them than experience rating.

Many share my skepticism that cost internalization in the funding of compensation in plans can make the economy significantly more efficient, but nonetheless they would argue that cost allocation is needed for reasons of fairness. As Ison puts it, it does not seem right to require "low risk occupations to subsidize those more hazardous."[29] Once more we are on familiar, and I think unpromising, turf. First, because we do not know who actually bears the incidence of such costs, even if initially imposed on certain activities, the usefulness of imposing these charges on fairness grounds is made dubious in the outset. Second, our Social Security disability system currently employs a financing strategy that ignores cost internalizing and one does not hear claims that these costs should be allocated according to the cause of the claimants' disability. To be sure, unemployment compensation in the United States is merit rated to some degree (a feature that would be eliminated by my short-term paid leave plan). Nonetheless, in many industries (such as construction) employees now make benefit claims that, according to the cost-internalization view, should call for considerably higher charges than many employers pay because they are at the maximum rate. Moreover, in many other countries, both workers' compensation and unemployment insurance systems operate through flat-rate financing without outcries of unfairness.

Besides, attempts at cost internalization through governmentally run plans would raise fairness considerations on the other side. To illustrate my point, consider drivers and insurance rates today. Young men in most states now pay substantial surcharges because, as a group, they are involved in more accidents. Many young men who are careful drivers naturally resent this practice. They claim that better categories for surcharge are categories such as immaturity, party going, consumption of alcohol, or even simply, miles driven. They could be right. But because current age-based categories are the result of the operation of the private market, they are tolerated (barely) on the ground that administrative efficiency directed the decision. Otherwise, one would expect other insurers to offer insurance based on those other categories. What if the government levied age-based charges? Official categorization such as "young men pay more" becomes less tolerable, I believe, especially because the administrative justification for such categorization becomes less demonstrable.

The same point applies when we examine Harris's and Ison's compensation plans that would assign costs by industry. To be sure, insurance companies today adjust premium rates by industry for both liability and workers' compensation insurance. Indeed, some costs probably do vary by industry because of inherent risks. However, I would think that large firms with good records would complain loudly about a publicly run, industry-based, cost-allocation plan that made no allowances for their individual records. Today, at least some firms can secure lower costs through experience rating or self-insurance, but that would not be available in a public plan. Maybe other factors, such as age of plant, type of worker, and nature of machinery, are more important determinants of accident rates, and those factors such as pricing variables presumably would get fair consideration in a competitive scheme. But there would be no competitive pressures on a state monopoly to shift off industry-based charges once the goverment began with those charges.

More broadly, once government begins to engage in differential treatment, due process values begin to push it toward even finer distinctions. The upshot is either complaints of unfairness, when highly individualized treatment is denied, or else high administrative costs, when it is granted. In the end, this is not to say that cost-internalizing finance of public-run compensation mechanisms that treated individuals and/or firms as members of larger groups would be fundamentally unfair. Rather, my point is that uniform charges would also be fair.

The concerns raised in this section generally pertain to all sorts of disability compensation plans, however broadly or narrowly cast. But a very broad disability compensation scheme raises yet additional cost–internalization problems. For example, to just what activities are the costs of illnesses and natural birth defects to be charged? Is recreation to be surcharged because of the colds it produces or perhaps subsidized because of its health benefits? Ison refers to possible surcharges on smoking. What of cholesterol, fat, and alcohol?

In sum, we should abandon the idea of channeling behavior through the funding of compensation mechanisms. Collective efforts to promote safety can focus on the regulatory and other strategies of separate safety agencies that should or could not wind up including cost-attaching charges, fines, or taxes.[30] Next, in Chapter 7, I turn to such strategies.

NOTES

1. D. HARRIS, et al., COMPENSATION AND SUPPORT FOR ILLNESS AND INJURY 328 (1984). Professor Michael Trebilcock asks, "can one ethically defend a system that creates a 'privileged' class of victims of one source of misfortune (accidents) and treats victims of other sources of misfortune (for example, illness, congenital disabilities, or desertion) that generate similar income deficiencies much less generously?" Trebilcock, *The Social Insurance-Deterrence Dilemma of Modern North American Tort Law: A Canadian Perspective on the Liability Insurance Crisis*, 24 SAN DIEGO L. REV. 929, 994 (1987).

2. O'Connell and Guinivan, *An Irrational Combination: The Relative Expansion of Liability Insurance and Contraction of Loss Insurance*, 49 OHIO ST. L.J. 757 (1988). For an earlier and more detailed translation, *see* O'Connell and Barker, *Compensation for Injury & Illness: An Update of the Conard-Morgan Tabulations*, 47 OHIO ST. L.J. 913 (1986). It is worth noting that O'Connell estimated that two-thirds of the tort payout was for auto-related claims. I should add that of the $40 billion a large share went to the claimants' lawyers, another substantial chunk to duplicate other compensation sources, and an even larger slice for pain and suffering, so that the amount of net economic loss represented in the $40 billion is considerably smaller—less than half.

3. For other descriptions of the many and uncoordinated public and private sources of compensation that are available to the disabled, and their tendency both to overcompensate and undercompensate, *see* REPORT OF THE RESEARCH SUBCOMMITTEE OF THE DISABILITY INSURANCE COMMITTEE, HEALTH INSURANCE ASSOCIATION OF AMERICA, COMPENSATION SYSTEMS, AVAILABLE TO DISABLED PERSONS IN THE UNITED STATES (1979) [hereinafter cited as COMPENSATION SYSTEMS] and E. BERNZWEIG, BY ACCIDENT NOT DESIGN 29–40 (1980).

4. P. MUNCH, COSTS AND BENEFITS OF THE TORTS SYSTEM IF VIEWED AS A COMPENSATION SYSTEM 37, table A–3 (1977) (Rand Corporation Institute of Civil Justice), for example, shows that about 90 percent of auto accident tort claimants had less than $1000 of economic losses. More than two-thirds of product injury claimants had less than $1000 of economic loss, *id.* at 14,

table A–7. More than half of medical malpractice claimants had less than $1000 in economic loss, *id.* at 81, table M–64. And these tables do not even include victims with minor injuries who do not bother to sue. According to a recent General Accounting Office (GAO) study, most malpractice claims are not for major permanent injuries. Rather 72.6 percent involved emotional harm, insignificant harm, temporary disability or minor permanent partial disability, GAO, MEDICAL MAL-PRACTICE CHARACTERISTICS OF CLAIMS CLOSED IN 1984 24, table 2.7 (1987). About 60 percent of claimants who received any payment had economic losses of less than $10,000, *id.* at 45, table 3.6.

5. *See generally* Price, *Income Replacement During Sickness,* 1948–78, 44 SOC. SECURITY BULL. 18 (May 1981) and O'Connell and Barker *supra* note 2, at 937.

6. For example, Bernzweig's data show that in 1978, 150,000 motor vehicle accident victims were permanently impaired, and over 50,000 were killed, E. BERN-ZWEIG, *supra* note 3, at 2.

7. *See generally* FINAL REPORT OF THE NATIONAL COMMISSION ON SOCIAL SECURITY, SOCIAL SECURITY IN AMERICA'S FUTURE 157, 207 (1981).

8. *See* COMPENSATION SYSTEMS, *supra* note 3.

9. *See* J. BURTON and W. VROMAN, A REPORT ON PERMANENT PARTIAL DISABILITIES UNDER WORKERS' COMPENSATION 2 (1978) (prepared for the United States Department of Commerce for use by the Interdepartmental Workers' Compensation Task Force); Burton, *Compensation for Permanent Partial Disabilities,* in SAFETY AND THE WORK FORCE (J. WORRALL, ed.) 18 (1983); and REPORT TO THE PRESIDENT AND THE CONGRESS, WORKER'S COMPENSATION: IS THERE A BETTER WAY? 14, 16, 27–30 (1977).

"From one-third to one-half of the benefits are used to pay permanent partial disability cases," Berkowitz, *How Serious Is Sugarman's "Serious Tort Law Reform"?,* 24 SAN DIEGO L. REV. 877, 881 (1987).

10. *See* Zeiter and Beedon, *Long-Term Disability Programs in Selected Countries,* 50 SOC. SECURITY BULL. 8 (Sept. 1987).

11. Noncoverage of such people is by no means inevitable, however. *See* for example E. BERNZWEIG, *supra* note 3, at 39–40, describing the Israeli scheme for compensating disabled homemakers.

12. This is not simply an American issue. Even in New Zealand, it has led to a call to merge the New Zealand accident-compensation plan with that nation's regular social security and retirement schemes, *see* Marks, *The Need for a Comprehensive Approach,* in THE WELFARE STATE TODAY (G. PALMER, ed.) 355 (1977). Marks is especially concerned about New Zealand's failure to deal well and consistently with the problems faced by what she calls nonearning groups, such as students and housewives.

13. *See generally* O'Connell and Barker *supra* note 2, at 935, O'Connell and Guinivan, *supra* note 2, at 762, and E. BROWN et al., CALIFORNIANS WITHOUT HEALTH INSURANCE (California Policy Seminar 1987).

14. The consequences of lack of health insurance should not be exaggerated, however. For example, Professor George Priest reports the results of a 1982 phone survey that suggests that, whatever the magnitude of inadequate advance arrangements, only 1.5 percent of families were actually denied medical care for financial

reasons, Priest, *The Current Insurance Crisis and Modern Tort Law*, 96 YALE L.J. 1521, 1586–87 (1987). On the other hand, many of those without health insurance or access to public programs probably fail to seek medical care that they would obtain were they protected.

15. *See* Sugarman, *Short-Term Paid Leave: A New Approach to Social Insurance and Employee Benefits*, 75 CALIF. L. REV. 465 (1987).

16. Henderson, *Should Workmen's Compensation Be Extended to Nonoccupation Injuries?*, 48 TEX. L. REV. 117 (1969).

17. *See* Zeitzer and Beedon, *supra* note 10, at 15.

18. *See generally* Sugarman, *Children's Benefits in Social Security*, 65 CORN. L. REV. 836 (1980).

19. *See* Zeitzer and Beedon, *supra* note 10, at 9–11. Israel, for example, provides benefits to disabled homemakers. The Netherlands, for example, provides benefits to those disabled from birth.

20. *See* M. Trebilcock, The Role of Conduct Variables in the Design of "No-Fault" Insurance Systems (1988) (draft on file with the author). In an article that is focused on the mass tort problem, Professor Kenneth Abraham argues in favor of expanded first-party benefit arrangements rather than expansive tort liability or tailored no-fault plans. At least as a means for providing income support, Professor Abraham, like me, favors the social insurance route over the mandated employee benefit solution. Although Professor Abraham rightly points to problems of adverse selection and moral hazard that have stood in the way of the more robust development of the private disability insurance market, the former, at least, is largely avoided by a mandatory and broad-based social insurance scheme. Moral hazard, of course, remains a problem that must be dealt with by controls on wage-replacement levels and rehabilitation cooperation requirements. While I certainly do not object to Abraham's suggestions that efforts be made to promote more private first-party disability income protection in the short run, in the longer run only a national social insurance scheme can provide comprehensive protection, *see* Abraham, *Individual Action and Collective Responsibility: The Dilemma of Mass Tort Reform*, 73 VA. L. REV. 845, 898–907 (1987).

21. *See* for example Rovner, *Senate Labor OKs Mandated-Benefits Measure*, 46 CONG. Q. 363 (Feb. 20, 1988).

22. *See* for example *Who Can Afford a Nursing Home?*, 53 CONSUMER REPORTS 300 (May 1988).

23. This is an idea commonly proposed in England. *See generally* P. Mitchell, *Constructing a National Disability Income* (The Royal Ass'n for Disability and Rehabilitation, London, 1987); DISABILITY ALLIANCE, POVERTY & DISABILITY: BREAKING THE LINK (1987); and *An Introduction to the Disablement Income Group* (London, 1985) (all on file with the author).

24. *See* Merrill, *Compensation for Prescription Drug Injuries*, 59 VA. L. REV. 1 (1973) and Havighurst, *"Medical Adversity Insurance"—Has Its Time Come?*, DUKE L.J. 1233 (1975).

25. England, *The System Builders: A Critical Appraisal of Modern American Tort Theory*, 9. J. LEGAL STUD. 27, 49 (1980).

26. Assigning costs in comprehensive compensation plans will also create vexing practical problems. For example, it might be argued that if auto manufacturers had to internalize the costs of car accidents, they would develop more effective seat belts

and/or air bags. *See* Latin, *Problem Solving Behavior and Theories of Tort Liability*, 73 CALIF. L. REV. 677 (1985). But it is by no means certain that an agency in charge of cost internalization would actually impose these costs on carmakers. Those accident costs could also be attached to liquor, driving, and designing highways. In other words, one can suggest many plausible candidates for behavior modification through the assignment of these costs.

27. In 1967, Ison cited a lack of evidence that firm differentials actually yielded a reduction in accidents, T. ISON, THE FORENSIC LOTTERY 93 (1967). I take this to be his assessment of empirical research at that time. In his 1980 book, Ison attacks the feasibility of the New Zealand statutory provision that allows linking firm level differentials with employee accident claims, *see* T. ISON, ACCIDENT COMPENSATION 130–34 (1980). As we saw in Chapter 5, this authority has been virtually unused to date by the Accident Compensation Corporation.

Professor Palmer offers an additional relevant insight based on the New Zealand experience. Under the New Zealand plan, although workers face a one-week waiting period before obtaining income benefits, when the injuries are work-related, employers are required to cover that week's pay through a mandatory employee benefit. As a result, employers do have some money at stake that could be saved if their workers were injured less. But there is little indication that anyone sees it that way or that this provision has in any way increased safety efforts by employers, *see* G. PALMER, COMPENSATION FOR INCAPACITY 372–74 (1979).

I also think it worth special explanation of how Palmer, who has been intimately involved in this issue at both the theoretical and practical level, has over time come to oppose pursuing cost-internalization goals through the funding mechanisms of a compensation plan. In 1978, he said, "I began as a firm believer in the validity of the theory; I have ended up a skeptic as to whether any scheme capable of implementation will achieve much by the way of economic deterrence, at least so long as it is attached to a compensation scheme," *id.* at 380. By 1981, he was even more negative:

There are many arguments heard as to why accident prevention is advanced by a system of differential premiums. It has never yet been empirically demonstrated. I am persuaded after years of trying to work through this issue in many different countries that it is better to finance the scheme by way of flat-rate levies. They are administratively simple, Palmer, *What Happened to the Woodhouse Report?*, N.Z.L.J. 561, 571 (1981).

Palmer recognizes that others, economists especially, cling to the ideal of cost internalization (referring, for example, to Professor Monroe Berkowitz's more recent New Zealand study calling for more accident prevention through cost-allocation strategies). In the end, however, he concludes that "[t]he argument is one of the most fascinating in the accident compensation sphere. It can never be defeated in theory and never proved to work in practice. I doubt whether the debate will ever end," *id.*

Other inquiries into the impact of the New Zealand scheme on accidents have mixed findings, *see* for example Brown, *Deterrence in Tort and No-Fault: The New Zealand Experience*, 73 CALIF. L. REV. 976 (1985) and M. BERKOWITZ, THE ECONOMICS OF WORK ACCIDENTS IN NEW ZEALAND (1979).

28. I am not persuaded by Pierce's solution either—one superagency for all safety problems, *see* Pierce, *Encouraging Safety: The Limits of Tort Law and Government*

Regulation, 33 VAND. L. REV. 1281, 1320–21 (1980). Such an agency would inevitably be balkanized into many different units, each addressing separate issues. Most probably, it would also split into regulatory and compensation divisions. An equally promising approach is to arm existing agencies with the power to impose fines and charges: This severs the ties between compensation and regulation—the result I favor.

29. T. ISON, THE FORENSIC LOTTERY, *supra* note 27, at 58.

30. For example, Professor Kip Viscusi, in addressing the occupational disease problem, argues that all disease victims should be treated alike, by expanding Social Security's disability income benefit structure, as I have proposed. With respect to workplace safety, he favors, not the tort system, but a combination of minimum regulatory standards and "penalty taxes based on the current hazards of the taxpayer's workplace," *see* Viscusi, *Structuring an Effective Occupational Disease Policy: Victim Compensation and Risk Regulation*, 2 YALE J. ON REG. 53, 77 (1984). *See also* Viscusi, *Compensating Workplace Toxic Torts*, in NEW DIRECTIONS IN LIABILITY LAW (W. OLSON, ed.) 126 (1988).

7

Safety Regulation without Accident Law

ACCIDENT PREVENTION THROUGH REGULATORY STRATEGIES, WITH THE INCREASED INVOLVEMENT OF CITIZENS, VICTIMS, AND CITIZEN GROUPS

In 1951 Professor Glanville Williams predicted that administrative regulations would supersede tort law in the deterrence of accidents.[1] In my view, regulation today is a far more dominant force in advancing safety than is tort law. Yet the occasion of the rollback of personal injury law is a good time to consider whether new regulatory strategies should be tried.

Greater efforts by regulatory agencies will not rid our society of unreasonably dangerous conduct and products. Indeed, many of the shortcomings of our tort system as a deterrent apply to administrative regulation as well. Moreover, regulation has it own special problems. Administrative agencies are subject to "capture" by those they regulate. They also tend to pursue their own bureaucratic objectives. Even when doggedly pursuing the public interest in safety, they face difficult policy choices and enforcement problems. In general, agencies may rely too heavily on regulatory standards that tell actors specifically what to do rather than combining incentives with leeway for individual situations.[2] Still, I cannot imagine doing away with regulatory agencies as the central protectors of our safety. Our challenge lies rather in developing better techniques to make agencies more responsive and more effective. Allowing them to focus on accident prevention, undistracted by concerns over compensation, is a good start.

In the first part of this chapter, I address the claim that eliminating tort law will seriously weaken existing regulatory efforts on behalf of safety.

Then I discuss the advantages regulation has over tort law and suggest ways in which agencies might more effectively promote safety. Next, I consider how agencies can provide constructive outlets for people's anger at and dismay with the unreasonably dangerous conduct of others. Finally, I conclude that in the long run we should do away with personal injury suits with the exception of claims for punitive damages where the injurer's conduct has been truly outrageous.

The Interaction of Tort Law and Regulation

Global Perspectives on Regulatory Agencies in a World without Tort

Some people view regulation as a menace. They fear that if people could not point to tort law as a behavior regulator, then agencies could become too powerful. In short, they see the existing tort regime as a buffer against undesirable, centralized decision making.[3] This argument is not realistic. During the last two decades, when tort law has thrived, there has also been an explosion in the use of regulatory bodies concerned with safety—agencies such as the Consumer Product Safety Commission (CPSC), the Occupational Safety and Health Administration (OSHA), and the Enviromental Protection Agency (EPA). Hence, one could as easily argue that vigorous tort law spawns regulation. The better explanation, I believe, is that courts and legislatures have responded in parallel to the same public distrust of the market. Thus, I conclude that, broadly speaking, regulation expands or contracts independently of whether one can sue in tort for accidental injury.

Conversely, there are fears that it is too precarious to rely on agencies to protect the public. The budget cutting and deregulation attitudes that have marked the Reagan administration have fueled these fears, because many believe that the effectiveness of existing safety agencies has been deliberately diminished. Although there is considerable merit to this concern, it should be recalled that most major deregulatory efforts have been aimed, not at reducing safety controls, but at increasing access to closed markets and promoting price competition, as illustrated by deregulation of airlines, trucking, and financial institutions.[4] Anyway, the answer to diminished support for effective agency safety efforts is renewed support, not support for tort law.

To be sure, the existence of tort arguably deters some political forces that would otherwise promote deregulation in order to be rid of all formal controls on safety. Moreover, it is possible that the abolition of tort law would discourage the proregulation political alliances that sometimes form between plaintiffs' lawyers, insurance companies, and regulatory bodies. Nonetheless, I believe that the contention that tort law keeps regulatory agencies alive is ultimately unconvincing. Indeed, the prime outside defenders of safety agencies are typically those who promoted regulation on the ground that the market and tort law have failed to achieve socially desired behavioral control.

A further notion is that tort serves as "insurance" against the risk that the opponents of regulation will succeed in sapping the strength of administrative authority. The problem is that this insurance is too expensive. After all, unlike a weapon held in reserve, our tort system cannot be placed in a warehouse; enormous administrative costs continue to accumulate. Ultimately, I suppose, it comes down to this. If one agrees with the arguments I made in Chapter 1 about the puny deterrent potential of tort (even in a world without safety agencies), then the idea of spending lots of society's resources on tort law as a backup safety device makes little sense.

Tort Law as "Partner" or "Ombudsman" [5]

Some would argue that the repeal of tort law could yield less-effective safety regulation by government. To the extent that these arguments are valid, agencies may need more power and manpower in a world without tort. But as I suggested earlier, society could provide a large infusion of support for agencies and still achieve a drastic net reduction in administrative costs by, in effect, transferring a modest proportion of the people who administer the tort system to the safety agencies. Let me turn to some specific arguments.

Tort suits can sometimes identify problems for agencies to pursue. I concede this point even if agencies only occasionally rely on litigation for this purpose. Thus, new strategies may be needed to inform agencies of safety problems as they develop.

By publicizing dangers and injuries, tort actions can pressure agencies to act. The few celebrated cases that demonstrate this point seem quite exceptional. Nevertheless, it would be desirable to give victims and citizen groups new powers to force agency action.

Fear of tort liability may cause voluntary compliance with agency regulations. The idea here is that because people realize that failure to conform to regulatory requirements is likely to lead to a finding of negligence or product defect, tort law adds to the cost of noncompliance with safety rules. This concern suggests that more powerful agency sanctions may be needed, or that agencies may have to deploy stronger sanctions that now go unused.

Tort lawyers may function as public prosecutors. They go after wrongdoers that agencies now ignore. In fact, surely, most plaintiffs' lawyers' hours are devoted to auto accident cases, where public regulation is already substantial. And clearly much litigation involves duplicate claims against the same defendant for the same conduct or product. Nevertheless, without tort law perhaps we will need to add more agency lawyers. Of course, a large number could be hired with the earnings of a few prominent personal injury attorneys.

Tort lawyers and their investigators can uncover dangerous practices before agencies do or that agencies would never detect. While the extent that this claim is true is probably quite limited, perhaps new incentives are needed to encourage private citizens to identify dangerous conduct and safer alternatives.

Even if it cannot prevent dangerous conduct at the outset, tort law may be able to curtail certain existing dangers. For example, fear of litigation could curtail further marketing. This suggests that agencies may need augmented powers to block discovered dangers not initially deterred. Also, there may be a continuing role for private litigation that seeks injunctions rather than damages.

Promising Agency Techniques and Their Enhancement

I have just noted a number of reasons why, if tort law is repealed, administrative agencies arguably might benefit from increased regulatory authority, manpower, or initiative. I will now discuss three promising regulatory strategies in some detail, explaining their advantages over tort law.

Learning About Dangers

I want to emphasize both the flexibility regulatory agencies already have and the potential for increasing the role ordinary citizens play in the exposure of dangerous conduct. The CPSC, for example, utilizes two noteworthy techniques. First, it has established an extensive system of accident reporting, triggered by the treatment of victims in selected hospital emergency rooms throughout the country.[6] Unlike tort law, which relies on the happenstance of privately initiated lawsuits often filed long after the fact, the CSPC reporting network supplies prompt, reliable data about accidents as they occur. This is not a perfect system, of course. For one thing, although the agency learns about frequency and severity of harms from various products and activities, it learns little about possible preventive measures. Nonetheless, this reporting system, together with CPSC staff follow-up of a selection of emergency room reports through telephone and on-site investigations, has identified products warranting further safety study. In addition, it has taught the CPSC and those concerned with consumer safety that administrative action simply will not eliminate the great mass of accidents. Rather, patterns of use must change, perhaps through consumer education.[7] The alternative would be to banish or transform products we now consider essential parts of our everyday lives—products such as bicycles, knives, and stoves.

In addition to emergency room reporting, the CPSC has a second important routine method for learning about dangers. The statute governing the agency imposes on individual firms the duty to inform the CPSC whenever it learns of a "substantial product hazard."[8] With full compliance the agency would know almost as much as individual firms about product dangers. Alas, in 1983, for example, the CPSC reported that of the twenty-five most serious hazards it addressed that year, only five came to the agency's attention in this manner.[9] As a result, the CPSC announced clearer and stronger guidelines for self-reporting and promised tougher enforcement.[10] Whether improved compliance can be achieved and sustained remains to be seen, but at least the CPSC's response illustrates how an agency tracking a problem can attempt new initiatives where old ones fail.[11]

Moreover, there are means other than penalties and staff increases to remedy a substantial nonreporting problem. One is to encourage consumers to report more dangers. For example, the National Highway Traffic Safety Administration (NHTSA) maintains an Auto Safety Hotline that yields more than 500 calls a day, and consumer complaints have initiated many auto recall drives. The CPSC also has a hot line. Giving informers who provide valuable information cash and other rewards might further promote reporting. Of course, such a program could also enhance the deterrent effect of the agency's regulations.

Finally, unlike courts, agencies can themselves engage in research and inspections to discover dangers.[12] The tort system, in contrast, must rely on the happenstance of private action.

Recalls

It is important to contain a problem once it has been identified. Although market and other forces would remain potent, agencies might find this a bigger job without tort law. As a result, they may have to rely more on the recall—an important tool already used by many agencies that deal with products, including the CPSC, the Food and Drug Administration (FDA,) and the NHTSA. Indeed, reports of auto, drug, and consumer product recalls are commonplace. I want to make four points about recalls.

First, an agency has a decided advantage over courts in that it can evaluate different enforcement strategies. It can experiment and decide to chart a new course. Courts, by contrast, basically have a single weapon in their arsenal—damage awards. There is little room for innovation. Whereas tort law addresses the final product, agencies can intervene, for example, with process requirements before the undesirable results occur.

Second, any evaluation of the recall strategy must pay attention to its deterrent potential. Fear of a recall should provide the same leverage as does fear of tort liability when safety-conscious production people try to restrain eager marketing people. Moreover, unlike a tort suit managed by the legal department, a recall usually more directly involves the very marketing staff who orchestrated the product's distribution. The effectiveness of the recall threat as a deterrent is probably dependent on the likelihood it will be imposed and its potential cost to the firm if it is. Unfortunately, I have been unable to find much research on this issue. I concede that the costs of a recall probably do not correlate well with either the probable harm if the product is not recalled or with the costs of enhanced safety measured by the burden of improving the product. Nevertheless, the basic point is that recall costs are usually substantial enough to command the attention of decision makers.[13] In short, while the threat of a recall may not produce perfect economic incentives, firms likely to respond to the threat of litigation will also probably react to the threat of recall. To be sure, because of ignorance or laziness, consumers may not act when recalls are announced, for example, by failing to return a product or to take their car in for repair. Firms may nonetheless fear a recall for several reasons. The firm's reputation may suffer, retooling and remarketing may result in unpredictable costs, and the recall campaign itself may be expensive and time consuming to negotiate and publicize.

The upshot is that an agency record of what one might describe as a modest level of recalls is susceptible to two interpretations.[14] Indeed, rather than demonstrating administrative ineffectiveness, a stable or declining recall record may reflect the power of the recall threat to nip danger in the bud.[15]

Third, tort law and recall efforts can sometimes work at cross purposes. Firms may be reluctant to negotiate voluntary recalls because they fear increasing their exposure to lawsuits. Thus, eliminating tort liability may produce a greater willingness to recall what may be time bombs in the possession of consumers.[16] On the other hand, I concede that to the extent that agencies such as the CPSC rely on the underlying fear of product liability suits in order to force negotiated recalls, agency settlements with manufacturers concerning recalls might become more difficult to achieve without the threat of private litigation.

Fourth, giving consumers greater power and incentive to initiate recalls might enhance the deterrent value of this threat. These innovations require granting consumers various participation rights—such as the right to petition agencies to consider a proposed recall and to receive a financial reward if the recall is then ordered. This, in turn, can also help victims of dangers who report those dangers to the agency achieve a sense of satisfaction from having protected others from the same risks.

Priorites

Agencies have an advantage over courts in that they can set priorities and attack problems in some sensible order. Courts encounter problems haphazardly. The CPSC, for example, announces "product hazards for priority status" and then accords such hazards special emphasis and funding. Presumably the agency thinks it can intervene effectively in these areas. In 1983, for example, it selected ten such hazards including chain saws, the smoldering ignition of furniture and bedding, children's exposure to carcinogens, heating-equipment fires, smoke detectors, formaldehyde released

from plywood and particle board, indoor air problems from fuel-fired ap-
pliances, and school laboratory chemicals.[17] In 1986–1987, its priorities included some new and some continuing concerns: electrocution hazards, fire
toxicity, gas heating-systems, portable electric heaters, riding mowers,
safety for older consumers, child drowning, poison packaging, and all-
terrain vehicles (ATVs).[18] Once again, citizens can be given an important
role in this process. For example, agencies could be made to publish proposed annual priorities and then to invite citizen groups to testify at open
hearings.

Unlike the tort system, whose only flexibility lies in the possibility of
settlement, agencies can choose from criminal sanctions, civil penalities,
warnings, recalls, injunction like remedies, negotiated solutions, and court
orders. They can move by rule making or by individualized adjudication.
They can selectively enforce regulations, putting resources where they believe deterrence is most effective and they can emphasize voluntary cooperation where that seems best.[19] Torts cases plod along regardless of their
deterrence potential. Thus, auto claims, though probably least important
from a deterrence perspective, take up the most time and money.[20]

Citizen Participation and Agencies Generally

If there is indeed a need for victim vengeance, it is poorly served by tort
law today. Perhaps agencies can deal with this need and redirect it in a
constructive way. Aggressive citizen involvement in agency proceedings
can provide an outlet for expressing anger and dismay.[21] It also can demonstrate official concern for a person's suffering. Citizen participation in
specific cases may be especially meaningful. Thus, it may be important not
only, say, to place selected lay people on professional quality-assurance
boards, but also more effectively to solicit and investigate complaints from
ordinary people about their doctor or lawyer or architect.

In the prior section I suggested at several places not only specific roles
for citizens, but also the possibility of public financial rewards for effective
citizen participation. The general point is that agencies should experiment
with methods of encouraging people to inform the agency about dangerous
products, conditions, and practices and to propose to the agency both problems for priority attention and products for recall (or practices for curtailment). These financial rewards could take the form of attorneys' fees and
client bonuses. Thus, perhaps that first lawyer who demonstrates to an
agency that some product or activity is too dangerous could still have the
sort of recognition and compensation that comes with bringing a successful
tort suit in a new problem area today.

I admit that people today often feel frustrated when they take their complaints to government officials or professional regulatory bodies. Merely
exhorting more people to use this route will not solve the problem.[22] None-

theless, techniques already in place do show promise of increasing governmental responsiveness. The institution of "the ombudsman" is an example.

Moreover, to guard against agency "capture," perhaps individuals and consumer groups should have private rights of action against injurers when agencies fail to act—not for compensation, but for injunctions against clearly unreasonable dangerous conduct. Defendant liability for attorney fees in such cases could provide the needed grease for the smooth operation of the injunction remedy.

In sum, society should promote safety with different instruments from those used to pay compensation. If, as suggested earlier, cost internalization was thought desirable as a behavioral control device, safety agencies should employ it through charges and tax mechanisms, not those bodies that pay benefits.[23]

ABOLITION OF TORT ACTIONS FOR ACCIDENTAL PERSONAL INJURIES

Supplanting Rather than Supplementing Tort

In Chapter 6, I described the social insurance and employee benefit arrangements that I think should serve the compensation goal now supposedly promoted by tort law. Once the tort victim's need for reasonable compensation has been met by those other systems, maintaining ordinary private rights of action would involve greater social costs than benefits. That was the broad message of Part I of this book. And, I believe it would not be right to preserve tort remedies for those with, say, very high incomes not routinely covered by the regular compensation plans. For the reasons given in my discussion of cost internalizing in Chapter 6, I would not want to maintain tort claims so as to allow collateral sources to obtain reimbursement from the tort-feasor's insurer.[24] As for behavior control, we should rely on regulatory agencies as discussed here, market pressures, moral inhibitions, and self-preservation instincts.

Intentional Wrongdoing and Punitive Damages

Elimination of tort suits for accidents plainly implies the end of personal injury claims now sounding in negligence or strict liability. But what of cases of outrageous conduct? Although I would oppose allowing law suits for compensatory damages in such cases, perhaps claims should still be allowed for punitive damages—even in the long run.

Admittedly, there are drawbacks to this strategy. For example, allowing such suits will create new borderline problems, pressuring courts to extend recovery to negligent but not outrageous wrongdoing. Before corporations were held liable, I could require proof of outrageous conduct high up in the organization. Yet, I realize that it is sometimes quite difficult to pinpoint individual responsibility in large organizations. On the other side, I also recognize that I would at least be allowing tort law to punish the deliberate, white-collar wrongdoer, knowing that as a practical matter, punitive damages will not touch many of society's worst actors—hardened criminals—because of their insolvency. Finally, I am aware that pursuing punitive objectives through civil litigation, as we do with punitive damages today, involves problems of its own, including the absence of such constitutional protection as the "beyond a reasonable doubt" standard, the potential for unfairly excessive awards, and the considerable possibility of uneven results from jury to jury.[25]

Nonetheless, perhaps it would, on balance, be wise to keep this part of tort law alive if certain conditions are met. For example, judges or legislatures could constrain both the availability and size of punitive damage awards. In Chapter 8, I propose as part of my first-step proposal simply that judges be given the duty to decide whether, and if so, how much to award as punitive damages. I would be content to see how this approach turned out before proposing any further formal constraint. In the end, even if punitive damages wind up doing nothing for deterrence, they might satisfy victim and society needs for retribution that the criminal justice and regulatory systems do not provide.

The New Zealand experience is instructive. Although the legislation establishing the accident-compensation plan was silent on the matter, most informed people initially thought that tort actions for punitive damages had been outlawed. An appellate decision held to the contrary, however, reasoning that because such damages are not compensatory but punitive, they are appropriately still available.[26]

Motivated by the goal of promoting the optimal level of accidents, Professor Jason Johnston has advanced a tort reform proposal that he calls punitive liability.[27] It is premised on the belief that under a negligence regime, juries too often find conduct unreasonable that is actually reasonable with the result that negligence law in action overdeters in a socially undesirable way. Johnston recommends that a higher standard of fault be required before liability is imposed (say gross negligence proved by clear and convincing evidence), but that, in turn, the damages awarded in such cases be punitive in amount (i.e., in excess of ordinary compensatory damages). In practice, Johnston assumes that under his system some defendants would be held liable when they are really only ordinarily negligent; but at least they would not be held liable when they are not negligent at all. In this way, would-be defendants are meant to see that in practice they face approximately the same effective threat, Johnston argues, as they would under an efficiently operating negligence regime, and the overdeterrence problems would be solved.

One implication of Johnston's approach is that it is all right for defendants who are only ordinarily negligent to have punitive damages imposed on them. I think that most would find this quite troublesome. This could probably be avoided if we up the fault requirement a bit further, say, from gross negligence to egregious conduct. But then, of course, we are back to punitive damages as I have supported them. Moreover, because Johnston envisions combining his punitive liability scheme with a nonfault compensation scheme like New Zealand's, it turns out that he and I are not so very far apart after all.[28]

Other Kinds of Tort Suits: Property Damage, Dignitary Injuries, Financial Loss, Contract Warranties, and Injunctions

As Professor Terrence Ison long ago pointed out, it would be possible to disallow personal injury actions while leaving the rest of tort law intact. However, this might not be well advised. For example, I believe that property owners should have to use first-party insurance to protect themselves against compensatory losses. Also other victims with medical expenses and provable income losses likewise would (under my long-run proposal) have to find suitable recompense through the compensation mechanisms set up for ordinary personal injury victims. This would include defamation victims. On the other hand, in line with my previous comments, I would allow suits for punitive damages in the case of intentional wrongdoing to property, intentional defamation, and other intentional dignitary harms.

Financial loss is a more complicated matter. Tort claims for such harm should be reevaluated in light of other parts of the commercial law system, a task I put aside here. In general, contract law would continue to deal with consumer warranties, but no warranty would be construed to provide compensation for personal injury unless this were so stated explicitly. Such a warranty would become, in effect, an intentional insurance contract.

Injunctive relief would remain available especially with respect to nuisances. Moreover, as noted earlier, injunction actions could backstop agencies where wrongdoing continues despite administrative attention to the problem. Like those who bring civil rights suits today, attorneys who litigate such cases would function as private attorneys general, and in appropriate cases, their fees would be paid by the defendants.

NOTES

1. Williams, *The Aims of the Law of Tort*, 4 CURRENT LEGAL PROBS. 137, 172–76 (1951).

2. *See generally* L. LAVE, THE STRATEGY OF SOCIAL REGULATION (1981) who criticizes many existing regulatory practices and offers recommendations for reform that focus on improved data collection and analysis.

3. Professor Joseph Little, for example, defends tort law, notwithstanding its imperfections, precisely because of his fear of its alternative—state control, Little, *Up with Torts*, 24 SAN DIEGO L. REV. 861, 864 (1987).

4. On the other hand, budget cuts imposed on agencies such as the CPSC can more directly lead to the curtailment of specific consumer safety programs. *See* for example *Hearings Before the Subcomm. on HUD—Independent Agencies, Comm. on Appropriations, U.S. Senate*, 99th Cong. 1st sess. (March 27, 1985) (statement of CPSC Commissioner Stuart M. Statler).

5. *See* Linden, *Tort Law as Ombudsman*, 51 CAN. BAR. REV. 155 (1973).

6. For a discussion of CPSC's National Electronic Injury Surveillance System (NEISS) data collection system, *see* Heiden and Pittaway, *Rebuttal to CPSC's Hazard Data System: Response to a Critique*, 6 J. PROD. LIAB. 217 (1983); Heiden and Pittaway, *Utility of the U.S. Consumer Product Safety Commission's Injury Data System as a Basis for Product Hazard Assessment*, 5 J. PROD. LIAB. 295 (1982); and Waksberg, *CPSC's Hazard Data System: Response to Critique*, 6 J. PROD. LIAB. 201 (1983). The CPSC also receives voluntary reports of product-related deaths from coroners as part of its Medical Examiners and Coroners Alert Project and from its collection of death certificates, *see* Consumer Product Safety Com'n, *Annual Report*, 15 (1985).

7. It has been said that more than two-thirds of consumer product injuries come from misuse or abuse of the product. *See* Owen, *Rethinking the Policies of Strict Liability*, 33 VAND. L. REV. 681, 710 n. 89 (1980).

8. T. SCHWARTZ and R. ADLER, PRODUCT RECALLS: A REMEDY IN NEED OF REPAIR 35 (1983) (prepared for the Administrative Conference of the United States).

9. *See* Statler, *Reporting Guidelines under Section 15 of the Consumer Product Safety Act*, 7 J. PROD. LIAB. 89 (1984) and Barsky, *Abandoning Federal Sovereign Immunity: Public Compensation for Victims of Latently Defective Therapeutic Drugs*, 2 J. PROD. LIAB. 20 (1983).

10. United States Consumer Prod. Safety Comm'n, *News from CPSC*, 84–19.

11. In 1987, Terrence Scanlon, CPSC chairman, claimed that self-reporting of product hazards was up. Former CPSC Commissioner Stuart Statler has proposed revisions in the self-reporting obligation designed to improve compliance. *See Consumer Product Safety Commission Reauthorization, House of Representatives: Hearings Before the Subcomm. on Commerce, Consumer Protection and Competition, Comm. on Energy and Commerce*, 100th Cong. 1st Sess. 22 (testimony of Terrence Scanlon) [hereinafter cited as Scanlon], 203 (testimony of Stuatrt Statler) [hereinafter cited as Statler], No. 120–47 (1987).

It seems sensible for other agencies, such as the FDA, to follow the CPSC and mandate the reporting of defects that firms discover in their own products, as recommended by T. SCHWARTZ and R. ADLER, *supra* note 8, at 56–57.

12. For example, the CPSC annually produces hazard analysis reports on selected products.

13. Schwartz and Adler point out that recall may often cost more than product liability claims, T. SCHWARTZ and R. ADLER, *supra* note 8, at 56–57.

14. According to the CPSC, its actions between 1973 and 1985 led to more than 1300 "recalls or other corrective actions," CPSC, *Annual Report*, 36 (1985). There were 172 recalls in 1986, *see* Scanlon, *supra* note 11, at 22.

15. The same point applies to data concerning the paucity of reports under the

rules calling for enterprise self-reporting of hazards. A lack of such reports may also indicate that the fear of effective enforcement has caused manufacturers to make products safer.

16. *See* Statler, *supra* note 11, at 205.

17. United States Consumer Product Safety Commission, *News from CPSC*, 82–32.

18. CONGRESSIONAL QUARTERLY, FEDERAL REGULATORY DIRECTORY 86 (5th ed. 1986). For discussions of what action the CPSC takes with respect to its priority items, *see* for example CPSC, *Annual Report*, 19–26 (1985) and CPSC, *Annual Report*, 7–11 (1986).

19. For an interesting analysis of the advantages of cooperative regulatory enforcement strategies (emphasizing flexible or selective enforcement) as compared with traditional deterrence approaches, *see* Scholz, *Cooperation, Deterrence and the Ecology of Regulatory Enforcement*, 18 LAW 7 SOC'Y REV. 179 (1984). These advantages apply to centralized regulation and not to tort law.

20. Professor Howard Latin has proposed employing tort law only in those settings in which actors who are classified as high-attention problem solvers either (1) injure low-attention actors or (2) negligently or intentionally injure other high-attention problem-solvers, *see* Latin, *Problem-Solving and Theories of Tort Liability*, 73 CALIF. L. REV. 677, 196–98 (1985). This reflects a "priorities" strategy—using tort where it is most promising from a deterrence perspective. It would mean the elimination of the tort remedy in some areas as well as its expansion elsewhere. His examples of where liability would lie include transportation-carrier injuries of passengers regardless of fault, product injuries of consumers regardless of product defects, and injuries from ultrahazardous activities. But in lauding tort solutions over regulatory solutions, does Latin really mean to do away with the Federal Aviation Administration (FAA), the FDA, the CPSC, zoning ordinances, etc.? I rather doubt it. Assuming he does not, then he has failed to convince me that the extra social benefits (both behavioral controls and activity-level changes), if any, arising from his proposed regime of liability would be worth their costs.

In addition, Latin's proposal, unless he also changed tort law's rules of damages, would exacerbate the horizontal inequality among claimants that now exists as between injured workers and tort victims. And finally, even if Latin were right that it would be socially worthwhile to target certain accident costs to certain high-attention problem-solving injurers, this could be done through a regulatory system. This system would employ accident-related charges that are divorced from the society's compensation arrangements for victims. Such a division of the behavioral control function from the compensation function is, of course, what I have proposed.

21. Citizen participation in legislative hearings, I should add, can often serve this same function.

22. For some evidence of the traditional unwillingness of the professions effectively to police themselves, *see* Trebilcock, *The Social Insurance-Deterrence Dilemma of Modern North American Tort Law: A Canadian Perspective on the Liability Insurance Crisis*, 24 SAN DIEGO L. REV. 929, 992 (1987).

23. Dean Calabresi has schematically identified the role for torts as lying in between those situations in which (1) either the collectivity is uncertain what behavior to demand of people or it costs too much to control behavior collectively and (2) contractual (market) solutions are either too expensive or not trustworthy,

Calabresi, *Torts—The Law of the Mixed Society*, 56 TEX. L. REV. 519, 526–27 (1978). What distinguishes torts from collective control in this scheme is that tort liability allows the actor, rather than the collectivity, to decide whether the injury-risking conduct warrants the costs. Calabresi's attraction to torts reflects his ideological position in favor of individual choice and against collective judgments. But the shortcomings of regulation in certain areas that argue against collective determinations of what is desirable behavior do not rule out the use of regulatory schemes that employ cost-imposition strategies on the injurers' side but are nonetheless divorced from the role of paying compensation on the victims' side. Indeed, Calabresi seems to concede this when he talks of the next century of tort law in terms that include regulatory strategies such as pollution licenses or taxes that are not compensatory, *id.* at 533. Besides, adherents of cost internalization through tort law entrust to a public agency—the courts—the responsibility to assign the costs. Finally, as I have argued throughout, tort law today does not well reflect the role assigned to it in Calabresi's schema. It is overboard in its application to areas where regulation and contract would seem to suffice; at the same time it is ineffective in the areas where Calabresi's mixed society scheme would want it to function, because the factors of liability insurance and the nature of tort damage calculations mean that would-be injurers are not actually put to the economic choice envisioned.

24. When Professor Ison talked with New Zealander accident victims, he found no one embittered over the lost opportunity for retribution through a personal injury action, T. ISON, ACCIDENT COMPENSATION 179–80 (1980).

25. *See generally* Ghiardi and Kircher, *Punitive Damage Recovery in Products Liability Cases*, 65 MARQ. L. REV. 1 (1981); Owen, *Problems in Assessing Punitive Damages against Manufacturers of Defective Products*, 49 U. CHI. L. REV. 1 (1982); Owen, *Crashworthiness Litigation and Punitive Damages*, 4 J. PROD. LIAB. 221 (1981); and Schwartz, *Deterrence and Punishment in the Common Law of Punitive Damages: A Comment*, 56 S. CAL. L. REV. 133 (1982). Professor Gary Schwartz offers some supportive questionnaire data from a survey of judges who clearly thought that jury handling of punitive damages was less sensible than is their handling of ordinary pain and suffering damages, Schwartz, *supra* at 146.

26. Donselaar v. Donselaar, 1 N.Z.L.R. 97 (1982). Professor Palmer had earlier endorsed the idea that punitive damage remain available even after the abolition of actions for personal injury, G. PALMER, COMPENSATION FOR INCAPACITY 175 (1979). For a brief discussion of the New Zealand developments on punitive damages, *see* Hodge, *No-Fault in New Zealand: It Works*, 50 INS. COUNS. J. 222, 228 (1983). For a lengthy analysis of how New Zealand wound up with punitive damages on top of its accident-compensation scheme, and an endorsement of this result, *see* Love, *Punishment and Deterrence: A Comparative Study of Tort Liability for Punitive Damages under No-Fault Compensation Legislation*, 16 U.C.D. L. REV. 231, 234–44 (1983).

27. Johnston, *Punitive Liability: A New Paradigm of Efficiency in Tort Law*, 87 COLUM. L. REV. 1385 (1987).

28. Johnston, however, favors funding the compensation scheme through a social cost-internalizing mechanism, *id.* at 1437–38.

8

A Substantial First Step

OVERVIEW

I argued in Chapter 6 that the long-run compensation strategy should be to improve our ordinary employee benefit and social insurance schemes, with the goal of providing to nearly everyone first-party income protection and medical (and related) expense benefits that are at least comparable to what those with good benefits have already. As we thereby use institutions other than the courts to provide basic compensation for most people, and as we address safety concerns in new ways as suggested in Chapter 7, we largely can roll back the existing personal injury law system—to the social gain of nearly everyone.

In this chapter, I offer a plan for taking a substantial first step in the direction I favor. Although my proposed changes here would hurt some people, including some segments of the personal injury bar, both accident victims as a class and consumers in general would be well served by them. Moreover, business interests and much of the insurance industry should support them. Hence, my package is meant to link together victim, consumer, and business interests against those who profit from the excesses of the current regime, thereby ending the traditional legislative fight that pits business and insurance against consumers and plaintiffs' lawyers.

My first-step plan treats personal injury victims in two groups—the 90 percent who suffer minor or moderate injuries and the 10 percent who suffer the most serious injuries. Therefore, before presenting my proposal in detail, let me explain briefly how both short- and long-term disabilities would be treated were the proposal enacted.

Neither tort law nor workers' compensation would provide benefits to replace the first six months of earning loss following the onset of a disability. Instead, short-term income replacement needs arising from both accident and illness would be generously dealt with by a combination of (1) a mandatory employer-provided sick leave benefit designed to deal with the first week of disability and (2) a strong statewide temporary disability insurance plan (based on the schemes now existing in five states) for the rest of the period.

Employment-based health care plans would take care of the medical expenses of more temporarily disabled people than they do at present. Non-earner families would, in general, continue to look to Medicare or Medicaid. Workers' compensation and the tort system, where they applied, still would be available as backup to compensate for medical expenses. Unlike the typical arrangements today, however, they would only be available to compensate for otherwise unreimbursed medical expenses. As a result, few short-term disabled victims would fall into this residual category.

For injuries causing less than six months of disability, only those suffering a serious disfigurement or impairment (later defined in some detail) would have access to the tort system for the payment of general damages. Through this threshold device, tort compensation for pain and suffering would be reserved for those with serious injuries. As a result of these various changes, the bulk of personal injury claims, those for disabilities lasting less than six months, would largely disappear.

Long-term personal injuries would remain covered by both the tort and/ or workers' compensation systems under this first-step proposal. On the tort side, however, the new method of determining damages would, pursuant to the following four principles, make the system less like a lottery and more like a compensation plan that is sensibly coordinated with other benefits schemes. First, in social insurance and employee benefit programs victims are usually able to obtain their benefits at relatively little administrative cost to them. Second, in such plans the victim's own conduct, apart from the rare situation of deliberate self-injury, is usually irrelevant both to his or her eligibility for benefits and to the amount awarded. Third, benefits provided by any one plan are usually sensibly integrated with those provided by other plans; normally, social insurance and routine employment-based benefits are treated as a core with respect to which other benefits relate. Fourth, to the extent that cash benefits are paid for non-economic losses (i.e., impairments), as in workers' compensation and certain kinds of accident insurance, they are limited in amount and restricted to those victims suffering the more serious and permanent injuries.

My tort reform proposals rest on the idea that the law of damages should generally reflect these same four features. To achieve this result, the proposal envisions that, on the one hand, tort law no longer would duplicate benefits provided by other sources and awards for both pain and suffering and punitive damages would be constrained. Yet, on the other hand, two changes would be made that benefit victims: successful tort plaintiffs would be entitled to compensation from defendants for their reasonable attorneys' fees and they would no longer suffer a reduction in the amount of their recovery because they were at fault.

THE FIRST-STEP PROPOSAL DETAILED

Social Insurance and Employee Benefit Provisions

Temporary Disability Insurance

A generous temporary disability insurance program (TDI) is at the center of my first-step proposal for short-term income replacement in cases of disabilities arising from both off- and on-the-job injuries and illnesses. After a one week waiting period, workers would recover through TDI nearly all of their lost net wages for up to six months, subject to a weekly ceiling of twice the state average weekly wage.

As noted already, less-generous schemes of this sort already exist in five states,[1] which currently provide some wage-replacement benefits for employees who must stop work temporarily due to nonjob-related disabilities. In such jurisdictions, a number of significant liberalizations of the existing provisions would be required by my proposal. In states without TDI plans, I advocate the adoption of a scheme like the expanded California plan proposed here. The discussion that follows focuses on the main features of the proposed TDI plan and, for ease of exposition, explains the changes that would be required in California.

The TDI plan should provide benefits, on an after-tax basis, equal to 85 percent of the employee's predisability earnings.[2] Assuming that the proposed TDI benefits would be subject to neither social security nor federal income taxes, my proposal plainly implies replacing less than 85 percent of an employee's prior gross income. For now, therefore, I will assume that a replacement rate set at two-thirds of pretax earnings would approximate the proposed 85 percent after-tax result.

A two-thirds rule would bring TDI benefits into line with what current workers' compensation plans now typically pay the temporarily disabled, under which programs income-replacement benefits also are not taxable. Hawaii already provides a two-thirds replacement rate in its TDI plan. Applying this standard to the TDI plan in California, however, would mean a twelve percentage point improvement or, in other words, a 20 percent increase in benefits, over the approximately 55 percent wage-replacement rate of the existing plan.

The maximum earnings level to which the TDI replacement percentage applies should be set at twice the state average weekly wage. The current California TDI plan's benefit formula applies only to earnings up to the equivalent of $21,900 annually, thus creating a weekly benefit ceiling of $224. Inasmuch as this earnings maximum is approximately the state average wage, a substantial share of the work force necessarily earns wages in excess of the TDI ceiling. Therefore, under the current plan, many moderate earners and their families may face financial disruption during periods of disability.

By establishing the covered earnings ceiling at twice the state average wage, California's TDI benefit formula would apply to annual earnings of up to more than $40,000 in current terms. This increase would bring the full wages of approximately 95 percent of the California work force within the plan. In turn, the maximum weekly benefit would exceed $500.

Those few people whose earnings are even higher than twice the state average and who, therefore, would not have such complete earnings protection provided by TDI, equitably can be asked to buy their own excess coverage for those first six months of disability. In many cases, such people already will have that sort of protection provided through their job as an employee benefit.

Clearly, even with these proposed liberalizations, the TDI plan would not benefit nonearners who remain uncovered by the program. Yet, of course, nonearners who are disabled for six months or less generally cannot count on receiving anything from the tort system for wage loss either. Their needs for income will continue to be met, if at all, through private arrangements, charity, and existing public income transfer programs. After all, if a person is a nonearner and has become disabled, he probably had been relying on some other nonwork source of income before his disability that should continue afterward.[3]

The TDI plan should cover work-related as well as nonwork-related disabilities. With respect to short-term disabilities, workers' compensation and TDI in California now complement one another in the sense that the former covers work-related disabilities while the latter covers non-work disabilities. By expanding TDI to deal with both groups, this change moves toward eliminating temporary disability cases not only from the tort system, but also from the workers' compensation system, which, of course, no longer would cover short-term income loss. This shift in the source of one's recovery from workers' compensation to TDI also would have the important benefit of eliminating the often difficult decision that must be made under the current arrangement of whether an injury was work related. Covering both sorts of injuries in a single plan also has the advantages of (1) reducing the administrative costs that come from running two parallel programs and trying to decide which program applies in borderline cases, (2) assuring socially desirable equal treatment to work and nonwork disabilities, and (3) helping to free workers' compensation of responsibility for short-term injury cases. As a result, workers' compensation, like tort law, could concentrate its attention on the relatively few serious disability cases.[4]

The ordinary waiting period before TDI benefits become available should be seven days and the benefits should last for up to at least six months. The phrase "waiting period" refers to the threshold period of disability with respect to which benefits are not paid, not the time when the first benefit check is due. Existing TDI plans, including California's, typically have a seven day waiting period, and I propose to continue this practice. The purpose of the waiting period is to exclude from the plan the relatively minor disabilities that only briefly keep the employee out of work. This saves the TDI administration a mass of paperwork and reduces the TDI caseload considerably. Nevertheless, my proposal would not leave victims completely on their own for that first week, as the upcoming discussion of sick leave makes clear.

Before turning to that, however, something should be said briefly about the other end—the duration of TDI benefits. Although any time period is somewhat arbitrary, traditionally six months has been seen as a reasonable dividing line between temporary and long term. Unemployment compensation benefits in most states, for example, typically last for six months. Even more relevant, long-term disability benefits under the Social Security system traditionally became available once a claimant had been disabled for six months—although this waiting period now has been reduced to five months. Nevertheless, states with TDI plans vary in their practices; for example, although six months is the minimum, some plans, including California's, currently pay benefits for up to a year.

While permitting states to do more, my proposal assumes that TDI benefits would be provided for at least six months, longer than the great majority of disabilities last.[5] At the end of six months, a person's condition normally will have stabilized sufficiently so as to permit a reasonable assessment of the person's long-term prospects and, hence, his or her eligibility for programs aimed at permanent disabilities. Moreover, as will be explained below, because those disabled more than six months are deemed to have suffered "serious injuries" for tort law purposes, and thereby automatically become eligible to include claims for pain and suffering damages in their lawsuits, a six month period of TDI benefits would dovetail nicely with this rule.

Mandatory Sick Leave

All employers, or at least those with more than some nominally small number of employees, should be required to provide their employees with paid sick leave benefits according to a reasonable schedule.

Although people who miss less than a week of work owing to a disability could, for example, dip into their savings or, if available, use up a paid vacation day in order to cover a brief period of lost income, this is not an altogether satisfactory arrangement. Not surprisingly, therefore, between two-thirds and three-quarters of jobs now carry with them some sort of sick leave benefits meant to keep most workers in full-pay status during the occasional short illness or short period out of work owing to a minor accident.[6]

Nevertheless, the current American practice makes sick leave a voluntary matter, something that employers may or may not offer—and many do not. My proposal would ensure that nearly all employees have this benefit—at least those working for employers with more than some small number of workers.[7]

As for the schedule of minimum sick leave required, I propose that employees earn at least one day of paid sick leave for every month worked. These days could be accumulated, beyond year end for example, until they are needed. This scale of sick leave benefits currently is routinely provided by many large employers.[8] This scale also reflects the sort of benefit guaranteed to workers in many European countries,[9] and, generally speaking, by our state and federal governments to their employees.

I realize that even with this level of sick leave benefit ensured, workers sometimes will not have sufficiently accumulated sick leave to cover fully the waiting period before TDI benefits become available. For example, people who regularly have been out sick for a day or two at a time may not have enough sick leave days saved up if they have to be out for a week. Nonetheless, the alternative of starting TDI on the first day of disability and not having a sick leave plan, on balance, is worse. The administrative burden aside, placing a finite limit on very short term sick leave encourages employees to avoid exaggerating minor illnesses and prevents abusers from taking off, for example, one paid TDI day every week. Hence, I conclude that workers themselves may be relied on to deal with the occasional very short term gaps in income that might arise from insufficient sick leave under my proposal.

I should emphasize that the generous TDI and mandatory sick leave programs I have proposed here serve two important independent functions. On the one hand, they are desirable for their own sake—for making routinely available to all temporarily disabled workers the sort of sensible and generous short-term income replacement benefits that many employees now have. That is, they represent the sort of first-step progressive changes in policy that I would propose were I looking only at employee benefit and social insurance reform and ignoring tort law.

At the same time the proposals permit me to argue in good conscience that the short-term income replacement function of tort law (as well as workers' compensation) would thereby become obsolete—a position that just is not tenable with any significantly less generous first-party scheme.[10] This permits me comfortably to urge tort law cutbacks, which, in turn, should generate a source of funds that can be redirected to the first-party benefits I have proposed.

Incentives for Providing Health Benefits

If an employer adopts an employee health care plan that meets certain minimum standards, that employer should be exempted from having to provide medical benefits under its workers' compensation plan to its workers who are temporarily disabled through a job injury.

As explained earlier, a very high proportion of employees already are covered by health care plans connected to their jobs.[11] At the same time, employers now are required by the workers' compensation systems to provide what is often duplicate coverage for medical benefits for those injured on the job.[12] The usual consequence is a cumbersome, expensive, and often ineffective subrogation system in which the health plan is supposed to be reimbursed by the workers' compensation plan for expenses incurred in treating job-injured workers. My objectives both are to reverse this arrangement and, to the extent possible, to get the workers' compensation system out of the medical expense business for those suffering only short-term disabilities.

As I argued in Chapter 6, it would be desirable if all employers had good health care plans. Such an arrangement, valuable for its own sake, would also readily permit streamlining the workers' compensation system. Yet, candidly, in contrast to my long-run aspirations, I find it too daunting as part of this first-step proposal to argue for requiring good health care plans of all employers. Hence, this proposal simply creates an incentive.

The key here is how and at what level those minimum health plan standards would be set. To work as an incentive the burden must not be too great. On the other hand, to serve the function of replacing tort and workers' compensation, the minimum quality scheme must be high. I do not propose at this point, however, to deal at length with the issue of standards. Rather, at least for now, I suggest that they be set so that the employer's health plan in California must be certified to be "substantially equivalent" to what is provided either by the state of California to its regular employees or by the University of California to its employees. Parallel minimum standards could be adopted in other states. In California, this would require, among other things, that the health plan cover the employees' families, and, pursuant to provisions of recent federal law, provide former employees with coverage under the employer's plan for a reasonable period of time or until the former employees obtain new coverage through new employment.[13]

In fact, a large proportion of employers in California currently provide health plan benefits that either would qualify already under my proposal, or could be made to do so with little change or added expense. Others, I hope, would find the incentive to avoid many workers' compensation medical claims a good reason to adopt qualifying health plans.

As was true in my earlier discussion of income-replacement reforms, these minimum standards for health care plans serve dual purposes. Initially, they specify sensibly generous medical benefits that are desirable for their own sake. In addition, they help move the society toward the point at which tort law (as well as workers' compensation law) simply would not have to worry about paying for medical expenses for temporary disabilities. Certainly, health plans covering state employees in California now provide full or nearly full coverage of medical expenses for the lion's share of those who are disabled for less than six months.

Tort Law Changes:[14] Restrictions on Recovery

No Suits for Temporary Income Loss

Tort victims should not be able to sue for the first six months of lost income. This change is made possible because of the proposed employee benefit and social insurance changes described above. Tort law is taken out of the short-term income-replacement business and is allowed to focus its attention on the income losses of the long-term disabled. Although any short-term income not replaced by the mandatory sick leave and TDI plans would be borne by victims, the only significant unprotected income losses would be those of high earners who had elected not to make private arrangements to guard against that risk. So long as the income-replacement threshold of tort law is restricted to income losses of six months or less, I believe that no important social function would be lost by denying recovery to such upper-middle class and upper-class victims.[15]

Collateral Source Rule Reversal

Tort law's "collateral source" rule should be reversed so that tort law no longer compensates losses covered by social insurance and employee benefit plans. As earlier explained, American common law ignores, and hence treats as collateral, compensation sources such as medical and disability insurance, Social Security, sick leave benefits, workers' compensation, and the like. The result is either the duplication of benefits or expensive subrogation arrangements through which the collateral source is reimbursed.

The common law regime, in short, operates on the principle that tort payments are to be "primary" and other sources are to be "secondary"— with those secondary sources sometimes having reimbursement rights. If the main goal is to achieve a sensible scheme of compensation, however, the existing system is very wasteful. Plainly, double payment is undesirable. From the viewpoint of administrative efficiency, having tort law serve only in a backup (that is, secondary) role, paying exclusively for losses that are otherwise uncompensated, is far more sensible. Reversing the collateral source rule, it will be recalled from Chapter 4, was also supported by the Reagan administration, and has been enacted in several states in the past few years, sometimes applicable to medical malpractice cases alone.

Under my proposal the key consequence of the reversal of the collateral source rule for the temporarily disabled, of course, is that they would not be able to sue for medical expenses paid for by health insurance, whether private or public—protection that, one hopes, would begin to verge on universal. Still, I should emphasize that those relatively few short-term injury victims who have out-of-pocket medical losses or other expenses traditionally covered by tort law (such as replacement homemaker services) could continue to seek compensation for those losses in tort.

This proposal also has the long-run advantage that, as other sources expand, tort law is eroded from within and increasingly is relegated to a peripheral role in the overall compensation package. Thus, specifically with respect to the long-term disabled, the stage will be set further to oust the tort system when programs such as Social Security disability begin to be liberalized and we move closer toward my proposed long-run solution.[16]

On the other hand, in this first-step proposal, I would continue to ignore those collateral sources that are not a part of large-scale collective arrangements for economic protection against the risk of injury and death. Hence, whereas tort law would not pay for losses already covered by Social Security, workers' compensation, employment-related health care plans, private pension plans, and group disability insurance, tort law would continue to ignore for now sources such as private savings and other forms of family income and wealth. The idea, after all, is not to make tort law a "means-tested" benefit that is available only to those who are impoverished by the accident in question.[17] It is, rather, to have our basic public and employment-based income and expense protection structure come first.

I recognize that, in order to perform the offset calculus required by my proposal, the torts process, whether in settlements or through formal adjudication, will have to estimate the future value of basic social insurance and employee benefits to which victims are entitled. This estimating will be difficult to do accurately. But, because estimating the victims' gross future losses is itself very problematic, only reasonable estimates are required. Directing fact finders to estimate reasonably seems far preferable to me than merely allowing the fact finder to do what it wants with the information it obtains about other sources, as some state laws now provide.

Some people respond to the general problem of future uncertainty by arguing that under tort law, damages meant to compensate for future losses should be payable as they accrue. After all, Social Security pays benefits periodically to the disabled with adjustments made if the beneficiary returns to work, and both public (Medicare and Medicaid) and private first-party health insurance plans also pay as medical expenses are incurred. I am not enthusiastic about putting tort law on a pay-as-needed basis, however, notwithstanding my wish to make tort damages resemble a long-term disability compensation plan. My reason is that the tort defendant is liable only for future losses and expenses properly attributable to the tort. If open-ended periodic payments were ordered in all serious cases, considerable future disputes would arise over causation. That, of course, is a shortcoming that does not apply to compensation plans not linked to specific sources of disability.[18]

Certainly, tort victims may be well advised to arrange to receive their award over time so as to avoid the risk of squandering a lump sum and winding up poor, or at least unable to pay for future medical needs. But surely, even under traditional rules, the victims' lawyers have the duty to explain that even if periodic payments are not conveniently negotiated with the defendants, an annuity certainly can be purchased by the victims. More-over, with the growth of structured settlements in large injury cases, it appears increasingly common that tort defendants also are pushing for pe-riodic payouts under the traditional regime. These arrangements typically will fix once and for all the total amount of the defendants' liability. Yet, where the victims' need for future medical treatment is quite uncertain and the causal problems noted above do not seem likely to be too troublesome, the traditional settlement system certainly permits the defendants to agree to become, in effect, insurers. That is, they may promise to pay, for ex-ample, for all reasonably attributable future medical costs, or at least all such costs up to an agreed on sum. However, whether or not that happens in individual cases, it seems to me, is best left to private ordering.

A Threshold for General Damages

Damages for pain and suffering, so-called general damages, should be barred in most personal injury cases involving temporary disability. Spe-cifically, a threshold requirement should be adopted of at least six months of disability or serious disfigurement or impairment.

This proposal is meant to eliminate pain and suffering recoveries in most cases—I estimate 80–90 percent of current personal injury claims—in which people are disabled for less than six months. It is modeled after general damages thresholds in some automobile no-fault plans. The basic argument here is that once the state has ensured that most people in the small and moderate injury cases have income loss and medical expense benefits, then most victims in this group in turn should be asked to forego tort damages that do not involve out-of-pocket losses.

In short, I see the pain and suffering threshold as a fair trade for the new first-party benefits I propose. Think about it as converting the pain and suffering recoveries of today's relatively less-injured tort victims into ex-panded income and medical expense recoveries for the temporarily disabled in general. In evaluating this trade as among victims, one should remember that temporary injury tort cases are the ones that now generate nuisance claims for pain and suffering. Therefore, although some obviously innocent victims of others' negligence will obtain less from this trade, so too will rather less-deserving tort claimants who (no doubt with the help, if not connivance, of their lawyers) now exploit the economically rational desire of insurance companies and large enterprises to close out the books on small personal injury cases.

Understandably, insurers prefer not to spend all the money that would be necessary to determine whether victims really are suffering in the way they claim, or indeed even to demonstrate that victims are exaggerating their loss in cases where the defendants are confident that is true. Moreover, even as to those quite innocent and nonexaggerating victims who would no longer be able to obtain general damages under my proposal, one must understand that what is at stake here is pain and suffering that largely is transitory. Put differently, these are victims whose pain and suffering under today's system typically are but a memory long before a settlement, let alone a trial, occurs. Indeed, I believe that most people, contemplating the possibility of a temporary disability, would not want more than the prompt payment of their out-of-pocket losses, especially if they realized the enormous administrative overhead that would be saved by my plan and that much of what such victims formally receive for pain and suffering actually goes to pay their lawyers and not into their own pockets.

An exception to the six-month threshold requirement for claiming general damages is made in this first-step plan for those who suffer what I call serious disfigurements or impairments. In general, by this expression I mean serious consequences to the victim's body that will extend beyond the six-month period even though the victim is otherwise essentially recovered and able to return to his or her preaccident activities. Examples include a large facial scar, the loss of a limb, the loss of fertility, and so on. Although such victims may not be permanently disabled from carrying on their regular work or normal activities, they are permanently impaired in other important ways and hence represent the strongest cases for general damages awards. Continuing to allow tort claims for pain and suffering in such cases also responds to rhetorical examples typically given by plaintiffs' lawyers in defense of the current system.

Obviously, some elasticity exists in the meaning of "serious disfigurement or impairment." Its interpretation could be developed in the reform statute or left to judicial interpretation. Experience with existing automobile no-fault statutes that impose somewhat similar thresholds on tort suits for pain and suffering is helpful. In view of the Michigan and Florida experience especially, care in the initial drafting seems quite important, even though great detailing in the statute probably is both unwise and unnecessary. On this basis, it might be better to include more than the phrase "serious disfigurement or impairment" that I have been using so far. For example, perhaps a sensible statutory definition would require "serious and permanent disfigurement, loss of a limb or organ, or serious and permanent impairment of an important bodily function."[19] For my purpose at this point, however, perhaps it is enough to have set out the general idea as well as my expectation that the threshold test would be designed and interpreted so that general damages claims would be restricted to a very small minority of those victims who essentially are able to return to their former activities in less than six months. As for the reliability of my prediction that a threshold of the sort described will eliminate about 80–90 percent of tort claims where people are disabled for less than six months, research indicates that the threshold in Michigan's automobile no-fault statute has eliminated an estimated 89 percent of all personal injury claims arising from motoring accidents.[20]

A Ceiling on Pain and Suffering Awards

Pain and suffering awards should be restricted at the upper end as well. Specifically, the legislature should impose a ceiling of $150,000 for general damages, to be adjusted regularly for inflation.

In no real way can money make up for the horrible suffering that seriously, often permanently, injured victims endure. For this reason, and because pain and suffering, however unpleasant, does not involve an out-of-pocket of funds, it is frequently argued that dollar awards for pain and suffering are an altogether inappropriate remedy and should be eliminated entirely.[21] Indeed, some find it indecent that people would ask for money when a loved one is lost, or that people would even suggest that their own pain and suffering should be given a price tag. Still others, noting that no real market exists for first-party pain and suffering insurance, have concluded that it is wrong to increase the price everyone pays for goods and services in order to transfer money for compensation of losses that people themselves apparently do not want to insure.[22]

Yet, because general damages currently are a central part of our tort system, they should not be barred precipitously in cases of serious harm. If nothing else, general damages arguably serve the function of soothing the outrage people can feel, especially in cases of major injury, at having their bodies negligently damaged by others. And while in other cultures remedies such as an abject apology from the company president whose employee or activity injured you might be more apt, dollars do have symbolic value in the individualistic, capitalistic United States. Hence, as already noted, under my first-step proposal those who suffer either what I have been calling a serious disfigurement or who are unable to return to their normal activities within six months of the accident remain able to sue in tort for pain and suffering damages. Damages for intangible losses also would be available in wrongful death cases if they currently are allowed under state law. As proposed in Chapter 6, for the long run, I favor equal treatment with respect to compensation for pain and suffering for all disabled people. And, as argued in Chapter 7, I would restrict outrage-based recovery to punitive damage suits.

Still, I find altogether inappropriate the enormous sums now sometimes given as general damages. They are unpredictably awarded—often, it seems, because of lawyer talent, jury idiosyncrasy, and the like—and, I believe, serve no useful social purpose that $150,000 would not serve as well. Greater sums serve to enrich the victims and their lawyers at the expense of the rest of us, taking an unreasonably disproportionate share of the total payout of the tort system. After all, $150,000 is a considerable sum even today, readily providing around $1000 a month to the victim, even if casually invested. This tidy amount, as well as any larger sum, I believe, should serve to soothe the seriously harmed victims' feelings of loss and/or insult. While the purpose of pain and suffering awards certainly should not be to make the victims wealthy, that is exactly what very large awards do.

To be sure, one may protest that the victims need money to pay for their lawyers. After all, even in medical injury cases in Califorina, for example, a $250,000 ceiling on pain and suffering awards has been used, rather than the $150,000 ceiling proposed here.[23] But, as I will explain shortly, my proposal takes care of the victims' lawyers' fees directly so that general damages no longer need serve as a hidden device for that purpose. Indeed, my $150,000 ceiling might be thought of as roughly comparable to a $250,000 cap where the victims' lawyers' fees must come out of that sum.

In contrast, as we saw earlier, the Reagan administration initially proposed a ceiling of $100,000 for the combination of both pain and suffering damages, my subject here, and punitive damages, which I take up later. Because that proposal, unlike mine, does not include additional compensation for the lawyers' fees, that ceiling comes close to proposing, in effect, that victims should in general net no compensation at all for pain and suffering. Although, as already noted, there is much to be said for such a view, my judgment is that, as part of substantial first-step package, it is too great a break from the current system. As a tactical matter as well, it would be wiser, I believe, to leave in the system the possibility of fairly substantial awards for serious injury or death cases resulting from clear negligence to victims whose hard damages are quite small. In view of the decisions by various state legislatures that have acted, the Reagan administration's Tort Policy Working Group subsequently endorsed a $200,000 cap on pain and suffering and separate limits on punitive damages. This solution is now closer to my proposed limit of $150,000 with attorneys' fees added on top.

The workers' compensation laws of most states provide for payments for what amounts to pain and suffering in serious injury cases, especially where a partially permanently disabled worker has suffered one of those specifically "scheduled" impairments such as loss of an eye or a limb. Although these benefits are quite small in some jurisdictions, limiting tort awards to less than what injured workers might receive for the same loss in the more generous workers' compensation plans probably would be inappropriate.

Another point of comparison is New Zealand, where, as noted already, even though ordinary tort law for personal injuries has been replaced by a general accident compensation plan, victims still are entitled, on a nonfault basis, to compensation for what we call pain and suffering. The maximum amount of such payments is restricted, however, to $27,000 N.Z.[24] Translating this figure to the United States is not easy, given differences in traditions and living standards, but I think it fair to say that someone wanting to import the New Zealand limit would settle on a limit of less than $100,000. Under the New Zealand plan, where it should be noted that most medical costs incurred by accident victims are covered outside the plan by the regular national health service, payments for noneconomic loss were approximately 20 percent of total benefits in 1985–1986.[25]

I have chosen to express my proposed limit on pain and suffering awards in the form of a fixed-dollar ceiling amount primarily because this is a familiar and easily understood idea. In fact, if the general principle of limiting pain and suffering awards gains acceptance, a more complex formula ought to be considered. The main point here is that, because the $150,000 limit would apply to the very young and the very old alike, its bite would be far greater for the former group. In other words, if people of quite differing ages both were injured enough to be thought entitled to the maximum, the annuity value of the award would be far greater to the one with the shorter life expectancy. This suggests the possibility of a limit on pain and suffering of, say, $50,000 plus the annuity value of $600 per month for the expected future duration of the victim's pain and suffering—on the assumption that the cost of a formula such as this in the aggregate would be more or less equivalent to the $150,000 cap.[26]

Still, it is worth noting that the age of the victim at the time of injury is not explicitly taken into account either in the system of payments for impairments under American workers' compensation plans or in the rules for payments for intangible losses for personal injury victims under New Zealand's general accident compensation plan. Moreover, considerable uncertainty exists as to exactly how a complex limit of the sort just imagined would function in practice. Therefore, for now at least, I am content with the simpler $150,000 proposal.

Indeed, and in further argument against too much fine tuning, one must appreciate that in practice a $150,000 limit would not be watertight. Juries still would have some leeway to boost victims' overall award in most serious injury cases by raising the estimated amount of the victims' lost future income and medical expenses, and settlement argangements will be made in light of this possibility.

In quite a different spirit, some states have enacted an overall limit (for example, $1,000,000) on the amount of total damages that one can obtain through the tort system, at least in medical malpractice cases[27] or in suits against the government. But because this sort of provision could limit a permanently disabled victim's ability to obtain compensation for otherwise uncovered medical expenses and income losses, it is not part of my proposal.

Judicial Determination of Punitive Damages Awards

Athough I suggested in Chapter 7 that I would support the long-run continued availability of punitive damage suits for cases of very serious wrongdoing, even in the first step, the legislature should attempt to restore some order to the field of punitive damages. Specifically, judges, rather than juries, should be given the duty to determine the amount of punitive damages, if any, that the plaintiffs recover.

Punitive damages are not entirely foreign to other compensation schemes. For example, workers' compensation plans commonly provide for an enhanced payment to victims whose injuries arise from especially culpable employer conduct. Nor do I propose the elimination of punitive damages from tort law because of the special role they can play in deliberate injury cases. However, I favor new limits on this type of award, because I am concerned both about the freewheeling way in which these damages seem to be awarded today (especially against corporations who as legal creations cannot really be punished in the way that jurors seem to want to punish them) and about the risk that they too often might be used by aroused juries to avoid the pain and suffering ceiling I propose in the first-step reform. While a number of different strategies for dealing with the problem are promising, the simplest seems to be to take the question entirely away from the juries and give it to trial judges. This remedy not only puts the matter in the hands of people who are both less likely to be carried away by passion and accustomed to imposing fines in other areas, but it also would keep otherwise irrelevant, yet inflammatory, evidence away from the juries as they consider the questions of liability and compensatory damages.

Many observers have concluded that the awarding of punitive damages, at least by juries, is now out of control.[28] Three major complaints are voiced. The first stems from the perception that juries are permitted to award punitive damages in what traditionally have been considered ordinary negligence cases. Many object not only to this outcome, but also believe it has negative effects on the torts process generally. That is, the prospect of winning punitive damages in such a wide range of cases, or at least obtaining a higher settlement award for nonpunitive damages, routinely spurs plaintiffs' lawyers to make escalating claims of defense wrongdoing, thereby further embittering the torts settlement process.

Second, juries now sometimes are awarding punitive damages of enormous magnitudes. The $125 million verdict against Ford in a 1978 Pinto crash case involving a fire[29] highlights the growing tendency of juries to award more than $1 million in punitive damages.[30] Moreover, because of the growth of mass tort cases and the current rule that one victim's recovery of punitive damages does not preclude the rights of others to recover, defendants now face an increased possibility of having to pay a large aggregate amount of punitive damages for a single act.[31]

This is not to say that punitive damages are being awarded in a large proportion of torts cases; they are not. Data suggest that only between 1 and 3 percent of plaintiffs win such damages.[32] Nor should one forget that punitive damages awarded by juries frequently are scaled back—first by trial judges, then by appellate courts, and yet again in the course of posttrial settlement negotiations.[33] Nonetheless, the fact remains that juries do award in excess of $1 million in punitive damages in a nontrivial number of actual cases.

Third, it is troublesome that enterprise defendants run the highest risk of having large punitive damage awards assessed against them. Even if the conduct of the individual employees who were involved has been very culpable—indeed, even if they were high-level management people—it seems misguided to anthropomorphize the enterprise by imagining that punitive damages serve to punish it. Instead, the innocent shareholders and employees at large bear the brunt of the punishment—and this seems highly inappropriate. As long as the individual wrongdoers in the enterprise do not feel the sting of the judgment or find themselves demoted or fired, punitive awards show no more promise as a deterrent of wrongful conduct than do ordinary tort awards.[34]

This leaves, most importantly, the private attorney general function offered in support of punitive damages—in which the victim is rewarded with a bounty for calling attention to and helping to condemn the bad conduct in question. This justification for punitive damages also helps explain why they would go to the plaintiffs—and the plaintiffs' lawyers—rather than to the state, as has sometimes been proposed.[35] This line of argument, which sees punitive damages as a reward for public service, leads nicely to the reform proposal I offer here. Currently, judges generally decide the amount of attorneys' fees (if any) to be awarded to plaintiffs' lawyers who perform important public service functions in bringing litigation in other areas.[36] Under my proposal, judges alone would make punitive damages awards in personal injury cases.

A different question is whether change should be made in the substantive standard that must be met in order to trigger punitive damages. The traditional requirement of malice or at least intentional wrongdoing first gave way to the weaker test that, as Dean William Prosser put it, it was sufficient that defendants have acted with "such" conscious disregard of or indifference to the safety of the victim as to be the equivalent of intentional wrongdoing.[37] In turn, the "such" seems to have been abandoned so that any "conscious disregard" might suffice, and that in turn may mean that the victims need show no more than knowing negligence.[38] In response, some have urged a retightening of the standard, for example, by requiring the jury to find a "flagrant" disregard of the victims' safety.[39] In this vein, California recently enacted stricter standards for punitive damages (1) requiring proof by "clear and convincing evidence" and (2) redefining malice to require intentional or "despicable conduct" carried on with a "willful and conscious disregard of the rights or safety of others."[40]

Recently, a number of states have enacted legislation limiting punitive damages in other ways. New Hampshire, for example, has barred them entirely, joining a few other states where this has long been the rule.[41] It seems to me unnecessarily abrupt, however, suddenly to bar even judge-made awards in states that now allow punitive damages. On the other hand, just as I consider it unsatisfactory under the present system to be content with trial judges' abilities to reduce a jury verdict, so too do I find insufficient the reform proposal that seeks initially to have the juries decide if punitive damages are appropriate and then has the judges determine their amount.

My hunch is that real change, in terms of both when punitive damages are given and how much is awarded, is far more likely to occur by leaving the standard as it is but giving the job of applying it to the trial judges. Judges understand and, I think, can be counted on to respond to, the context in which the change in decision-making authority was made.[42] Moreover, were it understood that rewarding the public service of uncovering wrong-doing is the prime function to be served by punitive damages, this probably would lead judges in mass tort cases to deny, or at least substantially limit the amount of, punitive damages awarded to second and subsequent plaintiffs who sue in regard to past conduct that already has been identified and condemned in an earlier case.

Tort Law Changes: Expanding Recovery

Attorneys' Fees

Successful plaintiffs should be awarded their reasonable attorneys' fees in addition to other tort recovery. It would be desirable if the transaction costs of obtaining a tort award could be cut dramatically. This, unfortunately, is unlikely. Under the current regime it often is argued that the collateral source rule and/or pain and suffering damages serve as a practical matter to pay for the victims' lawyers. Because I have proposed changing those rules significantly and cutting back on recovery in both instances, I think it only fair in turn that the victims' lawyers be paid openly in addition to the victims' other recoveries. Although other American compensation systems do not pay for the claimants' advocates, only the tort system effectively *requires* such expensive help. Therefore, as part of making tort recovery in the victims' hands look more like recovery under those other systems, I have concluded that the additional payment of the victims' lawyers is necessary.

My proposal may be viewed as undercutting any incentive victims now have to settle their cases without lawyers, because at present the victims can keep the fee the lawyers otherwise would take. But, in fact, under the present system, victims generally are ill-advised to pursue their claims themselves; that is, studies show that claimants are usually better off even after paying for their lawyers than they are trying to do it alone.[43] Moreover, because tort law would concentrate on the serious injury cases under my proposal, a lawyer would almost certainly have been involved anyway.

My proposal calls for the award of reasonable fees to successful plaintiffs. The meaning of reasonable could be left to case-by-case development or perhaps the judges could be asked to adopt regulations. I would favor, however, a statutory solution. More precisely, for cases that go to trial, I propose a strong presumption against the award of fees greater than those sliding-scale fee percentages currently used in California for medical injury cases. This scale allows attorneys to charge clients no more than 40 percent of the first $50,000 of the awards, 33 percent of the next $50,000, 25 percent of the next $500,000, and 15 percent of any amount in excess of $600,000.[44]

Thus, under my plan, plaintiffs' lawyers continue to take personal injury cases on a contingent-fee basis and the fees would continue to be a proportion of the recovery obtained. But, the fees would be added on to the plaintiffs' recoveries, rather than taken out of it as happens today, and the percentages allowed ordinarily would be restricted to the statutory schedule. The latter restriction, of course, would be of special importance in the very large cases, where the flat percentage fee now ordinarily demanded by lawyers (often 33 percent, sometimes 40 or even 50 percent) is widely viewed as creating a windfall.

The sliding-scale maximum fee arrangement currently seems to work in medical injury cases in California, still serving to provide victims with competent legal services. A reduced percentage recovery for the plaintiffs' lawyers as the stakes go up, at least in theory, might have some influence on the willingness of some lawyers to press on with a great deal of time and effort. But, underzealousness is hardly a trait that one would expect the plaintiffs' bar suddenly to adopt.

One must understand that the amount of the victims' lawyers' fees also would be diminished under my proposal because those maximum percentages generally would apply to a smaller total. This comes about because, as already explained, no recovery of the first six months of lost income would be allowed, the collateral source rule largely would be reversed, and limits would exist on both pain and suffering and punitive damages.

I expect that in most cases, the court would award fees according to the maximum allowable percentages. But this would not occur automatically. In class action cases, or in mass torts situations with many similarly situated plaintiffs, or indeed in any individual case in which it was demonstrated that the lawyer had to put in little time per plaintiff, the court could approve only a lesser fee. Generally, speaking, a lower fee award likely would occur in cases in which liability is clear.

On the other hand, trial courts would be able to award fees in excess of the ordinary maximum in unusual cases involving special service to the public at large that would not be recompensed adequately were the regular scale applied. Some lawsuits, for example, might require a truly extraordinary amount of investigation as compared with the recovery. Others might involve a truly extraordinary future benefit (for example, paving the way for many additional claims for similarly situated victims) yet produce little damages in the case in question. As with reductions from the fee schedule, the legislation should make clear that these upscale deviations are to occur only in exceptional cases.

Should the plaintiffs' lawyers and the clients be able to agree to a fee that is larger than the proposal envisions that defendants would pay? That is, should the law allow plaintiffs to agree to put up some of their own award as a supplement in order to obtain, say, better lawyers or harder work? Although this is a close question, on balance, I believe the answer should be no. No reason exists to think that the traditional contingent fee system functions in this way; that is, one does not read or hear about better lawyers regularly charging more. Nor, as just noted, does good reason exist to believe that the limitation imposed on lawyer-client freedom of contract in California medical injuries cases has deprived victims of the skilled and energetic representation that, under my plan, some might argue only could be obtained were the parties permitted to contract around the fee schedule. And even if the proposed fee limitation arrangement were to have some modest impact on the amount of pain and suffering awarded—which might occur—in view of the essentially arbitrary nature of that award, I would not be disappointed.

This proposed approach to the victims' legal fees, of course, would affect settlement negotiations as well, because the defense would have to agree to add on a sum for the claimants' attorneys. This is the routine practice in Great Britain today, for example, where the winning party is entitled to his legal costs, and it works smoothly.[45] In Great Britain, of course, the amount added on is supposed to be based on an hourly rate for efforts made. Thus, my proposal if anything, should be even easier to manage because there would be no debate over whether, say, the time that the victims' lawyers put in, and hence the total fees sought, were too great. In fact, settlement negotiations in the United States today are already carried on with both sides clearly aware of what part of the award is for the claimants' lawyers. My plan, in a sense, simply would have those negotiations occur in the shadow of a formal rule that provided for such fees.

It is fair to ask whether the maximum fee schedule should be lowered for those cases that are settled, at least if they are settled before the case reaches the courthouse steps, so to speak. Traditionally, personal injury lawyers take a different percentage of the award depending, loosely, on whether the case is tried or not. Perhaps, then, for cases settled reasonably early on in the litigation process, defendants should only have to pay the claimants' lawyers, say, 33 percent of the first $100,000, 20 percent of the next $500,000, and 10 percent of settlement amounts in excess of $600,000. I note by comparison that fees are now limited to 25 percent under the Federal Tort Claims Act[46] and that, as described in Chapter 4, the Reagan administration's Working Group proposed a sliding-scale fee limit (to be paid for by victims and apparently applicable to both tried and settled cases) that roughly is similar to what I have just suggested.[47]

Contributory Negligence

Contributory negligence in no way should affect the plaintiffs' recovery. If one accepts that the goal in reforming tort damage rules is to make recovery under that system more like recovery under social insurance and employee benefit plans, then contributory negligence by the victim no longer should count. It does not count either in the Social Security system or the workers' compensation system.[48]

With this change, tort law will have moved in the course of a couple of decades from a time when contributory negligence was a complete bar (at least formally), through the current era of comparative fault,[49] to a situation in which the victims' fault would not count officially against them at all.[50] Of course, victims still would have to show that the defendants are at fault or are properly covered by a doctrine of strict liability, but that would suffice. And the consequence would be a considerable benefit for a substantial proportion of tort plaintiffs.

At first blush, the existing comparative negligence regime appears even-handed. But the individual victims, out of whose pocket the money comes, and the defendants' insurers or employers, into whose pocket it goes, are hardly equally positioned in terms of need. Moreover, the victims, not the injurers, are the ones who bear the full physical burden of the injury.

This proposal is likely to be most controversial in cases where the victims are mostly at fault and the injurers, thus, only slightly at fault. In extreme cases, however, the courts can be counted on to use "proximate cause" (or even "no duty") rules to shift responsibility away from the injurers to the victims. Moreover, in an individual case that seems to entitle a wrongdoing plaintiff to an unjust windfall, the jury might well hold back on the victim's award.[51]

This brings me to the end of my package of tort reforms. Notice that none of these changes really goes to substantive law—such as new standards for product liability or medical malpractice that some have proposed. I firmly believe that the call of the Reagan administration's Working Group to return to the fault system is the wrong message. The long-run goal should not be to reinvest in the discredited idea that tort law can do somebody's idea of exquisite justice in individual cases, but rather to replace tort law with something better.

Financing the Proposal: Who Pays and Who Benefits

How much money will today's would-be tort defendants save under my proposal? How expensive are the new first party benefits going to be? Who, in the end, is going to pay more and who, less? Unfortunately, providing firm answers to these important questions is not easy, and at this point I am able only to provide some analysis about tendencies.

Clearly the cost of the tort law system would be cut back sharply as the mass of small personal injury cases disappear, the collateral source rule is reversed, and enormous awards for pain and suffering are curbed. Those savings would be offset somewhat by increases in tort costs owing to defendants' obligations to pay plaintiffs' attorneys fees and the elimination of the role of contributory negligence. On balance, therefore, the proposed package of tort reforms should yield a significant reduction in the cost of all forms of liability insurance that now cover bodily injury. Certainly, in states with common law rules still in place individual physicians and individual motorists should notice the difference. In large enterprises, although there of course would be dollar savings as well, perhaps more important would be the greater calm and stability that my proposal would bring: High echelon executives would be less distracted with tort liability problems, the scale of liability for most firms would become more predictable, and in turn, the problem of liability insurance unavailability with respect to bodily injury claims should be sharply reduced.

Public costs now associated with the processing of so many personal injury suits ought to decline as well. Yet, rather than an immediate savings in the costs of the judicial system, we probably first would see an improvement in the speed and care with which other legal problems were handled. I would count that as a significant benefit.

With respect to the proposed first-party benefits, I deliberately have left unresolved so far the extent to which they are to be financed formally by payments from employers as opposed to employees. Traditionally, sick leave and workers' compensation formally are funded by employers. California's TDI program, on the other hand, is funded formally by employee contributions, and the practice regarding employment-based group health insurance varies, sometimes fully paid for by employers, sometimes funded by shared employer and employee contributions.

As I suggested in Chapter 6, in the long run, which side makes the formal payment probably does not matter much. That is, whether they pay or the boss pays, employees ultimately really bear most or all of the incidence of employee benefit and social insurance programs in the form of lower wages.[52] To be sure, because of income tax advantages, some financing arrangements allow (or traditionally have allowed) employers and employees together to appear to shift costs onto the taxpayers at large. Yet even here, to the extent that a large overlap exists between the taxpaying pop-

ulation and the working population, these advantages ultimately are probably less than they appear to be.

Nevertheless, regardless of what the incidence theory says about the
bearing of these costs in the long run, the formal assignment of the burden
does matter. First, short-run–transitional impacts exist that may vary depending on who pays. For example, wage differentials may take time to
adjust, especially where collective bargaining contracts are in place or where
employees are working for minimum wages. Second, psychological factors
are at work. For example, it seemingly has been quite important for symbolic reasons that Social Security be funded by equal contributions from
employers and employees. Moreover, whether the money comes out of the
employee's paycheck or is paid out before determining the employee's gross
earnings seems to matter psychologically.

These considerations have led me to the following funding proposals that
seek to minimize the impact of the reforms as judged by who formally
pays. First, the expanded TDI program, which now ordinarily is funded
in California by what in recent years has been an employee contribution of
between .8 and 1.2 percent of the first $21,900 of wages,[53] instead would
be funded by equal employer and employee contributions. Exactly what
level those contributions would be requires more analysis that I so far have
not been able to do, but surely they ought to be less than 1 percent each.
One good reason for asking employers to pay at least half of the TDI costs
is that an important segment of workers' compensation costs, now formally
paid for by employers, would be shifted over to the TDI plan, thus generating substantial offsetting employer savings.

The mandatory sick leave program would be funded by employers—as
is, in a sense by definition, the practice today. As for qualifying health plans,
I would permit employers to ask employees to pay up to one half of the
costs and still have the plan qualify. But, of course, there would be no
requirement for any employee contributions. The flexibility created in the
financing of this part of the package would allow individual firms and their
workers to sort out what, overall, makes most sense for them.

Given these cost-sharing arrangements, let me turn to consider their
impact on various types of employer and employee. In enterprises in which
employees already have good benefits, the net new costs will be minimal
at most, and actual savings would not be uncommon. After all, in such
employment, broadly comparable sick leave already is provided. Supple-
ments to the existing TDI and workers' compensation programs already
are provided that are reasonably or nearly comparable to what would be
required under the reforms I propose. Also, health plans already are provided that at least closely approach what I would require of qualified plans.
Any additional costs of compliance with the new TDI and health plan rules
that such employers would face ought to be able to be paid for by the
administrative savings achieved from the merger of TDI and workers' com-

pensation for income replacement, plus the savings accruing from the elimination of the workers' compensation and health plan overlap for medical expenses. In sum, progressive employers and their employees, taken as a group, would not be seriously burdened by my plan. Indeed, because of the savings in liability insurance costs (or its equivalent) that these employers would enjoy, a net financial gain ought to result in the progressive employment sector. To be sure, different classes of progressive employers would fare differently, especially to the extent that benefits now funded through workers' compensation, which is somewhat experience rated, are shifted over to TDI, which, like Social Security, would be funded under my proposal by uniform contributions. But these gains and losses, on the whole, would be small.

Employees who now have poor benefits would fare quite differently. Many would get sick leave rights they currently do not have. Many would obtain substantial improvements in their temporary disability benefits. Perhaps many would obtain much better health plans. Of course, these improvements would have to be paid for. The TDI cost increase that would be charged to employees would be quite modest—although higher earners, of course, would face larger increases to go along with the increased ceiling on their protection. New employer costs for TDI generally ought to be offset by savings in workers' compensation and liability insurance. Health insurance improvements, of course, would be optional—where the incentive to have a qualified plan is taken up, employers could ask employees to contribute to the cost.

In the end, the mandatory sick leave portion of my proposal could well represent the most important financial burden on employers who offer no such benefits today.[54] In response to the financial concerns this requirement would raise, I have three comments. First, having some kind of sick leave benefit attached to one's work is a very good idea. In this respect, the United States' rules and practices are rather backward as compared with European countries, which at least suggests that our society can afford it. Second, as noted earlier, small employers, if necessary, could be exempted from this requirement. Third, firms might be permitted to include certain restrictions in their sick leave plans—at least if those restrictions would help make employers without sick leave plans today less fearful that this sort of benefit would generate abuse. For example, perhaps an employer would be allowed to provide that the sick leave benefit could not be used until the second day of any individual bout of disability, thus discouraging the use of Monday and Friday sick days when the employee really is just on holiday.

Overall, my proposal should not be viewed as asking more of employers than is fair for them to pay. Any increase in direct costs to employees should bring along benefits for which, I think, the great majority of informed employees would be happy to pay.

Finally, one must remember that the savings from my proposed restrictions on tort law would be enjoyed by others besides employers. Most importantly, at least where no substantial automobile no-fault plan is in place, motorists too could look forward to significant auto insurance premium reductions. If this was thought unnecessarily generous, however, and if money was wanted to subsidize generally the first-party benefits I have proposed, the financing package perhaps could include, for example, an increase in the gasoline tax that would offset half of the average motorist's savings in automobile liability insurance. In this way, although motorists as a class would benefit somewhat less than otherwise, the net financial shift of the burden of the proposal, as compared with the current regime, could be reduced. Some will be skeptical about whether even dramatic reductions in the cost structure of liability insurers will be translated, through competition, into appropriately lower liability insurance costs. Although I do not share that skepticism, if it were necessary to achieve passage of my plan, I would support required rollbacks in liability insurance premiums.

CONCLUSION

My proposal promises not simply cutbacks in tort recovery as the Reagan administration and defense interests have advocated, but a sensible package of tort cutbacks, tort expansions, and, most important, complementary expansions in employee benefits and temporary disability insurance.[55] Were this package enacted, the bulk of the personal injury tort claims would disappear from the judicial system. Most disabled victims would consider themselves better off. Enterprises and units of government would face much less uncertain prospects of tort liability. Defendants would not have to be so worried about the possibility of lightning striking them in the form of outlandish awards for either general damages or punitive damages, and, in return for reduced and more certain tort obligations, employers could be asked fairly to provide the better employee benefits mandated by my plan. We the public, as workers, consumers, and would-be victims, would get much more for our money.

Within the system, the main losers would be plaintiffs' lawyers and victims who under today's rules would have been lucky enough to win the lottery of giant pain and suffering and punitive damages awards. Other losers would be people who now receive duplicate recovery for their losses. On the other side, people who are badly hurt and whose fault contributes to their injury would gain. Having to live with a serious disability is, I believe, already plenty of punishment for these victims, if any at all is deserved. They should not suffer the further punishment of severely restricted payment for their losses.

For now, serious injury cases would remain in the torts system. This means, for example, that doctors' complaints that they are being unjustly sued when babies are born with serious birth defects are not likely to go away. Nevertheless, doctors should have their malpractice insurance bills cut somewhat and at least would have the satisfaction of knowing that, if large settlements are made in cases brought against them, most of the money would be aimed at the net out-of-pocket costs of the victim. Moreover, one should appreciate that other tort reforms now being seriously discussed are not likely to be any better in serving those doctors and others who see themselves as facing a crisis of insurance affordability. Furthermore, keeping the serious injury cases in the tort system should blunt for now the criticism of those who still believe that tort serves important deterrence and punishment functions. Although I have explained why I am highly skeptical about the claims that tort significantly deters or punishes, for those who think otherwise, under my first-step proposal the specter of a substantial tort award (including punitive damages awarded by the judge) would for the meantime continue to hang over the heads of those who are responsible for a serious injury.

Indeed, with both tort law and workers' compensation law concentrated on the problems of the seriously disabled, society could better focus on that population as a whole and the next step toward achieving my long-run solutions could be formulated and discussed. Is there any reason for tort victims to be singled out for more generous benefits than are provided to other seriously disabled people? Should the pain and suffering benefits paid to seriously injured tort victims be extended to others? Should a series of tailored no-fault plans, such as the Vaccine Injury Act, be adopted for various groups of the seriously disabled? How can Social Security and Medicare begin better to serve the needs of the seriously disabled?

NOTES

1. The states are California, Hawaii, New Jersey, New York, and Rhode Island. For a recent general description of temporary disability plans, *see Social Security Programs in the United States*, 49 SOC. SEC. BULL. 37–41 (Jan. 1986) [hereinafter cited as *Social Security Programs*]. *See also* Price, *Cash Benefits for Short-Term Sickness: Thirty-Five Years of Data, 1948–1983*, 49 SOC. SEC. BULL. 13 (May 1986).

2. An 85 percent after-tax wage-replacement rate is a necessary, but suitably generous, proportion to make recipient reasonably whole—and to justify removing from the tort system the responsibility for short-term income replacement. The 85 percent figure rests on the assumption that those on disability leave save work expenses, such as commuting costs, and the judgment that a small gap between prior net wages and replacement income is justified on grounds of incentives for rehabilitation and against malingering. Although economists and others are correct in principle to worry about possible undesirable incentive effects produced by high wage-replacement programs, no great cause for alarm exists here. For example, I have seen no evidence that automobile no-fault plans (with at least as generous short-term wage-replacement benefits as are proposed here) have caused temporarily disabled victims to malinger. Nor do employers with voluntary plans having gen-

erous wage-replacement benefits appear to have serious concerns about shirking. They seem satisfied that nonprivacy-invading, routine, medical-monitoring arrangements sufficiently can ensure that those employees on temporary disability leave indeed are disabled.

3. I favor one exception to this general point about nonearners. Anyone who becomes temporarily disabled while receiving unemployment compensation benefits would be eligible for and would move over to the TDI system. In short, such people would have a recent earnings record sufficient to qualify for TDI. This provision tracks the existing California scheme under which a disabled person with sufficient earnings in his or her "disability base period" [*see* CAL. UNEMP. INS. CODE § 2610–2611 (West 1986)] generally will qualify for TDI so long as he or she is not eligible for unemployment compensation benefits, CAL. UNEMP. INS. CODE § 2628 (West 1986).

4. Professor Monroe Berkowitz is worried that if temporary disability cases are taken out of the workers' compensation system, that system would not be viable as a mechanism for handling long-term work-related disabilities because of the difficulty of determining six months after the injury whether it was work related or not, Berkowitz, *How Serious Is Sugarman's "Serious Tort Law Reform"?*, 24 SAN DIEGO L. REV. 877, 882 (1987). This fear seems exaggerated to me. Surely, most cases that are going to lead to permanent disabilities are evident at the time of the accident so that administrative requirements could easily be imposed on employers in such instances to provide and preserve the relevant evidence.

5. For example, in California's workers' compensation system more than 70 percent of claims are for medical expenses only, about 20 percent include temporary income loss, and less than 10 percent are for permanent partial disability, permanent total disability or death. *See* WORKERS' COMPENSATION, A STAFF REPORT ON SUBJECTS SELECTED FOR STUDY BY THE JOINT STUDY COMM. ON WORKERS' COMPENSATION, CAL. SENATE INDUS. RELATIONS COMM. AND ASSEMBLY WORKERS' COMPENSATION SUBCOMM. 5, figure 1–1 (Feb. 1986) [hereinafter cited as WORKERS' COMPENSATION STAFF REPORT]. Thus, in that system more than 90 percent of all cases, and two-thirds of cases involving income loss, are relatively short-term disability claims.

6. *See Social Security Programs, supra* note 1, at 37 (estimating that in 1982 about two-thirds of private sector employees had such protection). One recent survey found that 78 percent of large- and medium-sized firms in the United States provide sick leave benefits, CHAMBER OF COMMERCE OF THE U.S. SURVEY RESEARCH CENTER, EMPLOYEE BENEFITS, 1985, 20–21 (1986).

7. I reluctantly would exclude such employers for the usual administrative burden reasons that are used to excuse small and often unsophisticated employers from otherwise applicable governmental requirements. Perhaps a suitable minimum number in this case would be eight employees.

8. *See* DEP'T OF LABOR, BUREAU OF LABOR STATISTICS, EMPLOYEE BENEFITS IN MEDIUM AND LARGE FIRMS, 1985 (Bull. 2262) table 18 (July 1986) [hereinafter cited as EMPLOYEE BENEFITS].

9. *See* DEP'T OF HEALTH AND SOC. SEC. INCOME DURING INITIAL SICKNESS: A NEW STRATEGY (H.M.S.0. Cmnd. 7864) (1980), a British government "green paper" that describes in Annex B the practices of many European countries.

10. Obviously there is room for debate over the details. Some might argue that a mandatory sick leave plan providing, for example, eight rather than twelve days a year is sufficient. Others might argue for a TDI wage-replacement ceiling of only, say, 150 percent of state average wages, and so on. Chiseling away at the generosity of my proposals is not the the only way that things might go, I should add. For example, some might push to reduce the TDI waiting period to, say, three days or to require that sick leave is earned at the rate of one and one half days a month as is now the case in some jobs.

11. Department of Labor surveys suggest that 96 percent of all employees working in large- and medium-sized firms are covered by some form of health insurance, *see* EMPLOYEE BENEFITS, *supra* note 8, at 25.

12. In California at present, medical benefits account for more than 40 percent of total workers' compensation benefits, *see* WORKERS' COMPENSATION STAFF REPORT, *supra* note 5.

To be sure, shifting costs from workers' compensation to health plans will not make those costs disappear, although significant administrative savings should result. But for individual employers who are not fully experience rated, the savings from reduced workers' compensation premiums may well be considerably in excess of the increase, if any, in their health plan costs attributable to such cost shifting because of the way that many group health plans and health maintenance organizations (HMOs) price their programs.

13. The recent federal requirements are contained in Title X, section 10001 of the Consolidated Omnibus Budget Reconciliation Act of 1985, Pub. L. No. 99–272, 100 Stat. 82, 223 (1986) [adding/amending I.R.C. § 162K (1978 & Supp. 1986)] [hereinafter cited as COBRA]. The COBRA provisions are meant to deal, at least in part, with the general problem that, in the past, many employees and their families have been without health insurance when the family breadwinner is between jobs.

I should remind the reader here that there are some benefits that workers' compensation plans and tort law now, at least in principle, may provide to the temporarily disabled that should not be ignored in the rush to keep the nonserious injury cases out of both the tort and workers' compensation systems. One is the cost of rehabilitation programs. A second is additional cost that may accompany disability, even short-term disability, that is not necessarily seen as a medical expense. These expenses may have to be incurred for things such as attendant care, a special and costly diet, or enabling the person to become mobile. As I discussed in Chapter 6, these sorts of costs, of course, are by no means restricted among the disabled to tort victims and the job-injured. Frankly, and parallel to my solution in Chapter 6, I see no good solution to the efficient payment of reasonable expenses for such purposes other than to insist that they be included benefits in any qualifying health care plan. Surely their medical necessity usually would be a prerequisite to their reasonableness, thus making their linkage to health care providers sensible in a perhaps analogous way to the fact that modern health care plans typically pay for prescription drugs.

A different problem, also discussed in Chapter 6, is the need to replace the in-home services previously performed by someone who becomes disabled. Because these services may well be, and stereotypically are, now done by housewives who are not in the paid labor force, one could not easily attach the payment for replacement services to the TDI plan. Although hooking them on to the health care plan would be plausible, this is well outside what traditionally is thought to be the responsibility of health insurance. Yet the fact remains that when someone who used to clean, cook, care for children, and the like temporarily is unable to do so on account of a disability, this is a consequence of the medical condition. Certainly in most instances, other household members, friends, and more distant relatives can pick up the slack at least for a time. Additionally, many social services agencies are ready to step in where need is acute and agency resources are sufficient. These factors provide support for a fairly substantial waiting period before providing cash benefits that would be designed to permit the disabled person to pay for replacement costs. Yet, six months may be too long to wait. Hence, I would propose giving serious consideration, as part of the first step, to requiring qualifying health plans to provide cash benefits for such purposes of a certain fixed amount per day (for example, $50) commencing once adult beneficiaries under the plan are disabled for at least six weeks. Such benefits would last for at least six months of disability, after which this need ought to be treated individually and, as discussed in Chapter 6, is more suitably the responsibility of the long-term disability schemes.

As a final note on health care plans, it should be pointed out that one problem with requiring family coverage is that when two family members are working in covered jobs this gives them unnecessary double coverage. Indeed, one reason for an employer not to provide a health plan today is that a significant portion of the enterprise's work force may already be covered through their spouses' work. Moreover, the problem of double coverage already is an increasing irritant to many two-earner couples. Perhaps, therefore, in such cases, double-covered workers would have to be given the right to elect some alternative employee benefit. I anticipate that many two-earner, double-covered couples would be happy if one could elect a child care benefit, or more pension benefits, in lieu of the double health care, and not at all resentful that they did not get the value of the health care plan as an increase in salary. Moreover, a cash out arrangement could jeopardize the current tax-free nature of the health care benefit to the rest of the work force. Another solution, of course, would be to provide for family protection as part of the health care plan, but to make the employee bear the cost of adding family members. I will have more to say about this in the section on funding.

14. These proposals are, in important respects, broadly modeled after some "trades" earlier proposed by Professor Jeffrey O'Connell, *see* O'Connell, *A Proposal to Abolish Contributory and Comparative Fault, with Compensatory Savings by Also Abolishing the Collateral Source Rule,* U. ILL. L. REV. 591 (1979); O'Connell, *A Proposal to Abolish Defendants' Payment for Pain and Suffering in Return for Payment of Claimants' Attorneys' Fees,* U. ILL. L. REV. 333 (1981) [hereinafter cited as O'Connell, *Pain and Suffering*].

15. I recognize that American automobile no-fault plans have come to the opposite conclusion, however. That is, they permit victims to sue in tort for lost earnings in excess of the internal weekly or monthly wage-replacement limit of the no-fault plan. *See* for example N.Y. INS. LAW art. XVII § 673(1) (McKinney 1985). For further discussion of the possibly desirable role of tort in compensating income losses of high earners, in a piece otherwise quite supportive of the types of reform proposed here, *see* Pedrick, *Perspectives on Personal Injury Law,* 26 WASHBURN L.J. 399, 414–15 (1987). *Cf.* Abel, *A Critique of American Tort Law,* 8 BRIT. J.L. &

SOC'Y 199 (1981), who strongly objects to tort law replacing the income of high earners. Professor Monroe Berkowitz, on the other hand, worries about the "high school graduate injured in an automobile crash the night of the prom [who] would receive no income replacement since he had no income to replace, even though, had he not been injured, he would have begun his work career on Monday morning," Berkowitz, *supra* note 4 at 887. This strikes me, however, as a very small problem that under my plan would mean that the graduate would, at most, lose what would have been his or her first six months of income—and would, as a result, have to be supported for that period by the same sources, presumably his or her parents, that had provided support for so many years up until then.

16. For a British call to reverse the collateral source rule as a step toward the eventual replacement of tort by the social insurance system, *see* Davies, *State Benefits and Accident Compensation*, J. SOC. WELF. L. 152 (1982).

17. Because some kinds of life insurance really are savings plans in important respects, and private savings are not one of the collateral sources I would count against a victim, for the sake of simplicity, I would not reverse the collateral source rule at all as to life insurance, at least at the outset.

18. For discussions of periodic payments, *see generally* R. KEETON and J. O'CONNELL, BASIC PROTECTION FOR THE TRAFFIC VICTIM 351–58 (1965) and Henderson, *Periodic Payments of Bodily Injury Awards*, 66 A.B.A.J. 734 (1980).

In 1975, California adopted a provision permitting (at the election of either plaintiff or defendant) the payment of periodic payments for future losses where there is an award in excess of $50,000 in medical injury cases, *see* CAL. CIV. PROC. CODE § 667.7 (West 1980). With one exception, however, this provision fixes the amount and duration of the payments at the time of the judgment. The exception is that if the plaintiff dies before the sums allocated for future medical expenses and future pain and suffering have been paid out, those remaining payments revert to the defendant. The justifications for the California rule are said to be to protect the victims and their families from the victims' possible improvident early expenditure of a lump sum award and, through the rule governing early death, to prevent the victims' heirs from obtaining a windfall. *See generally* American Bank & Trust Co. v. Community Hosp., 36 Cal. 3d 359, 683 P.2d 670, 204 Cal. Rptr. 671 (1984) (upholding this section against constitutional attack). Of course, this sort of provision does nothing about unexpected increases or decreases in the victims' losses or expenses that appear as the future unfolds—apart from victims' unexpectedly early deaths. Put differently, it deals with but one of the prediction problems faced at the time of trial or settlement. Section seven of the Uniform Law Commissioners' Model Periodic Payment of Judgments Act, 14 U.L.A 32 (West Supp. 1987) [hereinafter cited as Model Act] also attempts to deal with the uncertainty of future inflation, but not with the basic uncertainty that the living victims' medical needs and/or income losses may be other than predicted, *see* Model Act, at 39–41 (§ 11 and comment).

19. This phrasing is taken largely from language defining "dignitary loss" contained in § 102 (a)(6) of the proposed Federal Product Liability Reform Act, S. 2760, *see* S. REP. NO. 422, 99th Cong., 2d Sess. 21–22 (1986). The language in the text is also fairly close to Florida's existing provision in its automobile no-fault law, *see* FLA. STAT. ANN. § 627.737(2) (West 1984).

20. *See* Hammitt and Rolph, *Limiting Liability for Automobile Accidents: Are No-Fault Tort Thresholds Effective?*, 7 LAW & POL'Y 1, 7 (Oct. 1985).

21. *See generally* Jaffe, *Damages for Personal Injury: The Impact of Insurance*, 18 LAW & CONTEMP. PROBS. 219 (1953). For evidence (admittedly now more than fifteen years old) that few successful tort claimants know or care about damages for pain and suffering, *see* O'Connell & Simon, *Payment for Pain and Suffering: Who Wants What, When & Why?*, U. ILL. L. F. 1 (1972). For more recent and broadly comparable British attitudes, *see* COMPENSATION AND SUPPORT FOR ILLNESS AND INJURY (D. HARRIS et al., eds.) 139–63 (1984).

In his proposal to trade the payment of attorneys' fees for the payment for pain and suffering, Professor O'Connell's preferred solution is to eliminate pain and suffering awards entirely. As a backup position, he supports continued payment of seemingly unlimited pain and suffering in serious injury cases, *see* O'Connell, *Pain and Suffering*, *supra* note 14, at 360–62. My proposal of permitting such damages, but subjecting them to a ceiling, falls between Professor O'Connell's two positions.

Were pain and suffering damages to be allowed in serious injury cases, Professor O'Connell would subject them to a deductible in the proposed amount of $10,000, O'Connell, *Pain and Suffering*, *supra* note 14, at 350. This follows the position of the Uniform Motor Vehicle Accident Reparations Act. 14 U.L.A. 64 (1980) [hereinafter cited as UMVARA]. In my judgment, no persuasive reason exists to subject anyone who satisfies the high verbal threshold I have proposed to the additional requirement of a deductible. The UMVARA comments argue that this deductible serves to discourage claimants with minor or trivial injuries from alleging that they nonetheless meet one of the verbal thresholds, thus creating additional undesirable costs and controversy. This strikes me as overly cautious.

22. Certainly there is no market today for first-party pain and suffering like benefits for temporary disabilities. Although not widely purchased, first-party accident insurance, however, typically does pay sums for certain listed serious impairments (such as the loss of an eye or a limb). But if a person suffered that sort of harm, under my plan, he or she still could sue in tort for general damages for that loss.

23. CAL. CIV. CODE § 3333.2 (West Supp. 1987). *See generally* Fein v. Permanente Medical Group, 38 Cal. 3d 137, 695 P.2d 665, 211 Cal. Rptr. 368 (1985) (upholding the constitutionality of this provision).

24. *See* New Zealand Accident Compensation Act Amendment (No. 2) 1973, § 119–120. *See also* T. ISON, ACCIDENT COMPENSATION 64–68 (1980) (reviewing the first few years of experience with these provisions).

25. ACCIDENT COMPENSATION CORP., ANNUAL REPORT 20 (1986).

26. For other discussions of this point, *see* Danzon, *Medical Malpractice Liability*, in LIABILITY: PERSPECTIVES AND POLICY (R. LITAN and C. WINSTON, eds.) 122–23 (1988) (where scheduled payments for pain and suffering, adjusted for age and severity, are proposed) and H. MANNE, ed., MEDICAL MALPRACTICE POLICY GUIDEBOOK 172–73 (1985). Washington's new ceiling on pain and suffering works similarly because it is a function of victims' life expectancies. *See* Donaldson, Hensen, and Jordan, *Jurisdictional Survey of Tort Provisions of Washington's 1986 Tort Reform Act*, 22 GONZ. L. REV. 47, 49 (1986–1987).

27. Provisions of this type have been upheld against constitutional attack in Indiana in Johnson v. St. Vincent Hosp., 273 Ind. 374, 404 N.E. 2d 585 (1980), in Louisiana in Williams v. Lallie Kemp Charity Hosp., 428 So. 2d 1000 (La. Ct. App.

1983), and in Florida in Florida Patient's Compensation Fund v. Von Stetina, 474 So. 2d 783 (Fla. 1985), but not in Illinois in Wright v. Central Du Page Hosp. Ass'n, 63 Ill. 2d 313, 347 N.E. 2d 736 (1976), nor in North Dakota in Arneson v. Olson, 270 N.W. 2d 125 (N.D. 1978), nor in New Hampshire in Carson v. Maurer, 120 N.H. 925,424 A. 2d 825 (1980). *See also* VA. CODE ANN. § 8.01–581.15 (1984); KAN. STAT. ANN. § 60–3407 (Sup. 1986) and WIS. STAT. ANN. § 893.55 (West Supp. 1986).

28. *See generally* Owen, *Problems in Assessing Punitive Damages Against Manufacturers of Defective Products*, 49 U. CHI. L. REV. 1 (1982); Schwartz, *Deterrence and Punishment in the Common Law of Punitive Damages: A Comment*, 56 S. CAL. L. REV. 133 (1982); and NAT'L ASS'N OF INDEP. INSURERS, PUNITIVE DAMAGES AND THE CIVIL JUSTICE SYSTEM: THE CASE FOR REFORM AND A PLAN OF ACTION (1985) [hereinafter cited as PUNITIVE DAMAGES].

29. Grimshaw v. Ford Motor Co., No. 19–77–61 (Orange County Super. Ct., Cal.) (Feb. 7, 1978), *aff'd as amended*, 119 Cal. App. 3d 757, 174 Cal. Rptr. 348 (1981).

30. Even by 1982 publicity had been given to many multimillion dollar punitive damages verdicts, *see* Owen, *supra* note 28, at 3–5. For two more recent examples of jury verdicts of $10 million in punitive damages against tampon manufacturers in cases involving toxic shock syndrome, *see* O'Gilvie v. Int'l Playtex, Inc., 609 F. Supp. 817 (D. Kan. 1985) and West v. Johnson & Johnson Prods., Inc., 174 Cal. App. 3d 831, 220 Cal. Rptr. 437 (1985). The Playtex $10 million jury verdict, originally reduced to $1,350,000 by the trial court, recently was reinstated by the 10th Circuit, *see* O'Gilvie v. Playtex, CCH PROD. LIAB. REP. ¶ 11,428 (Kan. 1987). For a report of a very recent jury award of $100 million in punitive damages, *see* Taylor, *Texas Jury Awards Record $107.75 M in Benzene Case*, Nat'l L.J., Dec. 29, 1986, at 4. col. 3. *See also* Ausness, *Retribution and Deterrence: The Role of Punitive Damages in Products Liability Litigation*, 74 KY. L.J. 1 (1985–1986).

31. *See* F. HARPER, F. JAMES and O. GRAY, THE LAW OF TORTS §§ 25.5A nn. 32–33 (2d ed. 1986). For a relatively early recognition of the problem, *see* Roginsky v. Richardson-Merrell, Inc., 378 F. 2d 832 (2d Cir. 1967). *See also* Owen, *Punitive Damages in Products Liability Litigation*, 74 MICH. L. REV. 1258, 1325 (1976).

32. *See* M. PETERSON, S. SARMA, and M. SHANLEY, PUNITIVE DAMAGES: EMPIRICAL FINDINGS (Rand Corp. Institute for Civil Justice 1987). That study found, however, that the trend in the frequency and amount of awards of punitive damages is upward.

33. *Id.* at 26–30. For evidence that large award cases in general eventually settle on average for less than half of the initial jury verdict, *see* I. BRODER, ANALYSIS OF MILLION DOLLAR VERDICTS (Assoc. of Trial Lawyers of Am. 1986). In the famous Pinto case, the trial judge reduced the jury award of $125 million to $3.5 million, which was affirmed on appeal, *see* Owen, *supra* note 28. So, too, the $100 million award in the benzene case (*see* Taylor, *supra* note 30) has since been overturned and a new trial ordered. *See $108M Monsanto Award Overturned*, Nat'l L.J., July 13, 1987, at 22, col. 1.

34. It is difficult for management first to deny wrongdoing and then, when found liable, to turn around and sack the employees said to be to blame. For a discussion of punitive damages in the context of modern conceptions of corporate decision

making, *see generally* Metzger, *Corporate Criminal Liability for Defective Products: Policies, Problems, and Prospects,* 73 GEO. L. J. 1 (1984).

35. *See* for example PUNITIVE DAMAGES, *supra* note 28, at 18; Sales and Cole, *Punitive Damages: A Relic That Has Outlived Its Origins,* 34 DEF. L.J. 429, 479 (1985); and recently enacted statutes in Colorado, COLO. REV. STAT. § 13–21–102(4) (Supp. 1986) (directing that one-third of a punitive damages award go to the water conservation board), and in Iowa, IOWA CODE ANN. § 668A.1 (West Supp. 1987) (providing that 75 percent of a punitive damages award may be required to be paid to the state's civil reparations trust fund).

36. *See* for example 42 U.S.C. § 1988 (1982). *See generally Court-Awarded Attorneys' Fees,* 14 REV. L. & SOC. CHANGE 473 (1986).

37. W. KEETON, D. DOBBS, R. KEETON, and D. OWEN, PROSSER AND KEETON ON THE LAW OF TORTS 10 (5th ed. 1984) and Taylor v. Superior Court, 24 Cal. 3d 890, 598 P. 2d 854, 157 Cal. Rptr. 693 (1979).

38. *See* for example West v. Johnson & Johnson Prods. Inc., 174 Cal. app. 3d 831, 220 Cal. Rptr. 437 (1985). In *West,* although the trial court found that the jury's $500,000 compensatory and $10 million punitive awards both were the result of passion and prejudice, the court nonetheless termed the defendant's conduct "reprehensible" and allowed a substantial award ($100,000 in compensatory damages and $1 million in punitive damages), 174 Cal. App. 3d at 875, 220 Cal. Rptr. 464. Yet, from the evidence reported by the court of appeal, the plaintiff's theory seems to be that although her disease was unknown at the time of her injury, the defendant could and should have discovered it earlier. While this might have been possible had the defendant initially tested better or responded more aggressively to complaints (points that the plaintiff's expert witnesses made much of), there is no indication that this defendant acted any differently from its competitors. And while that inaction may not excuse the defendant from a charge of negligence, why it amounted to "knowing" negligence is unclear. In any event it strikes me as a rather bold basis for awarding punitive damages.

39. This, for example, is the strategy of § 303(a) of the proposed Federal Product Liability Reform Act, S. 2760, *see* S. Rep. No. 422, 99th Cong., 2d Sess. 21–22 (1986). That section also would require the plaintiff to demonstrate the defendant's "conscious, flagrant indifference" by "clear and convincing evidence."

40. *See* Civil Liability Reform Act of 1987, ch. 1498 [adding/amending CAL. CIV. CODE § 3294 (West Supp. 1987)].

41. N.H. CCH PROD. LIAB. REP. ¶ 93,025 et seq. Apparently the other states generally prohibiting punitive damages are Louisiana, Massachusetts, Nebraska, and Washington, although some limited exceptions exist in some of them, *see* Sales and Cole, *supra* note 35, at 435–36.

42. This proposal parallels one of the recommendations put forward by Sales and Cole, *supra* note 35, at 477, and by Mallor and Roberts, *Punitive Damages: Toward a Principled Approach,* 31 HASTINGS L.J. 639, 664 (1980). For evidence that California trial judges surveyed by Professor Gary Schwartz probably also would favor my proposal, *see* Schwartz, *supra* note 28, at 146–47.

43. *See* for example COMPENSATION AND SUPPORT FOR ILLNESS AND INJURY, *supra* note 21, at 81–82.

44. *See* Civil Liability Reform Act of 1987, ch. 1498 [adding/amending CAL. BUS. & PROF. CODE § 6146 (West Supp. 1987)]. *See also* Roa v. Lodi Medical

Group, Inc., 37 Cal. 3d 920,695 P. 2d 164, 211 Cal. Rptr. 77 (1985) (upholding prior similar provision against constitutional attack). Under my proposal, provisions should be made so that the "bend points" in the fee schedule would be regularly upwardly adjusted for inflation.

45. *See* COMPENSATION AND SUPPORT FOR INJURY AND ILLNESS, *supra* note 21, at 128–32. I do not mean to defend the details of the British scheme, which turns out to be very expensive in the smaller cases.

46. 28 U.S.C. § 2678 (1982).

47. A different question is what to do about plaintiffs' costs other than legal fees. For the present, I would leave the rules about such costs as they are, with the liable defendants typically paying largely trivial sums and, therefore, the successful plaintiffs paying out of their awards what can amount to substantial sums. But making defendants pay for such costs is sure to generate some new disputes over their reasonableness. Moreover, when one remembers that workers' compensation claimants pay their own attorneys (typically 10 percent) and their own other costs, requiring tort claimants only to pay their other costs seems fair by comparison.

In his proposal to trade pain and suffering for attorneys' fees, Professor O'Connell was strangely silent on how the amount of the claimants' attorneys' fees would be calculated, but he did support having the defendants pay for the plaintiffs' costs as well, *see* O'Connell, *Pain and Suffering, supra* note 14, at 351–52.

48. Note that intentional self-infliction of harm precludes recovery in workers' compensation and would continue to preclude tort recovery, as today, under my proposal.

49. Most states now have adopted some form of a comparative negligence regime, *see generally* V. SCHWARTZ, COMPARATIVE NEGLIGENCE (2d ed. 1986).

50. In some jurisdictions ordinary contributory negligence currently is no defense at all in strict product liability cases, *see* RESTATEMENT (SECOND) OF TORTS § 402A comment n (1977). *See generally* V. SCHWARTZ, *id.* at § 12.1. Many find such a rule rather odd, under the existing regime, because it means that a defendant who is liable on the basis of his fault is able to reduce his liability because of the fault of his victim, whereas a defendant who is liable even without being at fault is not. The justification for that result must be that victim compensation is seen in such jurisdictions as the central purpose of strict products liability. My proposal would extend this rationale to all personal injury cases.

51. Just as juries well may have applied comparative fault rules at a time when contributory negligence was formally a complete bar, so too they might sometimes apply comparative fault in a no-bar world. If necessary, I would relent and agree to apply comparative negligence principles whenever the victim is more at fault than the injurer, and have no decrease for the victim's fault only when the injurer is as much as or more at fault.

52. *See generally* Woodbury, *Substitution between Wage and Nonwage Benefits*, 73 AM. ECON. REV. 166 (1983) and Smith, *Compensating Wage Differentials and Public Policy: A Review*, 32 INDUST. & LAB. REL. REV. 339 (1979).

53. I say "ordinarily" because some employers merely provide the TDI benefit and do not deduct any contribution from the employee's paycheck. The relatively wide recent swings in California's TDI contribution rate have been a product of both a poorly designed contribution formula and an unpredicted benefit growth. These problems now appear to have been solved and there is reason to believe that,

absent the changes proposed here, the contribution rate would soon settle down at about 1 percent of taxable wages, *see generally* CAL. EMPLOYMENT DEV. DEP'T, ANNUAL REPORT AND ACTUARIAL EVALUATION OF THE DISABILITY INS. FUND (1985).

54. For example, a Chamber of Commerce study, *supra* note 6, table 4, found that paid sick leave on average cost those companies surveyed that provided such benefits 1.3 percent of payroll.

55. For a brief summary of these recommendations, *see* Sugarman, *The Two Proposals on Tort Reform*, Nat'l L.J., July 4, 1988, at 13, col. 3.

9

Tort Reform by Contract

Under the current regime, potential accident victims have rights to bodily security that are determined by the contours of tort law. Actual accident victims, of course, have possible rights to compensation from their injurers. That both those categories of people have rights of value that might be exchanged through contract is the idea on which this chapter's approach to tort reform is based. Normally tort rights are only thought to matter following an accident. Typically in return for a financial payment (i.e., a settlement) from the injurers' insurers, the victims surrender their rights. Potential victims, by contrast, do not ordinarily do anything with their rights. Indeed, in unusual situations where potential victims have already transferred (waived) their rights through a preaccident exchange, many courts have been hostile to such deals and have refused to enforce the contract against the victims.[1] But what if preaccident exchanges could be entered into that clearly improved the position of both victims and injurers?

This chapter discusses a potential, preaccident market in legal rights to bodily security that could correct many shortcomings of existing tort law. In brief, it envisions that people who are otherwise adequately insured against accidents will transfer their preaccident rights to their employers, who would sell them to (i.e., presettle them with) liability insurers.

THE PROPOSED MARKET IN POTENTIAL TORT CLAIMS

Various previously described shortcomings in current law provide the basis for the proposed market in potential tort claims. First, as we have seen, when viewed as a system for compensating accident victims, tort law is inevitably incomplete. Yet, most potential victims, I have argued, would prefer to be assured of compensation whether or not their injurer is liable in tort and solvent. As a practical matter, however, it can be cumbersome to arrange for protection that merely fills in where tort law does not apply. Therefore, many people obtain broad first-party protection through their employer or through private insurance. At that point, however, tort law becomes largely superfluous in paying for their out-of-pocket losses. As a result, surely many potential victims with adequate first-party protection ought to be happy to sell their tort rights to redundant awards for less than injurers now spend to buy up those rights by settling lawsuits.

Second, because few victims seek to buy first-party insurance against pain and suffering, it is reasonable to assume that potential injurers also place a higher value on being rid of such claims than most potential accident victims place on their rights to sue for such losses (at least in less-serious injury cases). Finally, because the legal and related costs of tort disputes account for such a high proportion of the stakes, if these costs could be reduced or avoided, both injurers and victims could benefit. Together these deficiencies of the tort system afford considerable potential for a mutually beneficial exchange.

The primary participants in such a regulated market in potential tort claims, although not necessarily the only participants, would be employers and insurance companies. Employers, as agents, would sell potential tort claims of their employees to the insurers of potential injurers. Such a sale would effectively cause tort claims to be presettled.

If a victim were adequately insured, courts would no longer have a compensation-assuring reason to invalidate bargains in which he or she surrenders (waives) his or her tort rights. The major "regulation" of this market, therefore, would be to make the sale of potential tort claims conditional on the availability of other adequate compensation arrangements of a sort described below.

Here, more precisely, is how this proposed market might work on the employee side. An employer could offer its employees a choice between two options. One plan would leave tort rights in place as they are, along with whatever health insurance and income-replacement benefits the employer provides. In the other option, the employee would cede potential tort claims to the employer in exchange for either cash (in the form of higher wages or lower employee contributions to the benefit plan) or benefits, such as a higher income-replacement rate, lower health plan deductibles or coinsurance obligations, and added health care benefits such as outpatient mental health treatment and dental care. Details of the two plans would be worked out, as usual, with unions or other employee representatives.

Why involve employers in such a market? Why not have people negotiate directly with insurers? There are several reasons. First, employers have more bargaining power with liability insurers than individual employees would.

Second, employers could dispose of the rights in mass quantities, and so more efficiently. Not only could employers get more money for those rights than employees acting alone, but they might also be better able to demand that insurers police the safety efforts of the potential injurers who are their clients. Third, most employers already provide packages of health and disability benefits, and augmenting those benefits is the most sensible way to compensate employees for waiving their rights to sue. By integrating the added benefits into existing packages, employers could better approximate the kind of coverage their particular workers preferred.

The interests of employees would be protected in this system in several ways. First, the contemplated transfer of tort rights would be voluntary; courts would disallow arrangements in which the transfer of future tort claims against third parties is a requisite of employment. Second, the employers' bargaining power, together with potential competition in the market for tort rights, should help ensure that employees' rights fetch their full market value when sold.

Employers would be motivated by self-interest to make the plan work well. They would be allowed to take a commission as the employees' agents. The wish to maximize the number of employees who choose to sell as well as ordinary concern for employee satisfaction, would give employers reason to make sure workers wind up better off. Finally, employers are themselves defendants in tort cases involving other companies' employees. By participating in the grand scheme in which their own insurers would be presettling their tort liability by buying up other people's potential tort claims, they could foresee a reduction in the cost of their own liability insurance premiums and the burdens of defending against tort claims.

The advantage to liability insurance companies would be considerable. By presettling claims, insurers would reduce the uncertainty of their obligations and save the transaction costs that they would have incurred from handling claims. Both factors would give liability insurers an incentive to buy up as many claims as they could.

Injurers would still pay for the harms they cause, and, as they do when they buy insurance today, they would continue to pay in advance. But because of the savings in transactions costs, they would pay less under the proposed plan.

LESS-SERIOUS AND SERIOUS INJURIES

As discussed in Chapter 8, personal injury claimants can be classified into two groups—the 10 percent with serious injuries, and the other 90 percent. It seems clearest that if people could be ensured reasonable protection against the income loss and medical expenses caused by less-serious injuries (the 90 percent), then most would be prepared to dispose fully of their right to bring a tort suit for such harm. By selling their tort rights in such cases, people would mainly be surrendering rights to double recovery or compensation for pain and suffering, much of which would wind up in their lawyers' pockets.

In less-serious injury cases, moreover, there should be little difficulty showing that employees have adequate first-party protection, the precondition for upholding the sale of the tort claim. A rule of thumb might be to require that victims have substantially complete coverage for at least six months of out-of-pocket losses. Were the details simply left to common law development, courts might inquire as to what employee benefit and insurance company experts agreed were quality benefit packages, and uphold sales of tort rights when the victims had at least that level of coverage. Legislative or regulatory participation in the definition of "adequate insurance" could, of course, lead to quicker agreement on the precise minimum.

Plans with reasonable deductibles and coinsurance provisions would presumably be allowed. Regarding income replacement, for example, employees might be asked to use their accumulated sick leave for the first week of their disability; wages (after taxes) might have to be replaced only at, say, an 85 percent basis and up to only, say, twice the state average. For medical expenses employees might be made responsible for, say, a $100 deductible and 10–20 percent coinsurance payments. In short, as long as employees receive high-quality, first-party protection, courts would be justified in validating the sale of their tort rights, even if some small portion of those out-of-pocket losses that would have been compensated by tort law is left uncovered.

In fact, as we have seen, most employers (especially those of large and medium size) already guarantee their employees generous medical expense coverage for less-serious injuries and already have well-developed sick leave and temporary disability insurance plans. In such cases, employees do not need to be brought up to a higher standard of protection as part of their payment for waiving their tort rights. Rather they would be free to take more direct compensation by lowered employee contributions to the employee benefit package, outright cash payments (possibly as higher wages), or new benefits beyond the legal minimum.

Once the market is functioning, employers should not have too much trouble marketing employee tort rights for less-serious injuries. The appropriate buyers of potential medical malpractice claims, for example, would be easy to identify because in any single locale there are typically few active liability insurers of doctors and hospitals. Indeed, where employees belong to health maintenance organizations through their work place, the employers already have direct contractual arrangements with potential medical malpractice defendants. In such situations the health care providers could, in effect, reduce the premiums they charged employers for their health plan in exchange for waivers of tort liability from the participating employees.

In the case of automobile accidents, employers might also deal directly with the liability insurance carriers on behalf of their employees. Once again, in most locales relatively few auto-liability insurers dominate the market. Another possibility would be for employees with adequate work-based protection to deal directly with their own auto insurance companies. They could choose between an insurance policy that left their own tort rights intact and a policy that charged less in exchange for transferring to their own insurers their tort rights in less-serious automobile accidents. Where the latter option is selected, this would provide the insurer with potential claims to trade to (presettle with) other insurers. By this method, private agreement could largely dispense with the tort system for less-serious automobile accidents.

Separate consideration is required for the remaining 10 percent of injuries I have defined as serious. A traditional, otherwise generous, employee benefit package may not provide enough first-party protection for injuries that seriously disfigure, impair, or disable someone for more than six months. Therefore, a new and higher level of adequate insurance would be needed before sales of potential tort claims would be enforceable. There are two issues here.

First, when employees suffer long-term disabilities, their health and disability insurance plans may not provide a high degree of out-of-pocket protection. Many employers that now provide good income protection against short-term employee disability do not provide protection against long-term disability. Furthermore, a person with a serious disability may stop working and thereby cease to participate in the health plan routinely provided to in-service employees. Without such protections, courts would find it unfair for workers to waive tort compensation and refuse to uphold the sale of potential tort claims.

In view of these current practices, it is less clear that most employers would be willing to make the necessary new insurance benefits available to their employees. Still some employers currently provide or make available for purchase, both long-term disability income protection and continued access to the enterprise's group health plan for disabled former employees; such enterprises could thus satisfy this part of the adequate insurance condition with little change in their existing program. These employers might be good candidates to serve as selling agents for the potential claims of their employees for serious, as well as transient, injuries. An alternative arrangement might develop, however. While employers might be the ones to help sell the not-so-serious injury claims of their employees, insurers themselves (possibly working through unions or other employee groups) might organize efforts to help people sell their potential serious injury tort claims.

Second, in serious injury cases more people might insist on compensation that goes beyond out-of-pocket expenses before consenting to sell their tort rights. Therefore, at least at the outset, reasonable coverage for serious injury itself should probably be part of the adequate insurance definition for serious injury cases. People would probably not, however, insist on an individualized, after-the-fact benefit determination of the kind that tort law now makes. Most would likely be content with some predictable, predetermined, generous but not extravagant, schedule of benefits. One place to look for a comparison is in the accidental death and dismemberment policies that some employers sell or provide to their employees, which provide, as we have seen, so much for loss of a hand, so much for loss of an eye, and the like. Another place to look is to workers' compensation; as noted earlier, most states insist that, in cases of permanent partial disability, benefits be provided for the impairment itself. In general, therefore, insurance policies (or other arrangements) with payoff schedules similar to these examples ought to be deemed adequate to support the sale of potentially serious tort claims.

At least in the beginning, many people might be reluctant to presell more than their rights in less-serious injury cases. That is, the market in potential tort claims for serious injuries might be considerably slower to take off. Still, people might begin to sell portions of their stake in serious injury cases as part of the same transaction in which they sell rights concerning less-serious injuries. For example, people might agree not to claim damages for losses covered by other sources of payment, not to seek pain and suffering damages of more than $150,000, and to waive their jury trial rights with respect to punitive damages. Because giving up these rights would enhance the worth of what employees were otherwise selling, they should realize more value for them. But unlike the complete sale of potential tort claims for serious injuries, no additional first-party protection would be required when such partial rights were sold. For even after such a sale, seriously injured victims could still sue in tort for uncompensated income losses and out-of-pocket expenses and for substantial general damages; judges should consider this to be adequate protection. At the same time, the ability to buy up partial claims, especially of the most unpredictable portions of liability, could appeal to liability insurers.

Notice, now, were this to happen, the key actors, by private agreement, would have largely duplicated the first-party benefit regime and the tort law legislative trades proposed in my substantial first-step proposal set out in Chapter 8.

SOME ISSUES

One matter deserving brief mention is the quality of information that potential victims must be given about the potential tort rights that they sell. It is widely thought that consumers today do not have enough information to evaluate limitations on liability and waivers of tort rights that might appear in standard form contracts for the purchase of consumer goods. Indeed, the difficulty of properly informing consumers in such contexts is so great that courts quite rightly will not generally enforce such limits. A market organized through employers, however, would largely avoid these problems. Employees have a much better chance to sit down and rationally look over a single plan for injury coverage and better understand what they are gaining and forfeiting by the sale of their potential tort claims.

Some might be concerned that the presettlement of tort claims would erode existing incentives for injurers to take safety precautions. I have throughout expressed my doubts about the effectiveness of such incentives. But, for what it is worth, it should be understood that experience rating of liability insurance would remain available in the market proposed here. The value of potential tort claims, after all, would depend both on the probability that an accident will happen and its severity. If a manufacturer relaxed its quality control in response to the presettlement of its tort claims, so that more hazardous products found their way into the marketplace, it would soon find that the value of potential tort claims against it would increase. To presettle those claims, insurers would then have to pay more, and in turn could demand higher premiums from the manufacturer in future years. To the extent this feedback mechanism were employed, it would give a manufacturer a continuing incentive to maintain quality control.

A brisk market in potential tort rights depends on the parties' ability to determine the value of what is being exchanged. What ought the insurers be willing to pay to presettle tort claims? And how ought they allocate those costs to their insureds? Determining how much a large group of employees could gain from matured and pressed tort claims would enable employers to establish an estimate of what insurers should be willing to pay to avoid that liability. Once this market began, and as long as a significant part of the tort system were still functioning, there should be adequate information available on the worth of any large group of employees' potential tort claims.

Because some people are more likely than others to be tort victims, their rights are worth more, at least in principle. Yet highly individualized compensation between employers and employees is unlikely. Faced with standardized alternatives, the employees whose tort rights are most valuable will probably be the least inclined to sell them. Although the eager sellers would have thus relatively less-valuable rights to sell, this problem of adverse selection seems no more severe here than in other insurance markets.

The idea of selling potential tort claims through employers to liability insurers may see strange, but the notion of trading in tort rights has been advanced in many creative ways in recent years. As already discussed in Chapter 5, over the past fifteen years Professor Jeffrey O'Connell has proposed a great variety of elective no-fault schemes in which victims would trade their tort rights for a package of no-fault benefits that covered their out-of-pocket losses. As noted there, many of O'Connell's proposals, like the one I propose here, foresee exchanges made before an accident occurs. Among them, for example, O'Connell proposed a series of direct, voluntary, preaccident exchanges between potential victims and potential injurers, such as product sellers and physicians. In return for agreeing in advance not to sue, victims would be entitled to specified no-fault compensation from injurers if they are later hurt in ways covered by their contracts.[2] The most important difference between O'Connell's idea and the proposal of this chapter is that my proposal does not call for a postaccident payment from injurers to victims. Rather, the sellers get cash (or benefits) in advance and claim from a separate source once injured.

Another O'Connell proposal, like the proposal here, calls for victims generally to sell all (or most of) their potential tort claims to a single buyer. In his plan, the buyers would be first-party insurers who would offer, in exchange, a guarantee of income and medical expense protection that would cover all accidents.[3] Again, there is an important difference from my proposal. In the O'Connell plan, on the occasion of an injury, first-party insurers would still file tort claims against the injurers or their insurers. Even if these claims were expeditiously settled among insurers, the settlements would have to be reached after accidents occur, thereby reviving the same difficult individualized determinations of fault, cause, and damages that plague the current system. Moreover, whereas the O'Connell plan emphasizes private first-party insurers as the buyers of tort rights and the providers of compensation, I instead foresee employers performing those functions. Of course, under my plan employers might well call on the products and services of first-party insurers to put together and underwrite their employee benefit packages.

In one specific area, O'Connell has made a proposal that is even closer to the one advanced here. He has envisioned the pre-accident transfer of work-related products liability claims, from workers to product manufacturers, in a transaction that involves employers.[4] His basic idea there is that the manufacturers can pay for the potential tort claims with lower prices for their products, the benefit of which can be passed on, at least in part, to the employees. O'Connell assumes that, because employers already enjoy workers' compensation protection for such accidents, many of them would be willing to make this exchange. And where existing workers' compensation was considered inadequate, the employees could bargain for stronger across-the-board, employer-provided, workers' compensation benefits. This plan is designed only to cover job-related product injuries, not personal injuries generally as I propose here. Thus, the proposal outlined here goes farther in the direction envisioned by O'Connell, with a correspondingly more sweeping potential to end the need for postaccident wrangling between the injurers' side (including their insurers) and the victims' side (including their benefit providers).

Judges who find the arguments of this chapter persuasive could, acting on their own, fashion a doctrine under which adequate insurance against a loss would defeat the existing presumption against enforcing bargains to sell potential tort claims. This route, however, would be much slower than legislation. In most states, the courts would have to wait for an attempted sale of tort rights before passing on the idea. The haze of legal uncertainty, however, may prevent a market for tort claims from ever getting off the ground. A clear signal from the legislature, by contrast, might induce a quick response from markets. Furthermore, legislation can specify at the outset what will constitute "adequate insurance"—or at least establish an administrative agency that would adopt regulations to that end.

Serious political problems may interfere with such a legislative initiative, however. The coalition of insurers and manufacturers might favor the proposal, but they would have to turn their attention away from their current agenda of simply trying to roll back victims' rights. Many of them may feel sufficiently optimistic about the prospects of outright victory in that rollback campaign to dampen their enthusiasm for a plan that would merely provide more efficient compensation for existing rights. Moreover, even if most businesses and professional groups found the proposal an improvement of the current system, some, especially those that now have poor employee benefits, might fear that the plan would put new upward pressures on their labor costs. Finally, the interests of the defense bar might not coincide with those of the firms they represent.

On the other side, potential accident victims are not well organized politically. The plaintiffs' bar, which purports to represent them, will be the chief losers in the proposed market for tort claims and naturally can be expected to attack it in any public debate. Consumer and labor interests might be receptive to the proposal, but they must be separated from their current coalition with the plaintiffs' bar. Thus, as with all tort reform, there are substantial obstacles that must be overcome before legislation can be passed to facilitate the regulated market in tort claims proposed here.

CONCLUSION

The idea of an employer-mediated, regulated market in potential tort claims is worth consideration on its own merits. But it can also shed light on what society wants its injury compensation system to look like. As I have already noted, such a market, if it worked as outlined above, could soon come to resemble the tort reform package proposed in Chapter 8. If a consensus were to emerge that this is where an efficient tort claims market would quickly lead, that would perhaps provide more reason to achieve that result directly through legislative action. Such reform would leave both injured and injurers as well off as they would be in an efficiently functioning market, but with even more savings in transactions costs.

NOTES

1. *See* for example Tunkl v. Regents of University of California, 60 Cal. 2d 92, 32 Cal. Rptr. 33, 383 P. 2d 441 (1963) and Henrioulle v. Marin Ventures, Inc., 20 Cal. 3d 512, 143 Cal. Rptr. 247, 573 P. 2d 465 (1978).

2. *See* for example O'Connell, *Expanding No-fault beyond Auto Insurance: Some Proposals*, 59 VA. L. REV. 749 (1973).

3. *See* O'Connell, *Harnessing the Liability Lottery: Elective First-Party No-Fault Insurance Financed by Third-Party Claims*, WASH. U.L.Q. 693 (1978); O'Connell and Beck, *Overcoming Legal Barriers to the Transfer of Third-Party Tort Claims as a Means of Financing First-Party No-Fault Insurance*, 58 WASH. U.L.Q. 55 (1979); and O'Connell and Brown, *A Canadian Proposal for No-Fault Benefits Financed by Assignment of Tort Rights*, 33 U. TORONTO L.J. 434 (1983). *See also* O'Connell, *Transferring Injured Victims' Tort Rights to No-Fault Insurers: New Sole Remedy Approaches to Cure Liability Insurance Ills*, U. ILL. L.F. 749 (1977).

4. *See* O'Connell, *Bargaining for Waivers of Third-Party Tort Claims: An Answer to Product Liability Woes for Employers and their Employees and Suppliers*, 644 INS. L.J. 530 (1976); O'Connell, U. ILL. L.F. (1977) *supra* note 3; and O'Connell, *The Interlocking Death and Rebirth of Contract and Tort*, 75 MICH. L. REV. 659 (1977). *See also* Havighurst, *Private Reform of Tort-Law Dogma: Market Opportunities and Legal Obstacles*, 49 LAW AND CONTEMP. PROBS. 143 (1986) (proposing, for example, that patients be allowed to trade malpractice claims with their health maintenance organization in return for better benefits or lower premiums) and Schwartz, *Proposals for Products Liability Reform: A Theoretical Synthesis*, 97 YALE L.J. 353, 407 (1988) (proposing that consumers with adequate first-party insurance be able to buy products for a reduced price in return for waiving their potential tort claims against the product maker). *See generally* P. HUBER, LIABILITY: THE LEGAL REVOLUTION AND ITS CONSEQUENCES (1988).

Conclusion

To review, the key points are these:

1. Current personal injury law is failing. It is incomplete as a compensation device, terribly wasteful of legal and other resources, doubtful as a promoter of safety, the probable cause of significant socially and economically undesirable conduct, and generally unsuccessful as a mechanism for doing justice between injurers and victims.

2. Even if the burden of the personal injury law system is not currently enormous for most American enterprises, professionals, and municipalities, its many uncertainties are genuinely worrying, especially as they threaten a significant chilling of desirable activities that contain some risk of bodily harm.

3. Meanwhile, although some tort victims win the jackpot, many Americans who are victims of accidents (and disease and other disabling conditions) do not have adequate compensation protection through the existing set of benefit arrangements, including personal injury law.

4. It should certainly be possible, then, to redirect a considerable portion of the money that is now spent on administrative costs (including legal fees) and that is paid to personal injury victims beyond their out-of-pocket losses into other more efficient and more broadly based compensation programs—and to do so in a way that promises to reduce considerably the negative consequences of the personal injury law system.

5. I have proposed a detailed first step, designed to make significant progress toward that goal. It would promptly remove the bulk of the personal injury claims from the tort system and provide those victims with generous and efficiently paid benefits for their economic losses. At the same time, it would bring under control the tort law payments made to seriously injured victims, through changes that would refocus personal injury law on victim needs and away from trying to

punish injurers. In the alternative, I have proposed a way to achieve much of the same result by private agreement.

6. I have also set out a longer-run solution. The key to long-run reform is the complete uncoupling of compensation from deterrence. Benefits paid to tort victims would be provided as part of our regular social insurance and employee benefit system. The scheme I prefer would radically simplify and strengthen that system, with responsibility divided for income-replacement and medical expense (and other) costs. Employers would pay for short-term benefits using enterprise revenues. An expanded Social Security system would provide long-term income support benefits. The health care component would be provided through a combination of mandated employee benefits and public provision. Deterrence would be the domain of administrative agencies concerned exclusively with safety, the market, self-protection, and private morality. The regulatory agencies would be bolstered by new citizen participation roles. Actions in tort for punitive damage would remain for cases of egregious wrongdoing, and private injunction remedies would still be available to stop unreasonably dangerous activities. But we would do away with the core of modern tort law.

If either of the first-step plans I have described in Chapters 8 and 9 were adopted, then we could look forward to a time when personal injury law is concentrated on the problems of the seriously injured. That would then set the stage for the additional intermediate steps that might be necessary to reach a comprehensive long-run program that did not at all rely on private accident law.

Those in-between steps might include the adoption of various tailored no-fault schemes for the seriously disabled along the lines of Virginia's new plan for damaged newborns and the federal Vaccine Injury Compensation program. They might include, for example, plans aimed at air crash victims, victims of pharmaceutical drugs, victims of designated medical misadventures, and/or victims of certain recreational injuries. Notice that, unlike nearly all the American auto no-fault plans now in place that concentrate their awards on relatively little-injured victims, the no-fault plans I envision here would deal only with serious injuries.

Experience with these plans would help our society reach a consensus on a number of issues that would be critical features of any longer run comprehensive scheme for the permanently disabled, such as (1) the level of income support that seriously injured victims should receive, (2) whether or not some portion of the award to those victims (as in the vaccine-damaged children's program) should be for pain and suffering, and (3) the sufficiency of the nontort safety measures employed to deal with the dangers that have been removed from the tort system by the no-fault plans.

But this is perhaps placing the cart before the horse. The initial trick will be to achieve political agreement on one of my proposed first steps.[1] Adoption of my legislative proposals would require altering the terms of the current debate by realigning the coalitions now engaged in battle.

Joining together on behalf of my reform package, I envision a coalition of victim, consumer, and business groups—each of which would benefit. Although this proposal ought to hold considerable appeal for corporate interests, the initiative on its behalf realistically may have to come from the consumer and victim side. This is because the already formulated proposals of those who have been protesting most strongly against the tort law in the current debate—enterprise defendants, their lawyers, and their insurers—are now largely dominating the political agenda. Their active opponents, plaintiffs' lawyers and consumer groups, have so far mainly felt forced to assume a defensive posture by trying to stop what appears to be a potentially out-of-control steamroller. I say "mainly" because the plaintiff side has employed one major counterattack strategy by attempting to shift legislative attention to regulating the insurance industry. My proposal, of course, offers quite a different strategy.

If it continues, the polarization that has thus far characterized the current tort reform battle is likely to lead to quite unfortunate consequences. Either substantial tort victim rights will be swept away with nothing gained for the disabled as a trade-off, or else socially undesirable features of the current tort system will remain intact due to the efforts of self-styled friends of victims, who defend every aspect of the existing regime.

The belief that we are in the midst of an unhealthy litigation explosion is now widely held—whether or not it is true.[2] Moreover, because personal injury problems are in the news so much, tort law has become a convenient hook on which to hang dissatisfaction with lawyers generally. Indeed, the widespread and unfavorable publicity that many plaintiff personal injury lawyers received in the aftermath of the Bhopal disaster probably helped to reinforce the stereotypical negative view of lawyers held by many ordinary citizens. Although the benefits of healthy skepticism of professionals by laymen are not to be gainsaid, it is nonetheless potentially quite a bad thing for the public at large to hold both lawyers and the law in low esteem.

Finally, the effort on the part of some conservatives to transform tort law into a broad ideological issue is an additional aspect of the current situation that deserves attention. The main theme has been to link the current infirmities of personal injury law to the allegedly lawless and misguided decisions of liberal judges.[3] The message that an all too unaccountable judiciary is once more engaged in illegitimate social engineering is not simply being sounded within the legal profession or by those officials whose central responsibility concerns tort law. Rather, this is the common law counterpart to the broad conservative attack on the Warren Court's legacy in the field of constitutional law.

Casting tort law developments in broad ideological terms was apparent in the 1986 election battle involving former California Chief Justice Rose Bird and several of her colleagues.[4] To be sure, the campaign that overthrew three of the liberal incumbents was most importantly fought on the death penalty issue; yet, the court's torts decisions were also widely attacked.[5] This clearly partisan effort perhaps explains the equally fervent defense of tort law by the likes of consumer advocate Ralph Nader, who is ideologically committed on the other side to the idea that activist courts are needed to protect otherwise politically weak interests from powerful corporations and abusive government officials.[6]

In such a heated political climate there is room, at least potentially, for many legislative solutions to blossom. Before my proposal can succeed, there will probably have to be a decoupling of consumer and victim groups from the plaintiffs' trial bar and their joining together with farsighted business interests that have also distanced themselves from their personal injury lawyers.

Might this happen? One hope for these decouplings lies, ironically, in the hands of the legal profession as a whole. It is not so much that lawyers' own rapidly rising malpractice insurance rates might give attorneys reason to fear that they have unleashed a regime of private litigation that ill serves society as a whole. Rather, it is that many lawyers now worry that the practice of law is viewed far too negatively by the public at large and would welcome and support a dramatic change that promised to turn public opinion around. Surely a reform promoted by lawyers that promised to reduce dramatically the need to use lawyers by those suffering personal injuries would have a real chance of achieving that goal.[7]

In the end, Professor Robert Rabin is probably right when he observes that "comprehensive no-fault will come, if at all, only on the coattails of a broader renaissance of social welfare concerns."[8] Because outside of law schools and legal offices, it is becoming increasingly clear that the United States' social insurance and employee benefit system needs considerable overhaul, quite apart from tort law reform, perhaps things would fall nicely into place if we could get the lawyers to pay attention. I have tried to sound this theme here, especially in Chapter 6. It will also be the main focus of my next book.

NOTES

1. For Professor Monroe Berkowitz's doubts as to the political feasibility of my first-step proposals, *see* Berkowitz, *How Serious Is Sugarman's "Serious Tort Law Reform"?*, 24 SAN DIEGO L. REV. 877, 886 (1987).

Professor Robert Rabin, finding "shallow roots" in the current tort reform movement, predicts "incremental rather than comprehensive change," Rabin, *Some Reflections on the Process of Tort Reform*, 25 U. SAN DIEGO L. REV. 13, 19 (1988). Yet, at the same time, he suggests that "it is far from clear than *any* reform strategy based on incremental improvements in the substantive and remedial character of tort law will have a significant impact," *id.* at 37.

2. *Cf.* Galanter, *The Day after the Litigation Explosion*, 46 MD. L. REV. 3 (1986) *with* Civiletti, *Zeroing In on the Real Litigation Crisis: Irrational Justice, Needless Delays, Excessive Costs*, 46 MD. L. REV 40 (1986) and Saks, *If There Be a Crisis, How Shall*

We Know It?, 46 MD. L. REV. 63 (1986). For empirical support for the proposition that claims costs are way up but not because of an increase in the number of claims, *see* Nye and Gifford, *The Myth of the Liability Insurance Claims Explosion: An Empirical Rebuttal* 41 VAND. L. REV. 909 (1988).

3. *See* for example L.A. Daily J., Nov. 20, 1985, at 1, col. 2 (describing a speech by then Assistant Attorney General Richard K. Willard in which he blamed activist judges for "outrageous decisions" that are the result of their efforts "to destroy traditional tort law doctrines that limit liability so that the legal system can be used as a vehicle to restructure society and administer a massive scheme for the redistribution of wealth"); N.Y. Times, May 31, 1986, at 28, col. 1 (quoting then Attorney General Edwin Meese III's statement that "what some of the liberal attorneys and liberal judges did to criminal law in the 1960s and 70s they are now, in the 1980s, trying to do to the civil law"); and remarks made to the American Tort Reform Association on May 30, 1986 by President Reagan who offered Bigbee v. Pacific Telephone, 34 Cal. 3d 49, 665 p. 2d 947, 192 Cal. Rptr. 857 (1983) (someone who was hit by a careless driver while in a phone booth was allowed to sue the phone company) as evidence that "[t]wisted and abused, tort law has become a pretext for outrageous legal outcomes—outcomes that impede our economic life, not promote it," Remarks to Members of the American Tort Reform Association, May 30, 1986, 22 Weekly Comp. Pres. Doc. 720, 721 (June 2, 1986).

4. For the first time in California's history, the voters decided not to retain sitting justices—Chief Justice Bird, Associate Justice Cruz Reynoso, and Associate Justice Joseph Grodin.

5. *See* for example "Crime Victims for Tort Reform White Paper on the Supreme Court Confirmation Elections: The Civil Issues" (processed 1986). For earlier background, *see* Fairbanks and Deen, *Supreme Court Decisions Create Controversy over Damage Awards* 15 CALIF. J. 183 (May 1984).

6. *See* for example Nader, *The Corporate Drive to Restrict Their Victims' Rights*, 22 GONZ. L. REV. 15 (1986/87).

7. In this vein Professor Terrence Ison has written that "retention of tort liability . . . in the long run . . . may not even be in the interests of the legal profession. To attempt the preservation of a system that is so utterly indefensible must surely be a negative influence on public confidence in the profession," Ison, *The Politics of Reform in Personal Injury Compensation*, 27 U. TORONTO L.J. 385, 402 (1977).

8. Rabin, *supra* note 1, at 44.

Bibliography

Atiyah, P. S. *Accidents, Compensation and the Law* (3rd ed.). London: Weidenfeld and Nicolson, 1980.

Bernzweig, Eli P. *By Accident Not Design*. New York: Praeger Publishers, 1980.

Calabresi, Guido. *The Costs of Accidents*. New Haven, Conn.: Yale University Press, 1970.

Cooter, Robert, and Ulen, Thomas. *Law and Economics*. Glenview, Ill.: Scott, Forseman and Company, 1988.

Danzon, Patricia. *Medical Malpractice: Theory, Evidence and Public Policy*. Cambridge, Mass.: Harvard University Press, 1985.

Fleming, John G. *The American Tort Process*. New York: Oxford University Press, 1988.

Fleming, John G. *The Law of Torts* (6th ed.). Sydney, Australia: The Law Book Company, 1983.

Harper, Fowler V., James, Fleming, Jr., and Gray, Oscar S. *The Law of Torts* (2nd ed.). Boston: Little, Brown and Company, 1986.

Harris, Donald, et al. *Compensation and Support for Illness and Injury*. Oxford, UK: Oxford University Press, 1984.

Huber, Peter. *Liability: The Legal Revolution and Its Consequences*. New York: Basic Books, 1988.

Ison, Terrence G. *Accident Compensation*. London: Croom Helm, 1980.

Ison, Terrence G. *The Forensic Lottery*. London: Staples, 1967.

Keeton, Robert, and O'Connell, Jeffrey. *Basic Protection for the Traffic Victim*. Boston: Little Brown and Company, 1965.

Keeton, W. Page, Dobbs, Dan B., Keeton, Robert E., and Owen, David G. *Prosser and Keeton on Torts* (5th ed.). St. Paul, Minn.: West Publishing Co, 1984.

Landes, William M., and Posner, Richard A. *The Economic Structure of Tort Law*. Cambridge, Mass.: Harvard University Press, 1987.

Litan, Robert E., and Winston, Clifford, eds. *Liability: Perspectives and Policy*. Washington, D.C.: The Brookings Institution, 1988.

O'Connell, Jeffrey. *The Lawsuit Lottery: Only the Lawyers Win*. New York: Free Press, 1979.

O'Connell, Jeffrey, and Kelly, C. Brian. *The Blame Game: Injuries, Insurance & Injustice*. Lexington, Mass.: Lexington Books, 1987.

Palmer, Geoffrey. *Compensation for Incapacity*. Wellington, N.Z.: Oxford University Press, 1979.

Posner, Richard A. *Economic Analysis of Law* (3rd ed.). Boston: Little Brown and Company, 1986.

Schuck, Peter. *Agent Orange on Trial: Mass Disasters in the Courts*. Cambridge, Mass.: Harvard University Press, 1986.

Shavell, Steven. *Economic Analysis of Accident Law*. Cambridge, Mass.: Harvard University Press, 1987.

Special Committee on the Tort Liability System. *Towards a Jurisprudence of Injury*. Chicago: American Bar Association, 1984.

Stapleton, Jane. *Disease and the Compensation Debate*. New York: Oxford University Press, 1986.

Index

About the Author

STEPHEN D. SUGARMAN is Professor of Law at the University of California, Berkeley. He teaches in the areas of torts, social welfare law, and family law. Sugarman has published in the field of personal injury law and reviews books on that subject for the American Bar Association Journal. His other book include *Private Wealth and Public Education, Education by Choice: The Case for Family Control,* and *In the Interest of Children.*